Artificial Intelligence in Games

This book covers all the necessary topics that a professional game AI programmer needs to know, from math and steering behaviours to terrain analysis, pathfinding, and decision-making. Written to be easily accessible, each topic is accompanied by an example game that allows the reader to add their own code to see the effects their changes have.

Each chapter is split into two parts. The first part covers the necessary theory in a friendly, conversational manner, using visual examples and fictional game scenarios to give additional context. The second part is a coding tutorial in C# for the topic at hand. Each chapter has its own example game available to download, written in C# in the Unity Game Engine.

This book will be suitable for students and aspiring games programmers looking to gain a grounding in game AI techniques.

Paul Roberts is a Lead AI Games Programmer who has worked for companies such as Activision, Team17, Traveller's Tales and Sumo Digital. Credits include *Call of Duty: Strike Team, Pitfall!, Worms Revolution* and *The Lego Movie: The Video Game.*

Artificial Intelligence
in Games

Paul Roberts

CRC Press
Taylor & Francis Group
Boca Raton London New York

CRC Press is an imprint of the
Taylor & Francis Group, an **informa** business

Illustrations by Nicholas Dent

First edition published 2023
by CRC Press
6000 Broken Sound Parkway NW, Suite 300, Boca Raton, FL 33487-2742

and by CRC Press
4 Park Square, Milton Park, Abingdon, Oxon, OX14 4RN

CRC Press is an imprint of Taylor & Francis Group, LLC

Library of Congress Cataloging-in-Publication Data

Names: Roberts, Paul (Game programmer), author. | Dent, Nicholas (Illustrator), illustrator.
Title: Artificial intelligence in games / Paul Roberts ; illustrated by Nicholas Dent.
Description: First edition. | Boca Raton : CRC Press, 2023. | Includes bibliographical references and index. | Summary: "This book covers all the necessary topics that a professional game AI programmer needs to know, from math and steering behaviours to terrain analysis, pathfinding, decision making, and more. Written to be easily accessible, each topic is accompanied by an example game, where the reader can add their own code to see the effects their changes have. This book will be suitable for students and aspiring games programmers looking to gain a grounding in game AI techniques"-- Provided by publisher.
Identifiers: LCCN 2022005391 | ISBN 9781032305950 (hardback) | ISBN 9781032033228 (paperback) | ISBN 9781003305835 (ebook)
Subjects: LCSH: Computer games--Programming. | Computer games--Design. | Video games--Design. | Artificial intelligence. Classification: LCC QA76.76.C672 R6327 2023 | DDC 794.8/1526--dc23/eng/20220412 LC record available at https://lccn.loc.gov/2022005391

ISBN: 9781032305950 (hbk)
ISBN: 9781032033228 (pbk)
ISBN: 9781003305835 (ebk)

DOI: 10.1201/9781003305835

Typeset in Times LT Std
by KnowledgeWorks Global Ltd.

Access the Support Material: https://www.routledge.com/9781032033228

Contents

1 Introduction

ABOUT THE AUTHOR

My name is Paul Roberts and I am a Lead AI games programmer. I've worked on a variety of big releases over the years including titles such as *Call of Duty: Strike Team, The Lego Movie: The Video Game* and *Worms Revolution* and have developed quite a few smaller mobile games too, including *Power-Up, Pixel 8, Rituals and Captain CupCake* and *Donut Disaster.* I have worked at big studios like Activision, Sumo Digital, Team17 and Traveller's Tales and been an indie developer at my own studio too – Playing with Giants. I also spent around six years leading the Computer Games Programming undergraduate degrees and master's degrees at a UK university, where I was fortunate enough to rewrite all their game AI content and set our students on the right path.

I have been programming since the ZX Spectrum days and am currently dabbling in some assembly language programming for the Atari 2600 for fun. I also write novels as a hobby; so if you are a fantasy fan, check out my novel, *The Betrayer: Prophecy of the Dragon Book One* (Amazon, 2022).

WHO IS THIS BOOK FOR?

This book was written for anyone wishing to get a grounding in-game AI techniques. I have pitched everything at an undergraduate level, but that does not mean that if you are not currently studying that you cannot get anything from this book. Not at all. I feel that anyone interested in game AI that has never approached the subject before can work their way through this book and gain a lot. There are, however, coding tutorials in each chapter written in C#; so to get the most from these, it would be beneficial if you could already code at a basic level.

HOW TO READ THIS BOOK

Each chapter is split into two parts. The first gives an overview of the topic in a friendly conversational manner and there are a lot of visual examples and fictional game scenarios to give some context to the area being covered. The second part of each chapter has been written as a coding tutorial. It will guide you through how to code the techniques the first half of the chapter covered. It is recommended that you read both parts of a chapter in order, but if you already have an understanding of an area and wish to jump right into the code, then skip straight to the second half of the relevant chapter. Likewise, if you are not interested in coding the solutions and just want to get an understanding of the different areas of game AI, feel free to just read the first halves.

I have compiled the topics for this book in a way that each chapter builds upon the last. If you choose to read the chapters in order, at the end of this book you should

DOI: 10.1201/9781003305835-1

have a good understanding of the fundamentals of game AI programming. However, each chapter stands alone. Meaning you can jump into a particular chapter of interest and read it in isolation and still have a good understanding of that topic.

ACCOMPANYING FRAMEWORK

For you to jump right into coding the game AI, I have written a framework in the Unity Game Engine in the C# language for you to do just that. It can be found at www.routledge.com/9781032033228. Each chapter has its own example game, and you will be instructed in the tutorial part of each chapter which files to look at. Full solutions have also been provided, but I'd recommend giving everything a good go before you look at these.

It should be noted that the code has been written for readability, not optimisation. This book is about learning, so the focus is on you (the reader) understanding the code, rather than the code running fast. Such a decision can have an impact in places and does, for example the Chess project. When you have completed the code tutorial, the AI player will take a very long time to make decisions. This is an unfortunate consequence, but it is more important at this stage that you understand the first principles of the code. Optimisations can come later.

WHAT IS GAME AI?

There are two sides to the AI coin. On one side we have academic AI and on the other, we have game AI. The purpose of game AI is vastly different from that of academic AI, although the techniques used for both come from the same toolkit, if you will. The way we implement these approaches can be completely different depending on the purpose.

There are also some approaches that academic AI uses a lot, but game AI not so much … neural networks for instance. They are a great approach to pattern matching, and for things like facial recognition, but in games they are just not as reliable as you might think. That is not to mention the sheer amount of time it takes to train the things. That is another difference between game AI and academic AI – in game development, it is much more of a risk to attempt some approach that a year later proves to be the wrong choice, which then pushes back release dates and adds to the cost of development. And the worst-case scenario here could be the game being cancelled. So, in games we can be very risk averse.

What Is the Purpose of Academic AI?

Academic AI is about developing systems as clever as can be and pushing the boundaries of current research. You could add developing emergent behaviours to this as well, but then we are straying into artificial life, and we can leave that for another book. All science-based research is attempting to push boundaries, and to be able to publish your research, or achieve a PhD, you need to demonstrate how your findings move things along, and that your solution is novel or unique. It is no different in the field of AI, and this has been going on since before the term artificial intelligence was even coined, when AI was a mixture of computer science, robotics and cybernetics. It still is a mixture of these really, but we now have the catchall term – artificial intelligence, or AI for short.

An important thing to note is that academic AI has always used games as test environments. John Von Neumann wrote the Minimax algorithm in 1928 for zero-sum games – the exact algorithm we use for Chess AI and lots of other board games to this day. This can be quite a slow approach given the number of moves that can be made on each turn, and even incorporating improvements like AlphaBeta pruning only allows you to look a little further along. In a video game, the time it takes to decide on a move is crucial. In academic AI the main concern is the intelligence of the decision, not the time it takes. As an example of academic AI not worrying about processing speed, I can point to Alan Turing who wrote the first chess program in 1950. This was before we even had computers capable of processing the calculations. To test it, he had to play the part of the computer. A friend would make a move, and then he would step through the logic of his algorithm to determine the AI's response. It apparently took him half an hour to make a single move. As I understand it, his algorithm could look twelve moves ahead, which is impressive.

What Is the Purpose of Game AI?

Game AI is about creating AI that is fun to play, that creates the illusion of intelligence rather than actual intelligence and can be processed at a decent framerate (60 times a second would be good). If achieving these three things means pushing the boundaries of current research, so be it, that would be great, but this is not the focus. An example where this happened is in the creation of Behaviour Trees. These were developed for Halo 2 by Damian Isla as a way for enemies to make better decisions. As a game AI programmer, we do conduct research from time to time, but if a solution exists that can do the job, then we tend to use that solution. In academic AI, as I said, you are looking for a novel approach to solving a problem. Game AI is not. It is just looking for a solution. Pathfinding is a great example where academia has pushed the boundaries, but the games industry has largely ignored these advances. We always seem to use the A* algorithm. It works – to some degree, so we never go looking for an alternative, but there are loads of pathfinding solutions out there. I even published a research paper on an approach I created called *Directed Recursion Search (DRS)* in 2018. But in games, the A* algorithm works, so that is what gets used. It is not until it is not good enough, say in a dynamic environment or a huge environment, where the flaws of the A* algorithm get exposed, and the AI programmer goes looking for an alternative.

So, What Is the Illusion of Intelligence?

I would define this as AI that is believable to the player playing the game. It does not matter what anyone else thinks. If the individual playing the game does not buy into the decisions on display, we have failed to create the illusion of intelligence. And this is regardless of how smart your AI really is.

Game AI must consider the human psychology of the player, something academic AI does not really need to do. This is interesting as the player is not something we get to code. So, we need to keep in the back of our minds 'How do we keep the player immersed in the experience' and that has nothing to do with being clever.

To give you an example of AI that could be termed as 'dumb' AI, are games where you play as a sniper. In one such game I was playing, I got to a section where there were a bunch of enemies in this kind of dugout area. I fired a shot that missed, and all the bad guys became alert and ran to hide behind cover and started firing back. All good so far. But … and I appreciate there are very few people like me, but I just sat there and just watched them. The enemies that is. And they started to come out of cover and run to a spot where another bad guy was hiding. And that bad guy would then run to another location. Over the space of about a minute, all the bad guys had changed positions multiple times. Think about it. There is a sniper in the area, and you decide to expose yourself by running to another hiding place. It just looked daft. It is just not something you would do in that situation. Now I appreciate why the AI was coded this way. It was to give the player targets to shoot at, which is all about making the AI fun. And that is the problem right there. How do you make the AI both believable and fun?

A huge part of the solution is to avoid making the AI obviously dumb. Things like the AI running into walls or closed doors for example. If they do, you will instantly lose the 'illusion'. However, if you manage to avoid the obvious dumb behaviours, you can get away with a lot. Also, do not underestimate the magic of randomness. Players tend to explain away a lot of things for themselves.

What Do We Mean by Fun AI?

Clever AI is rarely fun. Who wants to play a game where the AI outsmarts the player every game? Imagine Chess where you lose every game. Now some people may find that fun, but the majority will not. Conversely, game AI can have the opposite problem too. People complaining that the AI is dumb. You can develop AI that does not destroy the opponent, and makes clever decisions, but if it acts in a way that the player does not understand, it gets labelled as dumb. AI that the player can understand is important in developing the 'illusion' we discussed above. So, it is important that agents behave in a way the player expects. When I worked on Call of Duty, it started as a third person strategy game, then became a first person shooter, then evolved into a hybrid of the two. You could play as any one of your squad in first person, or go to the strategy view and control them all like an RTS game. The third person AI was very in-depth with the agents working together to flush out enemies. But when it changed to include the first person element, the AI had to change too. The player's expectations have changed based upon the camera, and with it, so did the idea of what made the game fun. It was no longer necessary for enemies to run around, no matter how clever they were – they just needed to hide behind objects, stand up and shoot, and allow the player to shoot them.

A lot of the intelligence can be missed unless you shout it from the rooftops. If the player cannot figure out what the AI is doing, or why it is doing it, then the player just marks them down as stupid, and they lose the immersion. Alerting the player to the intelligence that is taking place can help to avoid this. In the COD example I just gave you, if we had continued with the smarter third person variant of the AI when playing in first person, the player would not understand why a particular bad guy just ran across in the distance – in third person you see he is trying to out flank you, but in first person it makes no sense. So, the AI just looks dumb. Then when that 'dumb' bad guy comes up behind you and kills you, the game is not fair, and it is no longer fun. It is hard to make a game feel fair with hidden intelligence.

How Do We Get a Decent Framerate?

Framerate is a huge problem for game AI, and when we talk about sixty frames per second, this includes other systems too – Graphics, physics etc. – not just the AI. As I said before, academic AI does not need to worry about the amount of time an action takes. It is more about the result. I appreciate there are areas such as self-driving cars that need instant decisions, but often when developing AI in an academic setting, time is not a huge factor, whereas the smartest game AI in the world will not look great if the player must wait even a second for a decision to be made. How do we achieve the desired framerate? I have a three-step mantra to achieving this. We need to either reduce the problem, spread the problem or remove the problem. This is easier said than done, and as every game is different, there is no single solution.

Reducing the Problem

For game AI this is a major consideration. This is where you as the programmer have to get creative. How do we use the same techniques to get good results in a fraction of the time? One way is to reduce the number of agents getting an update. In Call of Duty, we were originally updating the whole map, which took a long time. We ended up splitting the world into sections, meaning that there were less agents in each section to process and we saw a huge processing speed increase. Imagine any game where a path is required. If that agent stands around and does nothing whilst a path is calculated, you lose the player's immersion. Worse are pathfinding algorithms like A* that hold up all other systems whilst they process, so you get a lag effect. Here, we can simply reduce the search space to speed things up. Imagine calculating a route from London to Edinburgh by road. There are a lot of nodes in that map. How about the same problem, but via trains? There are far fewer considerations for train lines giving a huge reduction in the search space. Unfortunately, with the reduction of nodes in the search space, we get a reduction in the quality of the route as well.

Spreading the Problem

Can the problem be split over several frames or multiple threads? Using pathfinding again as an example, we could search for a set amount of time, and then pause the search until the next update. The decision can still look delayed for the individual agent, but it will allow all other systems to update. We also need to consider what we do with that agent whilst we are waiting for the path to be calculated. We could let her wander around until the path is calculated. But this has consequences. What happens when we return a path, but our agent is away from the starting node? Do we have our agent walk back to the starting node? Do we need to generate another path for that? Maybe she is already part way along the path and would look silly if she goes back to the starting node to then retread the same route. All these decisions can have an impact upon the believability of the AI again.

Removing the Problem

Maybe a different solution would get you the results you are looking for, but without the same level of processing. At times you may have to drop a feature altogether. Could you get by without pathfinding by using simple steering behaviours? A path-finding algorithm would be more accurate, but if the player is not going to notice, why add the additional processing?

To achieve these three areas of 'Illusion' of intelligence, fun AI and framerate, it is all about compromise and a lot of smoke and mirrors.

GAME AI AND GAME GENRES

We talked a little about the difference a first person camera and an RTS style camera had on Call of Duty: Strike Team above. Although the results were different, the underlying approach used was very much the same. We used stack-based Finite State Machines, very much in the vein of the MARPO methodology (Movement, Avoidance, Routing, Planning and Orders) created by Dr Brett Lamming for Grand Theft Auto: China Town Wars. So, I wanted to go through the different game genres that exist and have a quick look at specifically the AI approaches covered in this book to show the overlap. Take a look at Image 1.1. A tick in a cell suggests that the AI approach listed down the left-hand side may be used in that game genre. Not that it must be used, or even ever has been used, but that it could be.

The first two rows cover decision-making with Finite State Machines and Behaviour Trees. A game may use both or just use one of them. It really depends on the game.

AI Approach \ Game Genre	RTS	RPG	FPS	3rd Person	Adventure	Platformer	Shmup	Sports	Fighting	Racing	Board Games
FSM	✓	✓	✓	✓	✓	✓	✓	✓	✓	✓	✓
BT	✓	✓	✓	✓				✓			
Path Finding	✓	✓	✓	✓	✓	✓	✓	✓		✓	
Terrain Analysis	✓			✓				✓			
Movement	✓	✓	✓	✓	✓	✓	✓	✓	✓	✓	✓
Fuzzy Logic	✓	✓	✓					✓	✓	✓	
Mini Max											✓
* Neural Network	✓	✓	✓								
* Genetic Algorithms	✓	✓	✓	✓				✓	✓	✓	

IMAGE 1.1 Game genres cross-referenced with AI approaches.

The two approaches marked with an asterisk indicate that these, if used, are more likely used in development rather than in the released game. This will be covered in the relevant chapters of this book. Some games may use fewer or more approaches than detailed above, but that is not what is important here, what is important is to understand that each of these approaches can be used in a wide range of game genres. So, when you understand how to implement a particular technique, you can use it for a variety of game problems. To ensure full transparency here, I should state that these genres will use other approaches such as scripting systems and messaging systems too, but as these are not specific AI systems, they will not be covered in this book.

2 Math

Math can be quite daunting for people, and that is usually a consequence of those with the knowledge presenting some scary formula upfront. The learner can instantly feel like they cannot do this, and their walls are thrown up. I have always found that by presenting a problem to solve and then stepping through the solution brings the learner along with you on the journey. By the time you get to the formula, it does not look quite so scary. And that is because the learner understands what you are trying to achieve and has context to ground the problem. There is nothing worse than an abstract problem, where the learner wonders why they would ever need to do this.

With that being said, there are some mathematical approaches we need to understand, so let us work through them in a step-by-step approach. We will only be covering the areas required for this book though. Mathematics is a huge topic and there are many good books on the topic. And if you feel you already have a good grasp of the areas I am about to cover, go ahead and jump to the next chapter. You can always come back for a refresher if you encounter something later that you do not know.

WHAT IS A VECTOR?

We will use the term *vector* a lot throughout this book, and as some of you may be unaware what a vector is we will cover this first.

A vector can be summarised as a variable that has a direction and a magnitude. For example, when someone stops you and asks for directions, you could say something like, 'go north for one kilometre, then go west and continue for five kilometres'.

Ok that is very contrived and no one in the history of the world has ever said that but stick with me. What that sentence did, was provide two vectors. One with a direction of north and magnitude of 1 kilometre and another with a direction of west and a magnitude of 5 kilomteres.

Components of a Vector

A vector has a number of components that correspond to the world within which we are working. That is to say, if we are making a 2D game, that game has two dimensions, so our vectors will contain two components (X and Y). In a 3D environment, our vectors will consist of three components (X, Y and Z).

Take a quick look at Image 2.3. We have three vectors named A, B and C. These are the blue lines. Each of them is made up of two components. $A = (10, 0)$ as it takes 10 steps from the start to then end of the vector on the horizontal axis (or x axis) and no steps on the vertical axis (or y axis), $B = (0, -4)$ as it takes no steps on the horizontal axis and 4 steps up the vertical axis. The C vector has the

DOI: 10.1201/9781003305835-2

components (10, 4) as it moves 10 steps to the right (horizontal axis) and 4 steps down (vertical axis).

It is important to note that the component values in *A* described above were for the vector having a direction moving from P1 to the right. If we had started from the vector's end point and moved to the cell containing P1, we would have had the values (−10, 0).

MAGNITUDE OF A VECTOR

The length of a vector is called the vector's magnitude. The terms length, distance and magnitude are used interchangeably throughout this book when referring to the length of a vector.

At times we want to know how far away something is. This could be an item or simply a position we want to go to. In games you will quite often find your way blocked by walls, cars, and any other number of items, but it is still really useful to know the distance as the crow flies. Take a look at Image 2.1. We have a generic game environment, and we want to know the distance from P1 to P2.

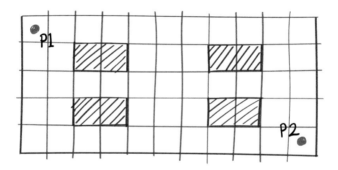

IMAGE 2.1   Generic environment.

With these two points, we can use a right-angle triangle to calculate the distance between them using the formula: $X^2 + Y^2 = Z^2$. Take a look at Image 2.2, where we are calculating the distance between points P1 and P2. In English, it simply means the distance on the horizontal is multiplied by itself, the distance on the vertical is multiplied by itself and the two results are added together. This will give us the squared distance between P1 and P2. This is shown in the image as Z^2 but is also known as the hypotenuse of the triangle. If you need the non-squared distance, you will have to get the square root of Z^2. In games programming, this is usually a step we do not need or want to do. When using this approach to check if something is within range, the range can be stored as a squared value too, meaning you never need to do the square root calculation. Distance checks can happen quite often and removing unnecessary calculations will help speed things up.

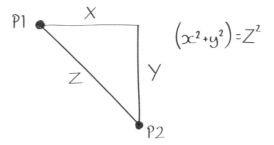

IMAGE 2.2   Pythagoras theorem.

Let us do this in our generic environment example. Take a look at Image 2.3. By drawing a line from P1 along the horizontal axis until we line up with P2 we get vector **A**. We can do the same to get the vector **B** by drawing a line from P2 along the vertical axis until we are in line with P1. The **C** vector is simply the line between P1 and P2.

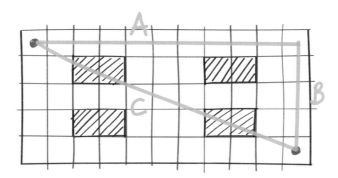

IMAGE 2.3   Applying Pythagoras to the game world.

To get the length of vector **C**, it is simply a matter of multiplying the length of the **A** component by itself and multiplying the length of the **B** component by itself and then combining the two results. We then get the square root to give us the length of the vector **C**. The following formula shows how we calculate this using the information seen in Image 2.3.

$$|V| = \sqrt{(10 \times 10) + (4 \times 4)}$$

$$= \sqrt{116}$$

$$= 10.77$$

In this formula, **V** is our vector (the line marked **C** in Image 2.3). The vertical bars at either side of a vector name are to represent that we are looking at the vector's length or magnitude. Take a look back at Image 2.3 and count the number of cells along the vector named **A**. There are 10, right? So, **A*****A** becomes 10*10. Look again and count the cells along the vector named **B**. I got 4. So, **B*****B** becomes 4*4.

|**V**| has a squared value of 116, but if we want the distance in the same context as the gridded distance we have been looking at we need to get the square root of 116. This gives us a value of 10.77. That is to say the vector **C** has a magnitude of 10.77, or the distance between P1 and P2 is 10.77.

Remember, we did not worry about obstacles, and a game character would need to navigate these. Do not worry about that for now, we will cover this in Chapter 5 – Pathfinding.

UNIT VECTOR

At times it is important for a games developer to know the direction of a vector capped at a length of 1. A unit vector is essentially your vector, but with a length of 1 unit. The process of calculating the unit vector is known as normalisation.

To normalise a vector, we simply divide each component of the vector by the magnitude of the vector. And lucky for us we just covered how to calculate the magnitude of a vector, but we will use another example to step through the process. Take a look back at Image 2.3. We want the unit vector equivalent of vector **A**. We know that the **A** vector has the components (10, 0).

If we put this through Pythagoras theorem, we get the following:

$$|A| = \sqrt{(10 \times 10) + (0 \times 0)}$$
$$= \sqrt{100}$$
$$= 10$$

Now we know our vector has a length of 10 units, we can use this in our normalisation process to calculate the unit vector. Simply divide each component of vector **A** by 10.

$$\bar{A} = \left(\frac{10}{10}, \frac{0}{10} \right)$$
$$= (1,\ 0)$$

A unit vector is often depicted by a little dash or ^ above the vector name. We will be using the dash format to differentiate our vectors.

Take a look at Image 2.4. We can see the unit vector of **A** clearly. It shows the same direction, but now it has been scaled to a length of 1 unit.

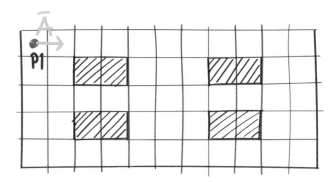

IMAGE 2.4   Unit vector **A**.

Unit vectors are useful for a variety of reasons, such as multiplying our speed by it to get a character to move in a particular direction at a particular speed, or when calculating the angle of rotation between two points. This leads us nicely into the dot product.

DOT PRODUCT

The result of the dot product is the cos of the angle between two vectors. To get the actual angle, we need to feed the dot product through the inverse cos function, but do not worry if none of this makes any sense as we have not gone through it yet and that is exactly what we are about to do.

Let us say we have two objects in the world, and we want to determine the angle between them. Maybe our agent is a sniper who is located some distance away and we need to know how far we need to rotate to face the other object. Take a look at Image 2.5 to get an idea of the problem. As you can see, we have two objects at different distances, but we do not know the angle between them. In the example, our sniper is located at (0, 0) on the graph.

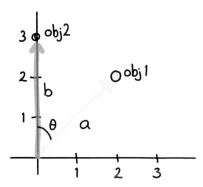

IMAGE 2.5   Vectors to object 1 and object 2.

This is where the dot product proves useful. The formula for the dot product looks like this:

$$\text{Cos }\theta = \frac{a \cdot b}{|a| \cdot |b|}$$

FORMULA 2.1   Dot product equation.

If this looks strange at the moment, that is ok. As with everything else in this book, we are going to step through it bit-by-bit, so we have a good understanding.

Formula 1 is actually a formula to get us the cos of the angle. So, to move the formula around a little to give us the actual angle, we get:

$$\theta = \text{Cos}^{-1}\left(\frac{a \cdot b}{|a||b|}\right)$$

FORMULA 2.2   Rearranged dot product formula.

The **a.b** part is the dot product, but before we look at this, we need to understand what **a** and **b** are. If you look back at Image 2.5, you will see that we labelled the arrows **a** and **b**. Each arrow is a vector, which has an x component and a y component. Obviously if we were working in three dimensions, there would be a z component, and everything we discuss here can be expanded to three dimensions.

$$a = \text{Vector to obj1} = (2, 2)$$
$$b = \text{Vector to obj2} = (0, 3)$$

TERMINOLOGY: SCALAR PRODUCT

Exactly the same as the dot product, just a different term used in many texts.

Now that we know what **a** and **b** represent, we can take a look at the **a.b** part of the equation. **a.b** is simply the process of multiplying the x components of multiple vectors together, multiplying the y components of the multiple vectors together and combining the results:

$$a \cdot b = (a_x \ b_x) + (a_y \ b_y)$$

So let us step through this. The x component of vector **a** is 2 and the x component of vector **b** is 0. The y component of vector **a** is 2 and the y component of vector **b** is 3. Placing these numbers into the above formulas we get the following:

$$a \cdot b = (2 \times 0) + (2 \times 3)$$
$$= \quad 0 \quad + \quad 6$$
$$= \quad 6$$

We now have the numerator for the equation, the next job is to tackle the |**a**||**b**| part. |**a**| simply means the magnitude or length of vector **a**. So, what we need to do is calculate the lengths of vectors **a** and **b** and then multiply the results.

To get the length of a vector, we will use Pythagoras Theorem. Given we already have vectors, the x and y components can be individually squared, added together and then the square root of the result is our magnitude.

$$|a| = \sqrt{2^2 + 2^2} = \sqrt{8} = 2.82$$
$$|b| = \sqrt{0^2 + 3^2} = \sqrt{9} = 3$$

Now that we have the magnitude of both vectors, we can multiply them together to give us the denominator of the equation:

$$|a||b| = 2.82 \times 3 = 8.46$$

Now all that is left for us to do is to put each of these results into Formula 2.1 and to calculate the result:

$$\text{Cos } \theta = \frac{6}{8.46} = 0.7$$

Remember we said that our formula gives us cos of the angle. Well, this is not what we were looking for. What we wanted was the angle itself. So, using the rearranged formula shown in Formula 2.2, we can plug our result of 0.7 into the inverse cos function to give us this. The result is 45.57°, which looks reasonable when you look back at Image 2.5.

$$\text{Cos}^{-1}(0.7) = 45.57°$$

SIMPLIFIED DOT PRODUCT

We can simplify the whole process if we choose to only work with unit vectors. This reduces our equation seen in Formula 2.1 to what we have in Formula 2.3. The little dashes above **a** and **b** signify they have a length of one (unit vectors).

$$\text{Cos } \theta = \bar{a} \cdot \bar{b}$$

FORMULA 2.3 Simplifi ed dot product equation.

To calculate a unit vector, we need to normalise the vector. We do this by dividing each component of the vector by its length. We already calculated the magnitude of our vectors. If you remember the vertical lines either side of a vector name signifies the magnitude. So $|\mathbf{a}|$ was equal to 2.82 and $|\mathbf{b}|$ was equal to 3.

Using these values, we can now calculate the unit vector of both of our vectors:

$$\bar{a} = \left(\frac{2}{2.82}, \ \frac{2}{2.82} \right) = (0.7, \ 0.7)$$

$$\bar{b} = \left(\frac{0}{3}, \ \frac{3}{3} \right) = (0, \ 1)$$

Next, we repeat the process we followed earlier to calculate the dot product, but this time we plug in the component values from the unit vectors:

$$\bar{a} \cdot \bar{b} = (0.7 \times 0) + (0.7 \times 1)$$

$$= \quad 0 \ + 0.7$$

$$= \quad 0.7$$

As you can see, this results in 0.7, which is the same as the original approach. This makes sense as all we have done is split out the normalisation of the vectors into a separate step. In games development you will quite often be doing this anyway, so if you are, then the reduced version of calculating the dot product is the way to go. Something to be wary of, however, is that if you do use the reduced version of the formula seen in Formula 2.3, you MUST use unit vectors otherwise the output will be garbage.

Unit Circle

One final thing to cover, which I feel is important, is to take a look at a unit vector on a unit circle. In the above equations, we came up with 0.7, which we then plugged into the inverse cos function to get us an angle. But what is that 0.7 value all about? Take a quick look at Image 2.6. You can see that our unit vector is pointing vertically up with a value of 1.0 in this direction. The opposite direction is −1.0 and at either side halfway around the circle we have 0.0. If our unit vector was to be pointing in another direction, the circle turns to match as our unit vector always points to 1.0.

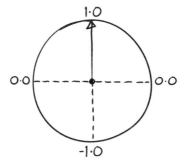

IMAGE 2.6   Unit circle with unit vector.

When thinking about the dot product and a unit circle, our first vector (vector **a** in the above examples) is the one that points to 1.0. If the second vector is also pointing in the same direction as the first vector, the dot product will result in 1.0, meaning the angle between the two vectors is zero. If we were to superimpose a second vector onto the unit circle, we would clearly see if it also pointed to 1.0, thus pointing in the same direction as the first vector. So, a dot product of 1.0 means the two vectors are facing the same direction. Another interesting point to note is that if the second vector is perpendicular to the first, that is, at a right angle, then the dot product would be 0.0. From this we would know that the angle would be 90° between the two. Go ahead and try. Choose a degree and map that to the circle in Image 2.7. This image already gives some key angles in red, with the dot product results in black, but feel free to add more.

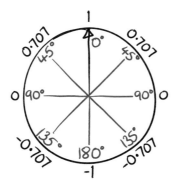

IMAGE 2.7   Unit circle with key degree segments and dot product results.

Notice how this approach does not actually inform us as to which direction we need to rotate. If the dot product returned 0.0 meaning a 90° turn, do we turn left or right? That is a good question, and if our agent was to turn in the wrong direction, it would look very silly.

DETERMINING LEFT OR RIGHT TURNS

We should store the right-facing vector for our agents. This is a vector that is perpendicular to the facing direction. In other words, it points out the right side of the agent (see Image 2.8). As the agent turns, the facing direction changes, and so does the right-facing vector – it MUST always be perpendicular to the facing direction.

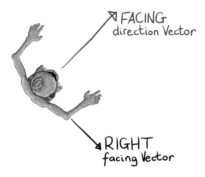

IMAGE 2.8   Right-facing vector.

Using the right-facing vector and the target direction vector, we can repeat the dot product to determine whether the rotation required is a left turn or a right turn. Remember, we need to ensure our vectors are normalised for this to work.

$$\overline{a} \cdot \overline{b} = \left(\overline{a}_x \, \overline{b}_x \right) + \left(\overline{a}_y \, \overline{b}_y \right)$$

The dot product will return a value greater than zero if it is a right turn, and a value less than zero if it is a left turn. So let us step through this. Take a look at Image 2.9, which shows the same zombie, along with a target to look at. I have taken the steps described in the previous section to determine that this is a 45° turn.

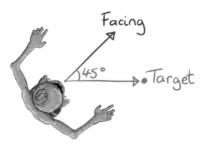

IMAGE 2.9   45° Turn to target.

However, let us place the target position to the other side of the zombie. We now have what you can see in Image 2.10 and this highlights the issue we are about to solve. We know we need to turn 45° to face the target, but we have no idea which direction to turn in.

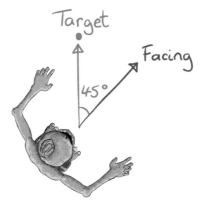

IMAGE 2.10   Also, a 45° turn to the target.

Let us place the unit circle around the zombie, but this time we will be using the right-facing vector. This is the vector that will be used first in our dot product calculation (the **a** vector in the formula **a.b**) and points to 1.0 on the circle. Take a look at Image 2.11.

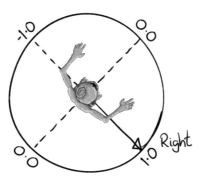

IMAGE 2.11   Unit circle based on right-facing vector.

Now take a look at Images 2.12 and 2.13. These images show the exact same zombie, with the unit circle oriented to the right-facing vector, but we have highlighted areas to indicate values greater than zero and less than zero. Take a look at the zombie in these images. Notice that it is still facing its original direction. It has not moved yet, and the highlighted areas are to the left and right of it.

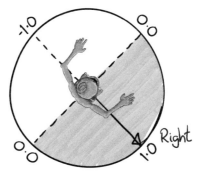

IMAGE 2.12   Right turn zone.

Whichever zone the second vector (the **b** vector in the formula **a.b**) falls into will
return a result greater than zero (Image 2.12) or less than zero (Image 2.13).

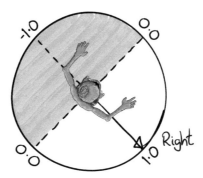

IMAGE 2.13   Left turn zone.

Hopefully you are still with me at this point. If not, it might make more sense when
we add those targets we saw earlier. So let us do that now. Images 2.14 and 2.15 show
the two different 45° turns and highlight the relevant zone that they fall within.

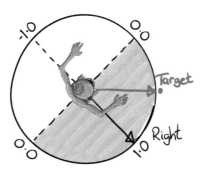

IMAGE 2.14   45° turn seen in Image 2.9.

If you plug in the vector components into the dot product formula, you do not need to care what the value is. All we need to know is if it is a positive or negative value. So, in code all you need is a simple if statement to determine whether you rotate left or right.

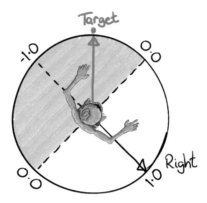

IMAGE 2.15   45° turn seen in Image 2.10.

ROTATION

At times you will want to rotate around a point. This may be around the origin or some arbitrary point in the world. To explain how to handle both situations, we are splitting the problem into two parts.

ROTATE AROUND THE ORIGIN

Rotating around the origin is the simplest form of the equation. We need to use both the cos function and the sin function along with the angle we wish to rotate by. This is done as follows:

$$\text{new } X \text{ position} = \text{Cos (angle)} - \text{Sin (angle)}$$
$$\text{new } Y \text{ position} = \text{Sin (angle)} + \text{Cos (angle)}$$

Using this approach, the rotated position will always be in the unit circle context. This means the rotated position is essentially the unit up vector rotated by the required degrees. Take a look at Image 2.16. Before the formula above is processed, the point is 1 unit up.

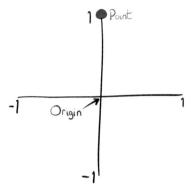

IMAGE 2.16   Starting position of point in unit space.

If we want to rotate by 45°, the point will be as seen in Image 2.17 after using the above formula.

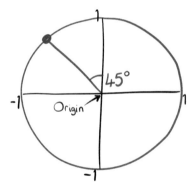

IMAGE 2.17   Unit vector rotation from up vector.

If we wanted to rotate an object around the origin, we can simply incorporate its world position into the above formula. This is done as follows:

$$\text{new } X \text{ position} = \text{Current } X \text{ position} * \text{Cos (angle)} \\ - \text{Current } Y \text{ position} * \text{Sin (angle)}$$

$$\text{new } Y \text{ position} = \text{Current } X \text{ position} * \text{Sin (angle)} \\ + \text{Current } Y \text{ position} * \text{Cos (angle)}$$

This saves us from needing to rotate around the origin and then scaling as it is all done in the same calculation.

ROTATE AROUND A POINT

What about if we wanted to rotate a position around an arbitrary point in the world, for example say we wanted to rotate a turret around a spaceship and the spaceship is not at the origin. It does not make sense to rotate the turret around the origin. Instead, we want to make our spaceship's position the rotation point.

Let us step through this with some images. Take a look at Image 2.18, which sets the scene. The object would be our spaceship and the facing vector is the direction of the turret.

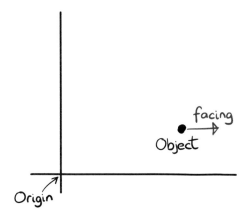

IMAGE 2.18   Object in world space.

The first thing we need to do is to calculate the local offset vector. This is the position we want to rotate minus the position we want to rotate around:

$$\text{Local Offset} = \text{Offset Point} - \text{Rotation Point}$$

If you take a look at Image 2.19, you can see what this vector looks like.

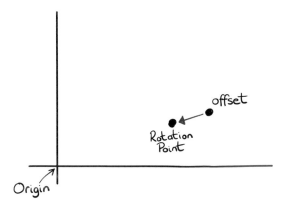

IMAGE 2.19   Offset minus rotation point.

What we are doing here is using the rotation point as a local origin around which we can rotate. Image 2.20 depicts the locality we are now working with.

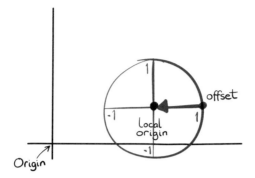

IMAGE 2.20   Rotation point becomes local space.

Now we can calculate the rotated offset position using the same formula we used previously, but this time we use the local offset position:

$$\text{Rotated Offset.x} = \text{Local Offset.x} * \text{Cos (angle)} - \text{Local Offset.y} * \text{Sin (angle)}$$

$$\text{Rotated Offset.y} = \text{Local Offset.x} * \text{Sin (angle)} + \text{Local Offset.y} * \text{Cos (angle)}$$

All that is left to do is to add the rotated offset position to the rotation point we started with:

$$\text{newPosition} = \text{Rotation Point} + \text{Rotated Offset}$$

If we were to rotate 45° from the scenario shown in Image 2.19, using the above process, the result would look something like Image 2.21.

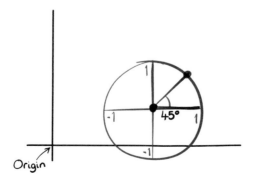

IMAGE 2.21   45° rotation.

MATH – PRACTICAL

PROJECT OVERVIEW

So, for this first project, we are going to start off small. We will only be coding a hand-ful of functions. One is to mathematically calculate the dot product for us, another is to calculate the magnitude of a vector, and another is to normalise a vector. I appreciate that the Unity game engine provides this functionality for us, but this book is about learning what happens under the hood. So we will be writing our own versions.

When running, this project will look like Screenshot 2.1. At the moment nothing happens, but when we have coded the required functionality, you will be able to click and hold the left mouse button to direct the red arrow. This is overlaid on a unit circle and the output on the screen gives us the dot product value, the number of degrees the arrow has rotated from the up direction and the equivalent value in radians.

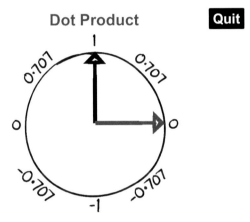

SCREENSHOT 2.1   Math project.

STEP-BY-STEP GUIDE

Open the Unity project named GameAi supplied with this book. Navigate through the folder structure to the Chapter2_Math folder. It is located in the Assets folder. Click on the Chapter2_Math scene. Run the application.

As you can see, nothing happens at the moment. So let us take a look at the code and make it work. Open the Scripts folder and locate the following two files: Arrow. cs and VectorMath.cs.

ARROW.CS

Looking first at Arrow.cs. No changes are required in this file, but it is worth just looking through and seeing what is happening. Locate the `Update()` function. As you can see, we first test to see if the left mouse button is being held. If so, we then calculate the vector from the centre of our unit circle to the mouse position. This could be a vector of any length, so we need to normalise it to get a vector in the same direction, but with a length of 1 unit. This is where our (yet to be coded) `VectorMath.Normalize()` function is used. Once we have the unit vector, we then get the dot product between the up vector (black arrow in our application) and our unit vector. Notice the use of `VectorMath.Dot()`. We will be coding that shortly. Next, we get the radians between the two vectors. This is done using the inverse cos function. To get the degrees, we need to convert from radians. This is done next by multiplying the radians by 57.29578 or the handy `Mathf.Rad2Deg` variable supplied.

At this point, we have a rotating arrow that has all the values we require. Unfortunately, the dot product does not tell us whether we need to rotate left or right from the up vector. So, we will handle that next.

We need to call our dot product function again, but this time instead of using the up vector, we want to use the vector pointing to the right of this. Conveniently for us this is simply the right vector. If we were to allow our black arrow to rotate and use this as our first vector in the dot product calculations, we would also need to calculate the corresponding right-facing vector to the black arrow. As I said, we are just using the up vector for the black arrow, so the right vector is simple for us to get.

As described in the theory part of this chapter, when we have the dot product between the right-facing vector and our unit vector, we can just test to see if it is positive or negative. We can then set the direction we want to rotate – negatively or positively. All that remains is for us to call the `RotateArrow()` function.

Right, let us code those functions and make all of this work. Open the VectorMath. cs file.

VECTORMATH.CS

There are a few functions in this file that will be used throughout this book. Some have already been coded, and others require us to add the code. Do not worry about those already coded for now, they will be used in subsequent chapters where we will go through them. If you have any problems, refer to the VectorMath_Solution.cs file located in the same folder as VectorMath.cs. This contains the complete solution, but all the code is commented out so it cannot cause any duplicate declaration issues for our project.

Step 1

So first, locate the `Magnitude()`function. We need to code this first as the `Normalize()` function will use it.

Where you see the following lines of code:

```
//Delete me.
return 0.0f;
```

Replace them with:

```
return Mathf.Sqrt((vec.x * vec.x) + (vec.y * vec.y));
```

Step 2

Next let us jump to the `Normalize()` function. Where you see the following lines of code:

```
//Delete me.
return Vector2.zero;
```

As we saw in the theory portion of this chapter, we need to use the magnitude of a vector to be able to get the unit vector. Lucky for us we just wrote a function to give us this. Add the following code:

```
float mag = Magnitude(vec);
return new Vector2((vec.x / mag), (vec.y / mag));
```

Step 3

Locate the `Dot()` function. Delete the following lines of code:

```
//Delete me.
return 1.0f;
```

Note that this function takes two vectors named **A** and **B**. The first thing we need to do is to ensure they are both normalised. I know we have normalised our vector in Arrow.cs, but we can never be sure, and if either **A** or **B** is not a unit vector, we will get very strange results.

To do this we will be using the `Normalize()` function we have just written. Add the following lines of code:

```
A = Normalize(A);
B = Normalize(B);
```

Finally, we need to do the actual dot product calculation. Add the following directly below the `Normalize()` function calls you just added:

```
return (A.x * B.x) + (A.y * B.y);
```

That's it! Now run the application and have a play with rotating the arrow. Be sure to watch the values as you rotate the arrow. It is important to understand what the dot product returns and how this relates to angles. Pay close attention to the angles. Notice they never go above 180°. That is because the value returned from the dot product is from 1 to −1 and this is mirrored on the left and right of the first vector in the dot product – the up vector in this example.

FUTURE WORK

Try modifying the project so you can rotate the black arrow, maybe by pressing and holding the right mouse button. Then calculate the dot product using this direction instead of the up vector. There is a handy `Perpendicular()` function in VectorMath.cs that will return the right-facing vector for you.

3 Steering Behaviours

How to move an agent across the game world is a simple enough problem to solve. We give them a target position, calculate a vector for the movement direction, normalise it and then use this vector, along with a movement speed to get us going. When we reach our target position, or at least a radius around our target position we stop. There are however a couple of things we have not considered. What if there is an obstacle in the way? What if our agent wants to avoid an enemy? Do we want the agent to abruptly stop when it reaches the target position, and look somewhat robotic, or to gradually come to a stop?

To answer these questions, we can turn to steering behaviours. There are a variety of tried and tested approaches, which when combined give us our desired behaviour. Steering behaviours will not navigate an agent through a complex environment, take a look at the pathfinding chapter for that, but they will help us to arrive at each node on a path, whilst avoiding obstacles enroute. We will be looking at some of the most commonly used steering behaviours, before we progress onto group behaviours.

STEERING FORCES

An individual steering behaviour will return a force to propel the agent through an environment in a particular manner. For example, you could have a steering behaviour that simply moves to a position, or a steering behaviour that evades an enemy. It may require multiple different steering behaviours to achieve the desired effect you are looking for, and the order in which these forces are applied can produce different results.

When coding your own steering behaviours, it is important that each behaviour does one thing. For example, do not try to create a behaviour that moves the agent towards a location *and* avoids obstacles. The returned force will achieve neither. Instead, create a behaviour to move towards a position and another behaviour to avoid the obstacles. We can then combine these behaviours to get the desired result. With all that being said, let us jump into some descriptions of the most commonly used behaviours. Take a look at Image 3.1. Our zombie is going to be used as the basis for the following explanations.

SEEK

First up is Seek. This behaviour will return a force that propels the agent to a particular location. This location could be static in the environment or a moving position. Either way, the process of calculation is the same. To Seek, we need to know the agent's current position, have a target location, the maximum speed a zombie can move at and the zombie's current velocity. And to achieve this, we will be using simple vector math.

DOI: 10.1201/9781003305835-3

IMAGE 3.1   A zombie to move.

Take a look at Image 3.2. We can see our zombie, but we can also see a target position we want to Seek. First, we need to deduct the zombie's current position from the target position and then normalise the resulting vector. This unit vector should then be multiplied by the maximum speed a zombie can move at to get the desired velocity. As the zombie is probably already moving, we also need to deduct the zombie's current velocity to get the required Seek steering force that will propel us to the target location.

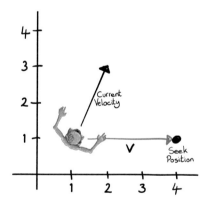

IMAGE 3.2   Vector to Seek position.

There was a lot of information in that explanation, so let us step through the process of calculating a desired Seek velocity. First, we need to get the numbers we will be dealing with. Take another look at Image 3.2. As you can see the zombie is located at (1, 1) and the position to Seek is located at (4, 1). The first step was to deduct the zombie's current position from the target position. This results in the vector labelled as 'v'.

$$V = (3,\ 0)$$

Next, we normalise this vector. We do this by dividing each component of a vector by the length of the vector. To get the length of a vector, we use Pythagoras Theorem.

$$|V| = \sqrt{(3\times3)+(0\times0)}$$
$$= \sqrt{9}$$
$$= 3$$

The mathematical depiction of a vector length is to have the vector name between two vertical bars. So, our vector **v** would become |v|. Obviously, you would not bother multiplying zero by zero, but for completion sake I have included this. We end up with a length of 3. This makes perfect sense as we are moving 3 on the horizontal axis and not moving on the vertical axis. To normalise the vector we now need to divide the *x* component by the length and divide the *y* component by its length. What we now have is a vector pointing in the same direction but scaled to a length of one. In this book, we will be using a little dash above the vector name to signify a vector with a magnitude of one.

$$\bar{V} = \left(\frac{3}{3},\ \frac{0}{3}\right)$$
$$= (1,\ 0)$$

As you can see, we end up with the unit vector (1, 0). This makes sense as we have no movement in the *y* component. All that remains for us to get our desired velocity is for us to multiply our unit vector by the maximum speed a zombie can move.

$$\text{Desired Velocity} = \bar{V} * \text{Maximum Speed}$$

This will scale the vector to a length which is as long as our fastest speed would allow us to move. Image 3.3 depicts this for us. Our desired velocity is now a vector with the values (2.5, 0).

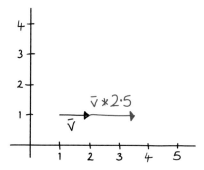

IMAGE 3.3   Unit vector scaled by a maximum speed of 2.5.

The final step to determining our Seek force is to deduct our current velocity from our desired velocity. We have to remember that if we are already moving, we need to incorporate this into the desired force.

$$\text{Seek Force} = \text{Desired Velocity} - \text{Current Velocity}$$

The current velocity of our zombie is a vector with the values (1, 2). Check back with Image 3.2 to confirm.

$$\text{Seek Force} = (2.5, 0) - (1, 2)$$
$$= (1.5, -2)$$

To depict the impact of this force on our current velocity, take a look at Image 3.4. This addition will move us in the right direction to the target position, but it is also clear that we do not quite reach the target. This is because we capped our movement to the maximum speed.

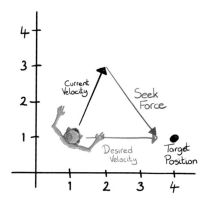

IMAGE 3.4   Seek force applied to the zombie's current velocity.

As the agent moves, the required Seek force will change. This will keep us heading in the right direction. This behaviour does not stop at the target location. Instead, it overshoots, meaning the Seek position is behind us, and as the force is recalculated, the agent will change direction and head back towards the target location, where it will overshoot again. If you have ever played the game Worms by Team17, you would have seen this in action when firing the homing missile.

FLEE

The Flee behaviour is essentially the opposite of Seek. This behaviour will return a force that propels the agent away from a target position. The position does not have to be static. If we were to use the location of a moving enemy as the position to flee from, the updated forces will continually force the agent away.

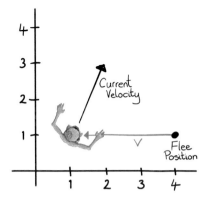

IMAGE 3.5   Vector from Flee position.

In the same way as we did for the Seek behaviour, let us step through the process of calculating a desired Flee velocity. First, let us get the numbers we will be dealing with. From Image 3.5, you can see the zombie is again located at (1, 1) and the Flee position is located at (4, 1). The first step was to deduct the Flee position from the zombie's current position. This results in the vector labelled as 'v'.

$$V = (-3, 0)$$

Next, we normalise this vector. We do this by dividing each component of a vector by the length of the vector. To get the length of a vector, we use Pythagoras Theorem.

$$|V| = \sqrt{(-3x - 3) + (0 \times 0)}$$
$$= \sqrt{9}$$
$$= 3$$

Next, we use the magnitude to get the unit vector for v. To normalise a vector, or in other words scale the vector to a length of 1, we simply divide each component of the vector by its magnitude. We know our magnitude is 3, and the components of vector **v** are (–3, 0), so let us go ahead and do that.

$$\overline{V} = \left(\frac{-3}{3}, \frac{0}{3} \right)$$

$$= (-1, \ 0)$$

As you can see, we end up with the unit vector (–1, 0). This makes sense as we have no movement in the *y* component. All that remains for us to get our desired velocity is for us to multiply our unit vector by the maximum speed a zombie can move.

$$\text{Desired Velocity} = \overline{V} * \text{Maximum Speed}$$

This will scale the vector to a length which is as long as our fastest speed would allow us to move. Image 3.6 depicts this for us. Our desired velocity is now a vector with the values (–2.5, 0).

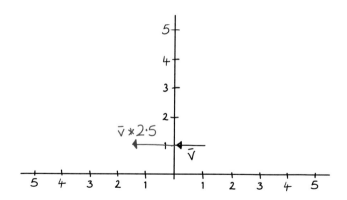

IMAGE 3.6   Unit vector scaled by a maximum speed of 2.5.

The final step to determining our Flee force is to deduct our current velocity from our desired velocity. We have to remember that if we are already moving, we need to incorporate this into the desired force.

$$\text{Flee Force} = \text{Desired Velocity} - \text{Current Velocity}$$

From our graph (Image 3.5), we can see that the zombie has a velocity vector with the values (1, 2). Check back with Image 3.5 to confirm.

$$\text{Flee Force} = (-2.5, 0) - (1, 2)$$

$$= (-3.5, \ -2)$$

To depict the impact of this force on our current velocity, take a look at Image 3.7. It is clear that this addition will move us in the opposite direction to the target position, but it is also clear that we do not quite reach the target. This is because we capped our movement to the maximum speed.

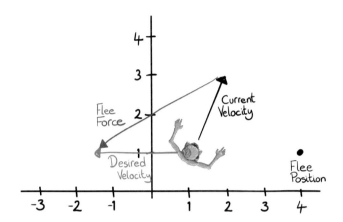

IMAGE 3.7   Flee force applied to the zombie's current velocity.

As the agent moves, the required Flee force will change. This will keep us heading in the right direction. This behaviour continually propels us away from the target location.

ARRIVE

Arrive is similar to Seek in that we move our agent towards a target; however, Arrive looks to slow our agent down and come to a gentle stop. To achieve this, we will be calculating a speed based upon a deceleration value. For the examples below, I have set DECELERATION to 0.5, meaning we will decelerate by a half. This value can be set to anywhere between zero and one, and, somewhere around 0.1 produces better results, but for this explanation, 0.5 makes things simpler to explain.

First, we need to calculate a vector from our current position to the location we wish to arrive at. Take a look at Image 3.8. On the left, you can see the calculated vector **v**. I have also included the max speed, which for this example is set to a magnitude of 20. This might be a little fast for a zombie but stick with me.

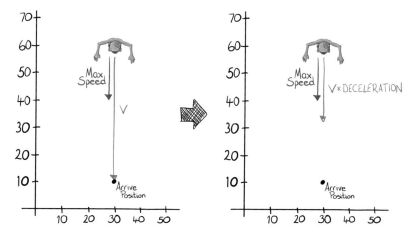

IMAGE 3.8   Calculated velocity greater than maximum speed.

Next, we need to scale **v** by our deceleration value to get our initial Arrive speed.

$$\text{Arrive Speed} = V * \text{DECELERATION}$$

As you can see from Image 3.8, on the right, this results in a vector with a magnitude that is still greater than that of our max speed, so we need to cap it. This means that if our Arrive speed is 27 (as in the image), we reduce it to 20 (our maximum speed). Image 3.9 gives us a visual representation of this.

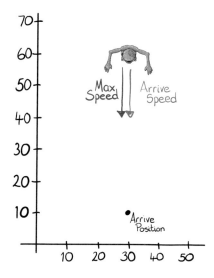

IMAGE 3.9   Capped at max speed.

To get our desired velocity using this information, we simply multiply **v** by our Arrive speed.

$$\text{Desired Velocity} = V * \text{Arrive Speed}$$

And then deduct our agent's current velocity to get the Arrive force.

$$\text{Arrive Force} = \text{Desired Velocity} - \text{Current Velocity}$$

And that's it.

But before we move on to the next behaviour, let us move our zombie a little and reassess the calculated speed. Take a look at Image 3.10, where our zombie has moved closer to the Arrive position.

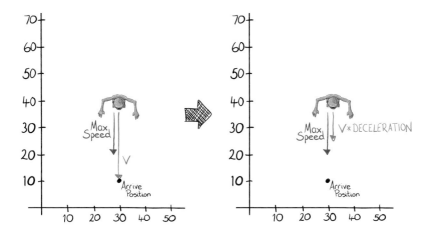

IMAGE 3.10   Calculated velocity decreased below maximum speed.

As you can see from the left image, **v** still has a magnitude greater than that of our maximum speed, but when it is multiplied by our deceleration value, we get a vector shorter than our maximum speed. This can be seen in the image on the right. This is the point we would cap our desired speed to the maximum speed, but since we have decelerated to less than the maximum speed, this is no longer necessary. Take a look at Image 3.11. As you can see, the arrow representing the arrival speed is not modified. It maintains its length, which is shorter than the maximum speed allowed. This is how our agent will slow down as it approaches the target.

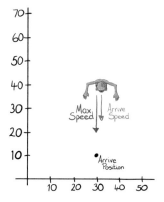

IMAGE 3.11   No need to cap speed.

Moving the zombie a little further, Image 3.12 shows the resultant vector to be dramatically reduced the closer it gets to the Arrive location.

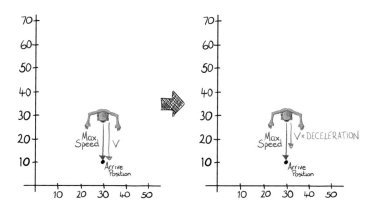

IMAGE 3.12   Calculated velocity slowdown increased.

A final thing to note with the Arrive behaviour is that if the magnitude of **v** (before
it is modified by the deceleration value) is equal to zero, that is, there is no distance
to the target, we just return an Arrive force vector with all components set to zero.

WANDER

A Wander behaviour returns a meandering steering force that gives the impression
of wandering through an environment. The difficulty with such an approach is that
we are generating a random position with each update, and the agent is continually
changing direction. If we are not careful the agent can look erratic or broken.

Let us take our zombie and place him at the centre of a unit circle. We will be orienting it to the facing direction of the zombie. Image 3.13 depicts our zombie. By generating a random number between −1 and 1, you can see we get the full 360° range. Well, you actually get 180°, we have to tell it to turn left or right, which gives us the full 360.

IMAGE 3.13 Zombie direction with unit circle.

Using the dot product formula described in the Math chapter, we can use this value to determine the angle of rotation required. It is a simple matter of plugging our value into the inverse cos function like this:

$$\theta = \mathrm{Cos}^{-1}\left(\begin{array}{l}\text{Random Value}\\\text{between } -1.0 \text{ and } 1.0\end{array}\right)$$

If you read the math chapter, you might be wondering what happened to the original dot product formula? Why are we not going through the steps of calculating vectors, normalising them and then performing the dot product itself?

$$\theta = \mathrm{Cos}^{-1}\left(\frac{a.b}{|a||b|}\right)$$

Well, nothing happened to it. We already have our −1 to 1 value, which is what the dot product would return, so we can go ahead and plug this into the inverse cos function to get the angle.

Remember that the angle returned does not indicate a positive or negative rotation. The simplest approach here is to randomly pick a left or right turn. Make it a 50:50 chance of doing either. This is done by generating a random number between 0 and 100, and if the result is less than 50, we leave the angle as it is. If the randomly generated number is greater than 50, then we add 180° to our angle to get the full 360 range.

Using this modified angle, we can now rotate the facing vector the required degrees like so:

$$X \text{ position} = \text{Cos (degrees)} - \text{Sin (degrees)}$$

$$Y \text{ position} = \text{Sin (degrees)} + \text{Cos (degrees)}$$

At this stage, we have a vector pointing in any direction with a length of 1. So let us scale this up to make our circle bigger. We do this simply by multiplying our vector by some radius value:

$$\text{Wander Direction} = \text{Unit Wander Direction} * \text{Radius}$$

Remember from the math chapter that the rotation formula above was around the origin, so we will also need to add the zombie's current position to get it located in the world correctly. We do not actually want it to be positioned on the zombie; otherwise, we would get a random seek position that could be in front of us as we want but could just as easily be behind us. We want to ensure this does not happen; otherwise, we end up with a behaviour that looks indecisive at best and broken at worst.

So let us move our wander position to a position ahead of our zombie. We can use the zombie's facing direction scaled by some scaling factor. When we have the projected position, all that is left for us to do is to add on our wander direction.

$$\text{Wander Position} = \text{Zombie Position}$$

$$\text{Wander Position} += \text{Facing Direction} * \text{Projected Distance Ahead}$$

$$\text{Wander Position} += \text{Wander Direction}$$

Let us take a visual look at each of these three steps. Image 3.14 shows the first two steps of the process. On the left, we calculate a random direction at origin. On the right, we then scale the vector to some predetermined radius. In this example, we have scaled the vector to a length of 2.

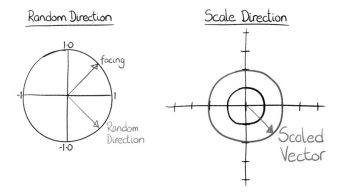

IMAGE 3.14   Scaling random direction.

We then added this scaled random direction to a position we projected ahead of the zombie. Image 3.15 shows the final step. Notice how regardless of the random angle and direction chosen it will always be ahead of the zombie? This ensures we do not calculate a direction to Seek that has our agent looking erratic. Be sure to have a radius smaller than your projected distance; otherwise, you will in fact end up with Wander positions behind you.

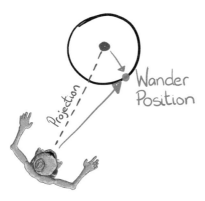

IMAGE 3.15   Final Wander position.

Now that we have a random Wander position, all that remains for us to do is to Seek towards it. Take a look back at the Seek section for details of how this is achieved.

COLLISION AVOIDANCE

We can now push our agent in the direction we want, but what happens if there is an obstacle in the way? Just using a Seek or an Arrive behaviour will not get us there, as it has no understanding of how to avoid obstacles. Similarly, Flee can see us running right into obstacles, rather than moving around them. So, we need another steering behaviour to handle this.

To ensure we do not enter the bounds of an obstacle, we will be projecting points around our agent to detect collisions. These protrude out like the whiskers on a cat and thus will henceforth be called whiskers. Take a look at Image 3.16. Our agent has five whiskers but could have fewer or more depending on your requirements. I have found that five is usually adequate but would not argue with anyone wanting more. Also, my agent can only move forward, so there is no need for whiskers to the rear but let us say you were coding a smart camera system that tracks a player in a three-dimensional environment; this will undoubtedly need to move up, down and backwards at times and as such should have whiskers all around it to ensure the camera never goes through the geometry.

IMAGE 3.16   Agent's whiskers.

Creating whiskers is simple enough. We use the facing direction, which as we know is a unit vector, and scale this by how far away we want the whisker to be. We then add this on to the agent's current position. For the whiskers that are not directly ahead, we just rotate the point around our agent by the required angle.

The distance we place a whisker ahead of the agent should be proportional to the speed with which our agent is moving. If we are moving fast, we want the whiskers further away from us to allow us to react earlier. If we are moving slowly, the whiskers do not need to be quite so far ahead, so we can bring them in closer to the agent. Image 3.17 depicts how a single whisker directly ahead would increase its distance from a zombie as the velocity increases.

IMAGE 3.17   Whisker position scaled with velocity.

When a whisker intersects with an obstacle, our agent needs to respond. It does this by calculating a force to repel the agent away from the collision. The faster the agent is moving, the further ahead the whisker will be, and thus the repelling force should be greater. Image 3.18 shows a zombie with a single whisker that has intersected with an obstacle.

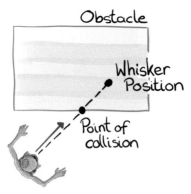

IMAGE 3.18   Collision with whisker.

Notice how the whisker is still at a location dictated by the speed of the agent? This is a good thing, because when we find our whisker is within the bounds of an obstacle, we can use both the whisker's current position and the point at which the whisker penetrated the obstacle to calculate a vector whose length will be equivalent to the force required to repel our agent. In other words, the distance within the obstacle that the whisker has managed to penetrate is the same as the distance required to scale our repelling force.

$$\text{Whisker Penetration} = \text{Whisker Position} - \text{Point of Collision}$$

Image 3.19 shows the vector calculated from the whisker position to the point of penetration.

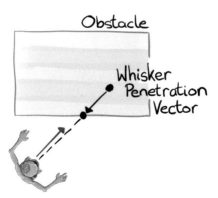

IMAGE 3.19   Whisker penetration vector.

You may think that we could just return the whisker penetration vector as our repellent force. This would work on many occasions but imagine the point we are seeking is directly ahead, but on the other side of an obstacle. The seek force would counteract the repel force and our agent would come to a standstill. Instead, we are going to use a repel direction for this obstacle. Simply put, we will calculate the vector from the centre of the obstacle to the agent and then normalise it. Take a look at Image 3.20.

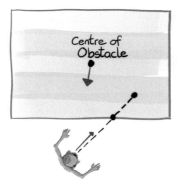

IMAGE 3.20   Determining repel direction.

When we have the relevant repel direction, we can scale this by the length of the whisker penetration vector, giving us a repelling force away from the obstacle, but not opposite to the desired seek direction.

$$\text{Repellent Force} = \text{Repel Direction} * |\text{Whisker Penetration}|$$

Image 3.21 shows the force calculated for Image 3.18 of the whisker when combined with the repel direction of the obstacle. We are still seeking to a position diagonally beyond the obstacle, but because the repellent force is coming from the centre of the obstacle, we should be gently pushed around it.

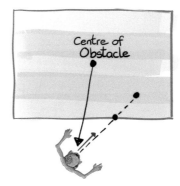

IMAGE 3.21   Repel direction scaled by whisker penetration length.

As described earlier, whiskers are projected at a distance scaled by the agent's current speed. As the obstacle avoidance force takes effect, the agent will slow down, and the whisker will move closer to the agent. This results in the repelling force reducing as we slow down.

   An agent with multiple whiskers has the possibility that more than one of them can be colliding with an obstacle at the same time. Rather than trying to combine all the repellent forces into a single force, it is more straightforward to handle the nearest intersection this frame and handle whichever is the nearest on the next frame. Eventually you will deal with all collisions as the agent slows and the whiskers move out of collisions. To determine which collision to handle, you should iterate through the list of whiskers and find the nearest point of penetration before calculating and returning the obstacle avoidance force.

EVASION

To evade an opponent, we could simply Flee from the opponent's current position. This will work to some degree, but it would look smarter if we predicted where the opponent was going to be and Flee from that position. This looks more intelligent as we are taking into consideration the fact that our opponent is moving and will not be at its current location for very long.

To do this we need to know the distance our agent is from the opponent, the direction the opponent is moving in and their speed. Using these details, we can predict where the opponent will be in a given time and then Flee from this position.

Deciding how much time ahead we use to predict the opponent's position can be a little tricky as we do not know when the opponent will change direction, and we cannot know the direction change until the opponent makes it. So, predicting where the opponent will be in 10 seconds is pointless, but so is predicting where they will be in 0.1 seconds– we may as well just use the opponent's current position and save ourselves the extra calculations. To address these issues, we should use a prediction time based upon the distance our agent is from the opponent and their movement speed compared to ours. The predicted position will be proportional to the distance between the two agents and inversely proportional to the accumulated velocities of the two agents.

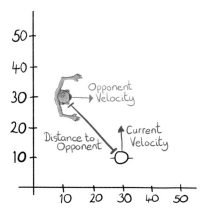

IMAGE 3.22   Agent at (30, 10) evading zombie at (10, 30).

If you take a look at Image 3.22, you can see that we have all the information we need to calculate the time ahead for our prediction. So, let us first get the vector to our opponent:

$$\text{Vector to opponent} = \text{Opponent Position} - \text{Agent Position}$$

Next, we use the magnitude of this vector and divide it by the accumulated speed of the two agents to get a floating-point time value.

$$\text{Prediction Time} = \frac{|\text{Vector To Opponent}|}{\left(\frac{\text{maximum}}{\text{speed}} + \frac{\text{opponent}}{\text{speed}} \right)}$$

All that remains is for us to calculate the position at the predicted time of the opponent, which we do by multiplying the opponent's velocity by the prediction time and add this to its current position.

$$\text{Flee Position} = \text{Opponent Position} + \text{Opponent Velocity} * \text{Prediction Time}$$

Now that we have a predicted position for the opponent, we can simply call the Flee behaviour, passing through this position. Take a look back at the section on Flee if you need to recap on what happens within the Flee behaviour.

INTERCEPT

Let us say we are now the zombie, and we want to close in on the opponent. We could simply Seek an opponent's position, but this can result in your zombie never reaching its prey. This will happen if the opponent is constantly moving. I appreciate this may be what you want from a zombie but let us say we have an especially clever zombie who wants to intercept its next victim rather than endlessly chasing. Instead of simply seeking, we should take into consideration where the opponent will be in a given time and head in that direction. This way we can cut the opponent off and the visual result is something more intelligent.

Determining the prediction time is done in the same manner as we did for Evasion. We need to take into consideration the distance we are from the opponent and how fast they are moving compared to us. Image 3.22 contains all the information we need.

To begin, we need to get the vector to our opponent:

$$\text{Vector to opponent} = \text{Opponent Position} - \text{Agent Position}$$

Next, we use the magnitude of this vector and divide it by the accumulated speed of the two agents to get a floating-point time value.

$$\text{Prediction Time} = \frac{|\text{Vector To Opponent}|}{\left(\frac{\text{maximum}}{\text{speed}} + \frac{\text{opponent}}{\text{speed}} \right)}$$

All that remains is for us to calculate the position at the predicted time of the opponent, which we do by multiplying the opponent's velocity by the prediction time and add this to its current position.

Intercept Position = Opponent Position + Opponent Velocity * Prediction Time

There is no need to try and predict where the opponent will be in a given time if we are directly behind them as the opponent's position is going to be closer. In this situation, we should simply call the Seek behaviour. To determine if we are directly behind the opponent, we use our trusty dot product again. Using our facing direction and the vector from our position to the opponent position, we can calculate the dot product, and if the value returned is greater than say 0.9, we know we are right behind them. Image 3.23 depicts this check.

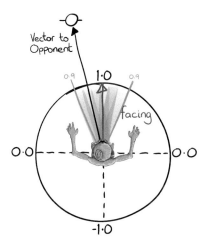

IMAGE 3.23   Determine if we are directly behind the opponent.

Note that we did not convert the result from the dot product into an angle. There is no need. We know that 0.9 is around the 25° range, which gives us a nice field of view.

OTHER BEHAVIOURS

There are a host of other behaviours that could be implemented, such as a Hide behaviour or an Interpose behaviour. These do not change much as the behaviour is really about figuring out the required position and then either calling Seek or Arrive to get you there. Just as you have seen with the Evasion and Intercept behaviours. Hide, for example, requires you to find a position on the other side of an obstacle to the opponent and Seek towards that. Interpose is about positioning your agent between two other agents. By getting a central position between the two agents, it is simply a matter of seeking it.

We are not going to spend any time looking at these behaviours as we have already covered the most difficult parts of these with Seek and Arrive. You can create behaviours to do all manner of things, just be sure to keep the idea simple though. You get an agent to Seek and Avoid by combining behaviours, not by creating a Seek and Avoid behaviour.

COMBINING BEHAVIOURS

Combining behaviours is not as simple as you may think. Not only do we need to consider which behaviours take priority, for example, avoidance is more important than seeking, but we also need to consider whether behaviours should be combined at all. Imagine having an agent that has both Seek and Flee behaviours. This is not a problem if you are seeking a different position than you are fleeing, but if these are the same position, then they will cancel each other out. Additionally, we need to weight each steering behaviour to ensure each behaviour enacts its force to the required amount.

MAXIMUM FORCE

Determining an overall steering force from all the active behaviours can be tricky. We do not want to simply add them all together and apply that to our agent; otherwise, we will get some very strange results. Instead, we want a vector returned for our accumulated steering force that is capped to a maximum length. When we have reached this maximum length, no further steering behaviours need to be calculated as we have no space to use their result.

So, let us decide on a maximum force. Visually depicted it would look something like Image 3.24. However, in practice the maximum force is simply a floating-point value which is used to compare against the magnitude of the accumulated force vector.

IMAGE 3.24   Maximum force allowed.

Next we will apply our obstacle avoidance steering behaviour. In this example, it falls below the maximum force allowed, so it is applied to our accumulated force in its entirety. See Image 3.25, which also shows the remaining force allowed.

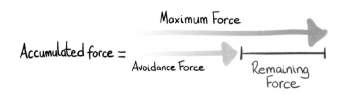

IMAGE 3.25   Avoidance force applied.

The remaining force is a floating-point value that is updated each time we add a steering force to our accumulated force. In this scenario, we deduct the magnitude of the avoidance force from the maximum force.

$$\text{Remaining Force} = \text{Maximum Force} - |\text{Avoidance Force}|$$

The next steering behaviour we want our agent to use is Seek. Image 3.26 shows the returned Seek force visually. As you can see, when it is added to the accumulated force, it goes beyond what is allowed. We check this by testing if the magnitude of the Seek force is less than the remaining force.

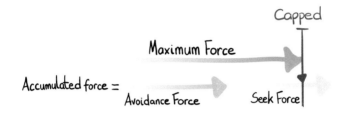

IMAGE 3.26   Seek force capped to maximum force.

As the Seek force in this scenario is greater than the remaining force allowed, we need to cap it at the length of the remaining force allowance. We do this by normalising our Seek force and then multiplying it by the remaining force.

$$\text{Modified Seek Force} = \overline{\text{Seek Force}} * \text{Remaining Force}$$

We now have an accumulated force at our maximum and there is no remaining force to fill. There is no point calculating any further steering behaviours as none of them will be applied. Image 3.27 shows our final accumulated force that will be applied to our agent this frame and the proportions made up of our individual behaviours.

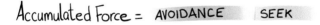

IMAGE 3.27   Accumulated force.

ORDER BY PRIORITY

The order in which we process the behaviours becomes very important, as those higher up the priority list have a greater chance of being used in the accumulated force described above. Deciding the order is the difficult part. You need to consider which behaviours are more important than others. Ensuring an agent stays out of collisions is always going to be more important than seeking or fleeing a position, so this should be processed first.

Prioritising them in code is a relatively trivial problem to solve. We simply process them in the order we want them handled.

WEIGHTING

To give us the ability to tweak the strength with which steering behaviours push our agent around, it is a good idea to incorporate some form of weighting. It can be difficult to get the values for the weights you find acceptable, and this is a trial-and-error task to accomplish. By having weights though, it gives us that ability to effect change without modifying the underlying code. To weight a force, we simply set a weight:

$$\text{Seek Weight} = 0.75$$

Then modify the corresponding steering force by the weight, before applying it to our accumulated force.

$$\text{Seek Force} = \text{Seek (Position)}$$
$$\text{Seek Force} * = \text{Seek Weight}$$

To add the force to the accumulated force, we need to call the function described above.

$$\text{Accumulate Force (Seek Force)}$$

It is up to the AI to decide which behaviours should be active at a given time. In later chapters, we will look at decision-making, and it will be in these states that different steering behaviours will be turned on or off.

GROUP BEHAVIOURS

If you have ever seen a flock of birds, you will know what we are going for with group steering behaviours. In 1987, Craig Reynolds described the approaches required to create to flocking behaviours [1]. This forms the basis of what we will be doing in this section, and lucky for us it builds upon what we have already covered.

There are three parts to achieving good flocking, and these are Separation, Alignment and Cohesion. Each will be covered in detail below, but to give you an idea of what this means, it is simply that we need our agents to stay away from each other, whilst maintaining a unified movement direction, whilst at the same time keeping them together. These behaviours in isolation do little. It is when they are combined that the magic happens.

There is no lead agent when flocking, all agents respond to each other within their own radius of awareness. Reynolds deemed this an agent's neighbourhood and looks something like Image 3.28. As you can see, the agent in the centre of the neighbourhood is our focus and it is aware of those within the highlighted arc.

We are sticking with zombies for the moment as they give us a great game scenario to work with. What we are going for is lots of zombies all meandering around, but generally heading in the same direction. There is no lead zombie, and all of them react to those around them. But how do we determine if another zombie is within our neighbourhood?

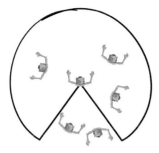

IMAGE 3.28   Agent in the centre's neighbourhood.

To create our neighbourhood we will be using the dot product again. The facing direction of the agent will be the first vector in the calculations and the second vector will be the vector to each of the other agents. If the dot product between these is greater than −0.5, then we include it in our group's behaviour calculations, if not, we just ignore it. Image 3.29 shows the same agents as in Image 3.28, but now at the centre of a unit circle. The red line to each zombie gives an estimate as to the value returned by the dot product. The area greater than −0.5 has been highlighted.

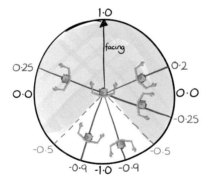

IMAGE 3.29   Agents within the neighbourhood.

SEPARATION

We do not want all our agents to occupy the same position, so we need to calculate a force that will keep them apart. Image 3.30 gives an example of what this force will do to our zombies. Compare this to their positions in Image 3.28.

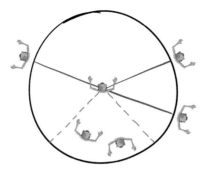

IMAGE 3.30   Separation.

To do this we need to go through each agent and check if they are within our
extended field of view and within a set distance. We do not want to include agents
that are too far away, otherwise you get strange results. For each valid agent, we
need to normalise the vector to them (**v** in this case) and divide it by its original
length.

$$\text{Force To Add} = \frac{\overline{V}}{|V|}$$

We then add this to our accumulated separation force.

$$\text{Accumulated Seperation Force} += \text{Force To Add}$$

When all valid agents have been processed, the accumulated force is returned.

ALIGNMENT

We generally want our agents to move in the same direction as those within the
neighbourhood. That is not to say every agent should be moving in the same direction. Not at all. Agents further away may be heading in a different direction, which
is fine; if they get within our neighbourhood, then their direction will have an impact
upon us and ours will in turn affect them. This is how we get the natural flow of
movement we see in flocking birds.

   The result we are looking for is shown in Image 3.31. This shows how we would
like all our zombies to align.

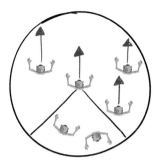

IMAGE 3.31 Alignment.

To achieve this, as with separation, we only consider those agents within our neighbourhood. For each valid agent we accumulate their facing direction and store it in an accumulated heading.

$$\frac{\text{Accumulated}}{\text{Heading}} += \text{Agent Facing}$$

When all valid agents have been processed, we then divide the overall total by the number of valid agents. This will give us the heading we want to move in.

$$\text{Alignment Force} = \frac{\text{Accumulated Heading}}{\text{Number of Valid Agents}}$$

The alignment force is reached by subtracting our current facing direction.

COHESION

To ensure our agents do not just move away from each other when using Separation, we need some way to keep agents coming back together. Image 3.32 shows the agents being pulled towards the agent in question.

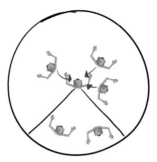

IMAGE 3.32   Cohesion.

To achieve this, we need to iterate through the other agents and for those considered valid, we accumulate their positions.

$$\text{Accumulated Position} += \text{Agent Position}$$

When we have processed all valid agents, the accumulated vector is divided by the number of valid agents to give us a position that resides central to all agents.

$$\text{Cohesion Force} += \frac{\text{Accumulated Position}}{\text{Number of Valid Agents}}$$

We then call the Seek function described earlier to move us to this position.

SUMMARY

As with steering behaviours, our agents can only move at a maximum speed, which means they can only have a maximum force applied to them. This means the forces returned by the separation, alignment and cohesion functions will probably not all take effect. So, the order in which these are applied is important. In general, separation is more important than alignment, and alignment is more important than cohesion. In other words, it is more important that our agents stay apart than having them head in the same direction, but it is also more important that they head in the same direction than moving them together.

FINAL THOUGHTS

You will use steering behaviours a lot when developing games. So, it is important to understand how they work. When developing your own behaviours, just make sure you keep them simple. They should only do one thing. We get complex agents by combining simple behaviours.

You probably will not be using flocking behaviours too much, but if you do, it is good to have the knowledge to draw on. In the next section, we will be coding a horde of zombies chasing the player around a shopping centre. This will bring together everything we have covered in this chapter.

REFERENCE

1. Reynolds, C. W. (1987). Flocks, Herds, and Schools: A Distributed Behavioral Model, in *Computer Graphics*, 21(4) (SIGGRAPH '87 Conference Proceedings) pp. 25–34.

STEERING BEHAVIOURS – PRACTICAL

PROJECT OVERVIEW

This project takes the form of the player being trapped in a shopping mall. Zombies will spawn every so often and give chase. The player can avoid the zombies and shoot them using the arrow keys and spacebar. Eventually the sheer number of zombies will overwhelm the player. When running, this project will look like Screenshot 3.1.

To enable the zombies to do this, we are going to be coding the various steering behaviours required. These include Seek, Arrive, Flee, Avoidance, Wander and Flocking. We will also need to code a function to combine the various active steering behaviours and return a single vector.

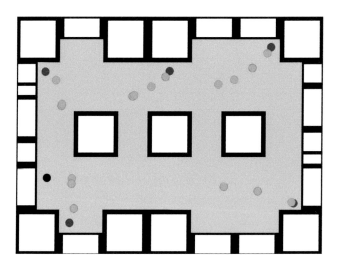

SCREENSHOT 3.1   Steering behaviours project.

From an under-the-hood visual perspective, you will be able to see what each zombie character is doing if you look at the Scene view in the Unity game engine. Lines are drawn to show the direction each zombie is heading as can be seen in Screenshot 3.2.

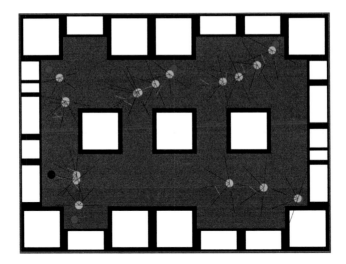

SCREENSHOT 3.2   Debug output.

STEP-BY-STEP GUIDE

Open the Unity project named GameAi supplied with this book. Navigate through the folder system to the Chapter3_SteeringBehaviours folder. It is located in the Assets folder. Click on the Chapter3_SteeringBehaviours scene. Run the application.

The black circle is the player, the blue circles are the zombie spawners, and the green circles are the zombies. As you can see, the zombies do not do anything at the moment, but you can move the player around and fire your weapon. You probably cannot see the blue circle either, this is because zombies have spawned on them and are yet to move. Let us take a look at the code and make those zombies come to life. Open the Scripts folder and locate the following file: SteeringBehaviours.cs.

STEERINGBEHAVIOURS.CS

This file is where all the different steering behaviours are found and where the functionality to combine behaviours is located. As you progress through the various examples below, if at any time you have any problems, please refer to the SteeringBehaviours_Solution.cs file located in the same folder as SteeringBehaviours. cs. This contains the complete solution, but all the code is commented out, so it does not cause any duplicate declaration issues for our project.

GetCombinedForce()

So first, locate the `GetCombinedForce()` function. Remove the following lines of code:

```
//Delete me.
return Vector2.zero;
```

The first thing we need to do is to create a vector to store our accumulated force:

```
Vector2 vAccumulatedForce = Vector2.zero;
```

Next, add the following to store how much force remains of our maximum allowance. The maximum force is set at the top of the file and stored in the variable fMaximumForce.

```
float fRemainingForceAllowance = fMaximumForce;
```

Avoidance is our primary concern, so we will deal with that first. We need to check if it has been enabled, otherwise we skip this behaviour. Find the following if statement:

```
if (bEnabled_Avoidance)
{
   //Add Avoidance code here.
}
```

Remove the comment in between the brackets. All subsequent code relating to avoidance is added between these brackets.

Next, we can call the Avoidance() function to get the desired avoidance force. We need to multiply this by the weighting in variable fAvoidanceWeight set at the top of the file:

```
Vector2 vAvoidanceForce = Avoidance() * fAvoidanceWeight;
```

As this is the first force we are calculating, we can simply see if this is greater than the allowed maximum force. We do this by getting the magnitude of the avoidance force. If it is greater, then we need to cap it to the maximum. This is achieved by getting the unit vector in the direction of the avoidance force and scaling it by the maximum force allowed. Add the following to achieve this:

```
if (VectorMath.Magnitude(vAvoidanceForce) >
fRemainingForceAllowance)
{
     return VectorMath.Normalize(vAvoidanceForce) *
fRemainingForceAllowance;
}
```

Now we can safely add the avoidance force to the accumulated force vector:

```
vAccumulatedForce += vAvoidanceForce;
```

We need to refresh the variable storing the remaining force allowed. This will be used to check against all other behaviours. As avoidance is always the first behaviour to be processed, we can guarantee that fRemainingForceAllowance is equal to the maximum force.

```
fRemainingForceAllowance = fMaximumForce - VectorMath.
Magnitude(vAccumulatedForce);
```

The Flocking check comes next. This follows the same process as the avoidance explanation given above. The only differences are that the flocking enabled variable is used, the `Flocking()` function is called and the flocking weight is used. I'm not going to repeat everything but have included the code. Find the following if statement:

```
if (bEnabled_Flocking)
{
   //Add Flocking code here.
}
```

Remove the comment in between the brackets. All subsequent code relating to flocking is added between these brackets:

```
Vector2 vFlockingForce = Flocking() * fFlockingWeight;

if (VectorMath.Magnitude(vFlockingForce) >
fRemainingForceAllowance)
{
    vAccumulatedForce += VectorMath.Normalize(vFlockingForce)
* fRemainingForceAllowance;
    return vAccumulatedForce;
}

vAccumulatedForce += vFlockingForce;

fRemainingForceAllowance = fMaximumForce - VectorMath.
Magnitude(vAccumulatedForce);
```

The Seek check comes next. This follows the same process as those described above. The only differences here are that Seek specific variables and functions are used. Find the following if statement:

```
if (bEnabled_Seek)
{
   //Add Seek code here.
}
```

Remove the comment in between the brackets. All subsequent code relating to Seek is added between these brackets:

```
Vector2 vSeekForce = Seek(targetTransform.position) *
fSeekWeight;

if (VectorMath.Magnitude(vSeekForce) >
fRemainingForceAllowance)
{
   vAccumulatedForce += VectorMath.Normalize(vSeekForce) *
fRemainingForceAllowance;
    return vAccumulatedForce;
}
```

```
vAccumulatedForce += vSeekForce;

fRemainingForceAllowance = fMaximumForce - VectorMath.
Magnitude(vAccumulatedForce);
```

The Arrive check comes next. This again follows the same processes as above. Find the following if statement:

```
if (bEnabled_Arrive)
{
   //Add Arrive code here.
}
```

Remove the comment in between the brackets. All subsequent code relating to Arrive is added between these brackets:

```
Vector2 vArriveForce = Arrive(targetTransform.position) *
fArriveWeight;

if (VectorMath.Magnitude(vArriveForce) >
fRemainingForceAllowance)
{
   vAccumulatedForce += VectorMath.Normalize(vArriveForce) *
fRemainingForceAllowance;
   return vAccumulatedForce;
}

vAccumulatedForce += vArriveForce;

fRemainingForceAllowance = fMaximumForce - VectorMath.
Magnitude(vAccumulatedForce);
```

Flee is the next behaviour to handle. Find the following if statement:

```
if (bEnabled_Flee)
{
   //Add Flee code here.
}
```

Remove the comment in between the brackets. All subsequent code relating to Flee is added between these brackets:

```
Vector2 vFleeForce = Flee(targetTransform.position) *
fFleeWeight;

if (VectorMath.Magnitude(vFleeForce) >
fRemainingForceAllowance)
{
   vAccumulatedForce += VectorMath.Normalize(vFleeForce) *
fRemainingForceAllowance;
   return vAccumulatedForce;
}
```

```
vAccumulatedForce += vFleeForce;

fRemainingForceAllowance = fMaximumForce - VectorMath.
Magnitude(vAccumulatedForce);
```

The final behaviour we are going to handle for this demonstration is the Wander behaviour. Find the following if statement:

```
if (bEnabled_Wander)
{
    //Add Wander code here.
}
```

Remove the comment in between the brackets. All subsequent code relating to wander is added between these brackets:

```
Vector2 vWanderForce = Wander() * fWanderWeight;

if (VectorMath.Magnitude(vWanderForce) >
fRemainingForceAllowance)
{
    vAccumulatedForce += VectorMath.Normalize(vWanderForce) *
fRemainingForceAllowance;
    return vAccumulatedForce;
}

vAccumulatedForce += vWanderForce;

fRemainingForceAllowance = fMaximumForce - VectorMath.
Magnitude(vAccumulatedForce);
```

Now that we have handed all the required behaviours, all that is left for us to do is to return the accumulated force that has been calculated throughout all the above blocks of code:

```
return vAccumulatedForce;
```

Seek()

Locate the `Seek()` function. The first thing to notice is this function takes in a target position as its only parameter. So, using this position we can calculate a vector from our current position to the target position.

Remove the following lines of code:

```
//Delete me.
return Vector2.zero;
```

And replace it with:

```
Vector2 vecToTarget = targetPosition - (Vector2)transform.
position;
```

We actually need a normalised version of this vector, so add the following line next:

```
vecToTarget = VectorMath.Normalize(vecToTarget);
```

Using this normalised vector, we can now calculate the desired velocity with the following line of code:

```
Vector2 desiredVelocity = vecToTarget * baseEntity.
GetMaxMoveSpeed();
```

As we are probably currently moving, we need to deduct our current velocity from the desired velocity:

```
desiredVelocity -= baseEntity.GetCurrentVelocity();
```

Finally, we return the desired force:

```
return desiredVelocity;
```

Arrive()

Locate the `Arrive()` function and delete the following lines of code:

```
//Delete me.
return Vector2.zero;
```

We need to specify what our deceleration will be. Add the following:

```
const float fDECELERATION = 0.1f;
```

Next we need to calculate the vector to the target position that was passed in as a parameter:

```
Vector2 vecToTarget = targetPosition - (Vector2)transform.
position;
```

To determine whether we should be slowing down, we need to know how far away we are from the target. We can determine this by calculating the magnitude of the vector we just got:

```
float fDistanceToTarget = VectorMath.Magnitude(vecToTarget);
```

The next step is to check if the variable `fDistanceToTarget` is greater than the desired threshold. For this, we are going to simply check if it is greater than zero:

```
if (fDistanceToTarget > 0)
{
```

Within this if statement bracket, we are going to calculate the desired velocity. The first step is to calculate the speed we wish to move at. This is where our deceleration variable is needed:

```
float fSpeed = fDistanceToTarget * fDECELERATION;
```

It may be possible that we are so far away, and the vector to the target we calculated is so long that the desired speed we just calculated is greater than our allowed maximum speed. So, we need to cap this:

```
fSpeed = Mathf.Min(baseEntity.GetMaxMoveSpeed(), fSpeed);
```

Before we can calculate the desired velocity, we need to normalise the vector to the target, so add the following line:

```
vecToTarget = VectorMath.Normalize(vecToTarget);
```

Now we can use our normalised vector and our desired speed to get the desired velocity:

```
Vector2 desiredVelocity = vecToTarget * fSpeed;
```

As we are probably currently moving, we need to deduct our current velocity from the desired velocity:

```
desiredVelocity -= baseEntity.GetCurrentVelocity();
```

Finally, we return the desired force:

```
return desiredVelocity;
```

Remember to close off the if statement bracket like so:

```
}
```

After the if statement we need to return a vector with a length of zero to indicate no force is required. Remember, we only process the above code if the length of the vector to the target was above the threshold. If not, we still need to return a Vector2. Add the following:

```
return Vector2.zero;
```

Flee()

Locate the `Flee()` function. Using the target position passed in as a parameter, we can calculate a vector from this to our current position.

Remove the following lines of code:

```
//Delete me.
return Vector2.zero;
```

And replace it with:

```
Vector2 vecFromTarget = (Vector2)transform.position
- targetPosition;
```

We actually need a normalised version of this vector, so add the following line next:

```
vecFromTarget = VectorMath.Normalize(vecFromTarget );
```

Using this normalised vector, we can now calculate the desired velocity with the following line of code:

```
Vector2 desiredVelocity = vecFromTarget * baseEntity.
GetMaxMoveSpeed();
```

As we are probably currently moving, we need to deduct our current velocity from the desired velocity:

```
desiredVelocity -= baseEntity.GetCurrentVelocity();
```

Finally, we return the desired force:

```
return desiredVelocity;
```

Did you notice how this works exactly like the Seek behaviour described above apart from one difference. Instead of calculating the initial vector from our current location to the target position, we calculated the initial vector from the target position to our current location. This gives us a vector away from the target. The opposite direction to the vector we calculated in the `Seek()` function.

Avoidance()

Locate the `Avoidance()` function. Notice that after we have checked if the obstacle manager has been set up correctly, we call a function called `SetUpWhiskers()`. This function sets up five whiskers. One to the front, one to the left, one to the right, and one between the front one and the left and right. Take a look at Image 5.16 for an idea of what this looks like. This function has already been coded, but if you decide you want more or less whiskers, feel free to modify as required.

Back to the `Avoidance()` function. Locate the following code and delete it:

```
//Delete me.
return Vector2.zero;
```

We need to iterate through all of our whiskers, so add the following:

```
for (int whiskerIndex = 0; whiskerIndex < whiskers.Count;
whiskerIndex++)
{
```

The important part of a whisker is where it is located. So get the current whisker's position:

```
Vector2 currentWhiskerPos = whiskers[whiskerIndex];
```

Now we need to iterate through all of the obstacles. So add the following loop:

```
for (int obstacleIndex = 0; obstacleIndex < obstacleManager.
zCollidables.Count; obstacleIndex++)
{
```

And the first thing we do inside the loop is to get the current obstacle and check it exists. We do not want any errors due to null pointers:

```
CollisionRect obstacle = obstacleManager.
zCollidables[obstacleIndex];
if (obstacle != null)
{
```

Now we need to determine whether this whisker is inside this obstacle. We are going to do this using line-to-line collision. If we find a collision, we will need to store how much penetration there was, so create a variable to store this:

```
float fPenetration = 0.0f;
```

`LineToLineIntersection()` was one of the functions provided in the VectorMath. cs file already coded. It takes as parameters the start and end positions of two lines. It also takes in a reference to a Vector2. If these two lines intersect, the function returns a Boolean value of true and internally sets the reference to a Vector2 to the position of the intersection. This is useful for what we are about to do, because it allows us to know whether an intersection happened, and if so, where. Feel free to take a look back at the VectorMath.cs file.

In the `Avoidance()` function, we want to know if the line from our agent to the current whisker has intersected with any of the lines that make up the edges of the current obstacle. Lucky for us that all our obstacles are rectangular. Add the following to check the first side of the current obstacle:

```
Vector2 vIntersection1 = Vector2.zero;
bool bLine1 = VectorMath.LineToLineIntersection((Vector2)
baseEntity.transform.position, currentWhiskerPos, new
Vector2(obstacle.vPosition.x, obstacle.vPosition.y), new
Vector2(obstacle.vPosition.x + obstacle.width, obstacle.
vPosition.y), ref vIntersection1);
```

Add the following to check the second side of the current obstacle:

```
Vector2 vIntersection2 = Vector2.zero;
bool bLine2 = VectorMath.LineToLineIntersection((Vector2)
baseEntity.transform.position, currentWhiskerPos, new
Vector2(obstacle.vPosition.x + obstacle.width, obstacle.
vPosition.y), new Vector2(obstacle.vPosition.x + obstacle.
width, obstacle.vPosition.y + obstacle.height), ref
vIntersection2);
```

We do the same again for the third side of the current obstacle:

```
Vector2 vIntersection3 = Vector2.zero;
bool bLine3 = VectorMath.LineToLineIntersection((Vector2)
baseEntity.transform.position, currentWhiskerPos, new
Vector2(obstacle.vPosition.x + obstacle.width, obstacle.
vPosition.y + obstacle.height), new Vector2(obstacle.
vPosition.x, obstacle.vPosition.y + obstacle.height), ref
vIntersection3);
```

And for the fourth and final side of the current obstacle:

```
Vector2 vIntersection4 = Vector2.zero;
bool bLine4 = VectorMath.LineToLineIntersection((Vector2)
baseEntity.transform.position, currentWhiskerPos, new
Vector2(obstacle.vPosition.x, obstacle.vPosition.y + obstacle.
height), new Vector2(obstacle.vPosition.x, obstacle.
vPosition.y), ref vIntersection4);
```

We only want to continue if we found an intersection with one of the four lines that make up the edges of the obstacle. To do this, we are just going to do a simple check:

```
if (bLine1 || bLine2 || bLine3 || bLine4)
{
```

Inside this bracket, we need to calculate how deep the penetration was. Add the following:

```
if (bLine1) fPenetration = VectorMath.
Magnitude(currentWhiskerPos - vIntersection1);
else if (bLine2) fPenetration = VectorMath.
Magnitude(currentWhiskerPos - vIntersection2);
else if (bLine3) fPenetration = VectorMath.
Magnitude(currentWhiskerPos - vIntersection3);
else if (bLine4) fPenetration = VectorMath.
Magnitude(currentWhiskerPos - vIntersection4);
```

Next we need to get the vector between the entity and the centre of the obstacle. First, we need to create a Vector2 that describes the position of the obstacle at its centre:

```
Vector2 vCentreOfObstacle = new Vector2(obstacle.vPosition.x +
obstacle.width * 0.5f, obstacle.vPosition.y + obstacle.height
* 0.5f);
```

Now we can calculate the vector between the entity and the centre of the obstacle:

```
Vector2 vObstacleToMe = (Vector2)baseEntity.transform.position
- vCentreOfObstacle;
```

For us to use this vector, we need to normalise it. We can then scale it later by the required penetration:

```
Vector2 vUnitObstacleToMe = VectorMath.
Normalize(vObstacleToMe);
```

Now that we have the unit vector pointing in the required direction and the penetration, we can calculate the repelling force:

```
Vector2 vRepellingForce = vUnitObstacleToMe * fPenetration;
```

All that remains for us to do is to return this vector:

```
return vRepellingForce;
```

Remember to close off all the above brackets. There should be four of them.

After the loop, we need to return a vector with a length of zero to indicate no force is required. The desired result from this function is to return a repelling force, but if there were no collisions, there is nothing to repel against. So, add the following:

```
return Vector2.zero;
```

Wander()

Locate the `Wander()` function and delete the following lines of code:

```
//Delete me.
return Vector2.zero;
```

The whole point of a Wander behaviour is to have the entity move in a random direction, but not flip backwards and forwards. So let us start by getting a random dot product with which to turn to face:

```
float fRandomDot = Random.Range(-1.0f, 1.0f);
```

We need the angle of rotation that this random dot product equates to. So, we will do that next. Remember that we are using radians rather than degrees:

```
float radian = Mathf.Acos(fRandomDot);
```

As has been discussed in the first part of this chapter, the dot product does not actually tell us if the rotation is a left or right turn. We are going to decide whether to turn left or right randomly. Add the following, which says 50% of the time we turn left and 50% of the time we turn right:

```
if (Random.Range(0, 100) > 50)
{
    radian += Mathf.PI;
}
```

To ensure our agent does not just flip around on the spot, we need to project ahead of us. Take a look back at Image 5.15. The distance of the projection is based upon a variable named `fWander _ DistanceAhead`, which is set at the top of the file. This is used to scale the facing direction of the agent:

```
Vector2 vWanderPosition = (Vector2)baseEntity.transform.
position;
vWanderPosition += baseEntity.GetFacing() *
fWander_DistanceAhead;
```

Using the radian we calculated, we are going to get a unit vector pointing in the desired direction:

```
Vector2 vWanderDirection = VectorMath.
RotateAroundOrigin(radian);
```

Now we scale the wander direction by a variable named `fWander _ Radius` that is set at the top of the file:

```
vWanderDirection *= fWander_Radius;
```

The last step to getting the actual position we want to aim for is to add our wander direction to the projected wander position ahead of our agent:

```
vWanderPosition += vWanderDirection;
```

Last but certainly not least is for us to calculate the force required to get us to this new position. As the code is exactly that already written for the `Seek()` function, it makes more sense to call the `Seek()` function and pass through our wander position as the target position parameter. We can simply return the result of the `Seek()` function to the `GetCombinedForce()` function that called the `Wander()` function:

```
return Seek(vWanderPosition);
```

GROUP BEHAVIOURS

First we are going to take a quick look at the `Flocking()` function. This has already been coded, but it will help us if we have an understanding of what is happening.

The point of this function is to collate together all other entities that are considered to be within our neighbourhood. We do this by iterating through all other zombies and calculating the magnitude of the vector between us and them. If they are too far away, there is no need to do the next step. For those that are close enough, we need to determine if they are within the desired field of view (dot product range). Take a look back at Image 5.29. This field of view is set at the top of the file and is called `fFlocking _ FOV` and is set to 0.5f. Feel free to change this. Any zombies that are close enough, and within the desired field of view, are added to a list that we will pass through to the `Separation()`, `Alignment()` and `Cohesion()` functions.

Separation()

Locate the `Separation()` function and delete the following lines of code:

```
//Delete me.
return Vector2.zero;
```

This function is going to accumulate a lot of vectors, one from each entity within our neighbourhood in fact. So let us create a vector to store this:

```
Vector2 accumulatedSeparationForce = Vector2.zero;
```

As we need to iterate through all entities in the neighbourhood, open a for loop to do just that:

```
for(int entityIndex = 0; entityIndex < neighbourhood.Count;
entityIndex++)
{
```

Get the current entity:

```
BaseEntity otherBaseEntity = neighbourhood[entityIndex];
```

Next, calculate the vector from our position to the other entity:

```
Vector2 vecToOther = otherBaseEntity.transform.position -
transform.position;
```

Retain the magnitude of this vector as it is required later:

```
float fMagnitude = VectorMath.Magnitude(vecToOther);
```

Normalise the vector:

```
Vector2 unitVecToOther = VectorMath.Normalize(vecToOther);
```

Add to our accumulation vector, the unit vector divided by the stored magnitude:

```
accumulatedSeparationForce += (unitVecToOther / fMagnitude);
```

Remember to close off the for loop with the following:

```
}
```

When the above for loop has completed, we can return the accumulation vector to the `Flocking()` function:

```
return accumulatedSeparationForce;
```

Alignment()

Locate the `Alignment()` function and delete the following lines of code:

```
//Delete me.
return Vector2.zero;
```

Alignment requires a vector to store the accumulated heading. Create this now:

```
Vector2 accumulatedHeading = Vector2.zero;
```

We are going to iterate through all entities in our neighbourhood, so let us do that now:

```
for (int entityIndex = 0; entityIndex < neighbourhood.Count;
entityIndex++)
{
```

Get the current entity:

```
BaseEntity otherBaseEntity = neighbourhood[entityIndex];
```

For the accumulated heading, we simply add the facing unit vector of each entity in our neighbourhood:

```
accumulatedHeading += otherBaseEntity.GetFacing();
```

That is all for the loop, so add a bracket to close off.

Now we have iterated through the neighbourhood, we can use the accumulated heading to calculate the accumulated alignment force by dividing the accumulated heading by the number of entities in our neighbourhood:

```
Vector2 alignmentForce = (accumulatedHeading / neighbourhood.
Count);
```

The final step for our accumulated heading is to deduct our own facing direction:

```
alignmentForce -= baseEntity.GetFacing();
```

We can now return the alignment vector to the `Flocking()` function:

```
return alignmentForce;
```

Cohesion()

Locate the `Cohesion()` function and delete the following lines of code:

```
//Delete me.
return Vector2.zero;
```

Cohesion requires a vector to store the accumulated position. Create this now:

```
Vector2 accumulatedPosition = Vector2.zero;
```

We need to take a look at each entity in the neighbourhood, so let us open up a for loop to do this:

```
for (int entityIndex = 0; entityIndex < neighbourhood.Count;
entityIndex++)
{
```

Get the current entity:

```
BaseEntity otherBaseEntity = neighbourhood[entityIndex];
```

Add to our accumulated position vector the position of the current entity:

```
accumulatedPosition += (Vector2)otherBaseEntity.transform.
position;
```

That is all for this loop, so add a bracket to close it off.

Now we have iterated through the neighbourhood, we can use the accumulated position vector to get an averaged position. We do this by dividing the accumulated position vector by the number of entities in our neighbourhood:

```
Vector2 averagedPosition = (accumulatedPosition /
neighbourhood.Count);
```

The final step to calculating our cohesion force is to get the force required to seek towards our averaged position. We can do this by using calling the `Seek()` function we already coded and passing in the averaged position as the target position parameter:

```
Vector2 cohesionForce = Seek(accumulatedPosition);
```

We can now return the cohesion vector to the `Flocking()` function:

```
return accumulatedCohesionForce;
```

FUTURE WORK

There is a lot more that can be done with this project. Try out some of the suggestions below to ensure you really have a handle on steering behaviours.

- Add Evade and Intercept behaviours.
- Add a scoring system. Could be points for each zombie killed or maybe a survival time.
- Create other types of zombies that act differently to those currently in the game.
  - Maybe have one that intercepts the player.
  - Another could hide from the player until they are close enough to attack.

4 Terrain Analysis

Terrain analysis comes in many forms, and it largely depends on the style of game you are developing as to which approach you would take. The analysis you would need to do in a real-time strategy (RTS) game is vastly different from what you might do in a third person shooter for example. In this chapter, we will be looking at two specific approaches, which will give you a variety of ways to analyse the terrain that will ultimately aid your AI agents in their decision-making.

INFLUENCE MAPS

Influence maps are an intuitive way of spatial analysis. They are usually found in strategy games but can be used in any game that requires some form of terrain analysis. As RTS games are the main beneficiary of such an approach, we will be using this genre in our examples. Within a game like Age of Empires, or Civilisation, influence maps can be used for a variety of reasons, such as accessibility of terrain (mountains, rivers, bridges etc.), identification of unexplored areas, the vulnerability of friendly or opposing forces, highlighting pinch points, creating a fog of war effect, and much more. Combined, this gives our AI an overall picture of the current state of the game and allows for more informed responses to a given situation.

At its most basic level, we split the world up into a grid of cells, with each cell representing the data required for our game. This could be a single value to represent the influence exerted by the units in the area, or something more complex, with each cell containing a structure that holds all the data we require – occupancy, terrain accessibility, visibility, units killed in this area and so on.

TERMINOLOGY: INFLUENCE

Influence is the level of impact a unit or agent has upon an area.

Let us run through a simple example so you get the gist of it. We are going to use a single value for each cell to represent the influence of each unit. This influence is going to be very basic, with each unit exerting a value of 1 in the cell they are in, and then this influence is propagated across the grid. In an actual game, we would calculate the influence exerted by a unit based on a variety of elements, such as attack strength, defence strength, attack range, health and so on. Take a look at Image 4.1, where we have a 20×10 grid and there is a single friendly unit located at cell (9, 4). As you can see, this unit exerts its maximum influence on cell (9, 4) and this influence disperses across the grid. Friendly units exert influence across the grid in a positive way and are depicted as red shaded cells.

DOI: 10.1201/9781003305835-4

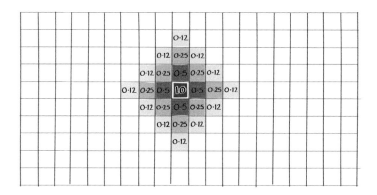

IMAGE 4.1   Single unit's influence.

The dispersal of influence is calculated using a drop-off function. For this example, the drop off is 0.5. That is to say, for each horizontal move, you take the current influence and multiply it by 0.5. Therefore, we go from full influence of 1.0, to an influence of 0.5, then 0.25 and so on. The drop off can be whatever you decide. A higher value, let us say 0.9, will exert influence further across the grid, whereas a lower value will restrict the influence exerted to near the unit.

An important thing to note is that you should have a cut-off point. I have a cut-off of 0.1. Any influence under this value is set to 0.0. This is important as you do not want to process the entire grid if you can help it. Using a drop-off function as described above will always give some influence to every cell; it is just that the values get smaller and smaller as you progress across the world.

Influence can be compounded if you have multiple units from the same team close enough that their influence reaches the same cells on the grid. Let us add a second unit and see how that impacts our influence map. Take a look at Image 4.2. Notice the two cells where the units' influence overlap. Together they exert a greater influence for their team. To calculate the influence for multiple units, we simply process each unit's influence in turn and then add their influence to the value already stored in a particular cell.

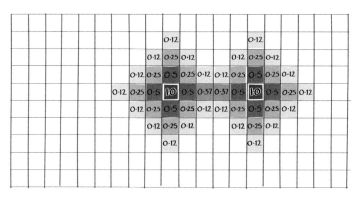

IMAGE 4.2   Two units' influence.

So what happens if there are also units from the opposing team? Let us add a few enemy units to our world and see the overall results. Take a look at Image 4.3. The influence exerted by the friendly forces has been removed for the moment, but their locations are highlighted. Calculating the influence exerted by the opposing force works the same way as it did for friendly units. The opposition will influence the map negatively, so when we add this influence to the current value stored in a particular cell, it will reduce the influence of the friendly team. If the value in a cell becomes negative, then the opposing force has a stronger influence in that area.

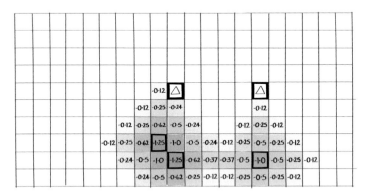

IMAGE 4.3 Opposing forces overall influence.

Now all we need to do is add both forces' influence together to get the combined influence map for the world. Remember positive values indicate an area where friendly forces exert control, whereas negative values indicate the opposing force has control. Take a look at Image 4.4, which has the final colour-coded influence map. The area between the two forces where neither team exerts control has been shaded green and represents a kind of 'no man's land'. The cells with 0.0 originally had influence, but the opposing force cancelled it out. Take a look back at Image 4.2 and compare the control they had over the grid. The influence exerted by friendly forces has not changed, but the opposing force exerts more influence, which has changed the dynamic of control.

IMAGE 4.4 Influence map considering all forces.

We can also identify the 'frontier' between these two forces. This is any area on the grid where the influence shifts from positive to negative values. If we were to have our forces act in a more aggressive nature, we could increase the influence of the friendly forces, which would push the frontier closer to the opposing forces. Likewise, if we want our AI to act in a more defensive manner, we simply reduce the influence friendly forces exert. This would bring the frontier closer to our troops.

TERMINOLOGY: FRONTIER

This is any cell within the grid that transitions from a positive influence to a negative influence.

Using the information gained, we can have our AI make smarter decisions. Now the decision we make is largely based upon what we want to achieve. For example, maybe we want to locate resources. How do influence maps help? Well, we can use the visibility values in a cell to determine when an area was last explored. Visibility can be a value representing when a cell was last explored. By ranking the nearest cells to our scout, we can choose the one with the highest visibility score as our target location. Each time our scout passes through a cell, the visibility score gets set to zero, meaning the next nearest high visibility scoring cell will be somewhere else. This way our scout continues to explore. Each time he comes across a resource or building, this can be stored within a database of our AI's understanding of the world.

When our scout has discovered resources, we would want to gather them. It makes sense for us not to send our workers into hostile territory. To determine if an area is safe, we can get the cells containing the resources we know about and rank them based upon influence. Those located in cells with the highest positive values are the safest. However, we can also send some of our troops to fortify the area as well. When our troops are close to the resources, they will exert influence on the area, pushing the frontier back and making the area safer.

The same approach could be taken with the defence of friendly buildings. If any are located in cells with a negative influence, they are vulnerable. Our AI should send some troops that way to fortify the area or build a wall to protect it. If we find that an enemy building is in a cell with a positive influence value, their building is vulnerable, and our AI should probably go and do something about this.

REFRESH RATE

There is a lot of data stored in an influence map, and updating every frame is not recommended. In an RTS game where the action is slower paced, an update every frame will not produce better results than if you refreshed the influence map once every two or three seconds. Something to consider is, do you have a shared influence map that all agents can access? This will reduce the processing hit dramatically than the approach of each unit or agent having their own version. This can lead to problems, however. It would appear that the AI is cheating if they were aware of resources that their own forces did not locate. You can expand the structure in each cell to allow for some values, such as visibility to be team specific, but bear in mind this increases the size of the influence map's memory requirements and the time it takes to process. We have said it before, but it is worth saying again. Everything is a balancing act. My advice would be to reduce the data required to an absolute minimum and have an influence map per team.

Hopefully you can see just how valuable this approach is in terms of giving us usable data and an up-to-date view of the environment, and just how extremely fluid this can be. Something else you might have noticed, especially with the gradient colours on the previous images is that influence looks very much like a heat map, which is something we are going to look at next.

HEAT MAPS

A heat map can also be constructed as a grid but is not restricted to this approach. As the heat map is very agent specific, it should serve a specific purpose. We could create a range of points rather than a grid, and this could be in any shape required. Possibly a circle of points like in Image 4.5 that moves with the agent, or a rectangle to fill a room like in Image 4.7 that is static, but gives us a clear route around the enemies, or for whatever purpose you require.

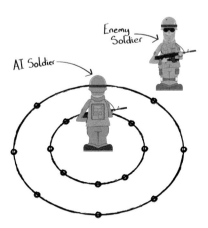

IMAGE 4.5   Circular points around the agent.

At each point, or cell if you are going with a grid structure, there should be a heat value. This should range from one to zero. One represents hot values, and zero represents absolute cold values. All values in between are a gradient on that scale of hot to cold. Depending upon your implementation, hot values are generally considered good and cold bad.

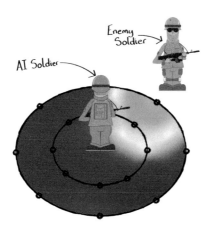

IMAGE 4.6   Blended values represented as colour.

So, looking at Image 4.6, you can see that the enemy soldier close by has cooled down the edge of the circular heat map. Our soldier will choose to move away from this enemy, giving us an alternative approach to obstacle avoidance that was discussed in Chapter 3 – Steering Behaviours.

Using another example, imagine a dungeon crawling game where we have an AI character navigating corridors and rooms filled with creatures. In this setting we could have the heat maps specific to rooms. An optimisation here could be to not process heat maps for rooms that have no AI characters present. Image 4.7 shows our character looking to navigate a room filled with zombies. The enemies in the room have cooled the heat map, and the hot points give us the best route.

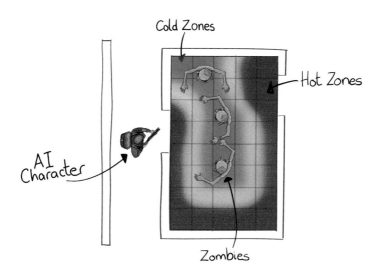

IMAGE 4.7   Rectangular heat map encompassing room.

Now Image 4.7 may look a little contrived. So, let us move those zombies around a little. Take a look at Image 4.8. The zombies have shifted positions and our heat map shows an alternate route through the room. As the zombies move, the heat map will change rapidly, giving our character up-to-date information as to the state of the environment changes and allow the AI to make better decisions. It is entirely plausible that there will be no route through this room, and in that case, the AI character will still seek to move to hot positions, which keeps them out of the zombie's reach. Assuming our character has a ranged attack, they can then pick off the zombies from a distance.

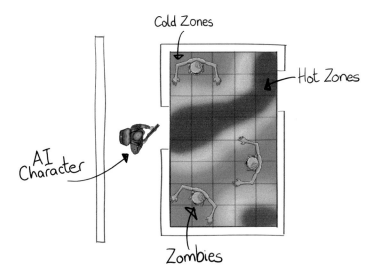

IMAGE 4.8 Zombies in different positions.

As an alternative approach to heat maps, let us say we want to create a heat map to aid a soldier on the field of battle. We do not really want to use pathfinding as the field is pretty much open space. The only obstacles are the other soldiers: friendly and opposing. Our AI-controlled character wants to make a run up the field, whilst avoiding everyone else. Well, that is where a heat map can prove useful. We could create an array of points ahead of the player and have a heat value for each. We then go through all the other soldiers on the field and cool down each point based on the distance the soldier is from the point. What we are left with is a range of values, that if drawn to the screen, it would look something like Image 4.9.

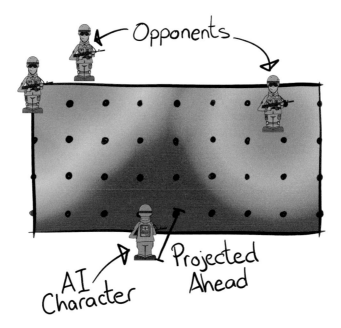

IMAGE 4.9   Heat map.

To get the colours seen in Image 4.9, we modify the colour based on the value stored at the point. High values are red (hot), and as the value decreases, it becomes blue (cold). As this heat map is projected ahead of our player, we then simply find the nearest hot position and move in that direction. If we project the heat map up field from our current position, as the character moves, so does the heat map. This means the AI will never actually reach the desired position and keep it continually moving.

TERMINOLOGY: HOT AND COLD

In the examples, hotspots are deemed good positions. Of course you could flip this in your implementation and have hot spots where the enemies are if you wish. Either way we get the same information from the heat map which allows us to make informed decisions.

REFRESH RATE

A heat map is a slightly different prospect to an influence map, especially if it is a small heat map and is moving with the agent in real time. You want the most up-to-date information you can get, but you do not want the processing hit. You may also want each agent to have their own heat map. You can still manage by having the maps update every one or two seconds. This can also have the effect of making the agents look like they are making slightly delayed decisions, which is more human-like than instantly reacting to changes in the world.

To improve processing times, it is a good idea to only use heat maps on agents when required. For example, do not have agents in another part of the dungeon using them. Have a more simplified behaviour and when they become important, switch the heat map functionality on.

CELL GRANULARITY

Something that affects both techniques described in this chapter is the size of the cells, although heat maps work perfectly fine with an array of points. If using a grid system, then the size of a cell can become an issue. If cells are too big, the information gained is not very useful, but if the cells are too small, then the memory requirements go up and there is a lot of processing every update to be carried out. This like many things is a balancing act and is very much game specific.

IMAGE 4.10   Unit sized cell size.

To some degree it can be trial and error to get the level of fidelity you want. However, having very small cells does not always produce a better knowledge of the environment. The best thing to do is to start at some arbitrary size and reduce it until you get results you are happy with. The absolute minimum size should be that of a single unit, but for most games this is not necessary. Take a look at Images 4.10 and 4.11. You are not gaining a great deal by having such a level of fidelity seen in Image 4.10. The cell size used in Image 4.11 requires less memory and processing and gives you the overall understanding of the world you need.

IMAGE 4.11   Larger cell size.

FINAL THOUGHTS

Influence maps and heat maps are extremely useful tools that provide you with an up-to-date analysis of the terrain. They give you the data required to make smarter decisions. How you use this information is crucial. It is also possible to have too much information. Imagine you have an influence map that contains multiple components: accessibility, visibility, pinch points, and more, but after lots of play testing, you find that the data gained on pinch points is not having a major impact upon the intelligence of the AI. What should you do? Simple, if you find that a particular analysis is not benefiting your AI, don't be afraid of removing it and saving yourself the processing hit.

TERRAIN ANALYSIS – PRACTICAL

PROJECT OVERVIEW

In this project, we observe the movement of a swarm of aliens. The nest is located at the top left corner of the environment and the food is spread out across the grid. The aliens are not very intelligent. They do not know where the food is located and have no knowledge of where the nest is.

When you click the Spawn button, an individual alien will leave the nest and go in search of food. Whilst the alien is searching, it will heat up each cell in the environment that it passes through. The amount of heat is determined by the number of moves the alien has made when it enters a cell. This results in the areas closer to the nest remaining hotter for longer. Once the alien has located a food source, it changes its behaviour. It stops heating up the environment and instead starts cooling it. The alien also stops moving randomly through the environment, preferring to move to the hottest neighbouring cell.

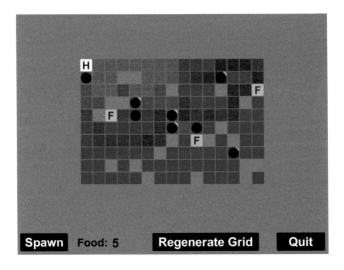

SCREENSHOT 4.1 Terrain analysis project.

Over time the heat value stored for each cell will cool by itself. If you take a look at Screenshot 4.1, you will see a range of colours. Red is the hottest a cell can be and blue the coldest. The aliens are the black circles. Those aliens that have located food and are transporting it back to the nest have a green slither to indicate them carrying something.

It is extremely easy for an individual alien to get lost in the environment and die. An interesting facet of this project is that the more aliens there are in the environment, the greater the influence they spread across the grid. It is this influence that allows the aliens to return to the nest with the food they have found. This is a simple form of emergent behaviour.

TERMINOLOGY: EMERGENT BEHAVIOUR

A behaviour observed in an agent that is not coded for is termed 'emergent'. In the given example, none of the aliens work together, but their impact upon the environment results in a kind of coordination that was not programmed.

STEP-BY-STEP GUIDE

Open the Unity project named GameAi supplied with this book. Navigate through the folder system to the Chapter4_TerrainAnalysis folder. It is located in the Assets folder. Click on the Chapter4_TerrainAnalysis scene. Run the application.

You can click the 'Regenerate Grid' button to see different random environments, but when you click the 'Spawn' button all that happens is a black circle appears over the H cell. This black circle is an alien. Unfortunately, at the moment it does not do anything. This is because we need to code the `MakeMove()` function. Before we get to this, it is worth taking a moment to have a look through a couple of files. Open the Scripts folder and locate Heatmap.cs and HeatmapCell.cs.

HEATMAP.CS

This file is extremely basic. It is static to allow all files to get at the data and consists of the locations for the food, an array of GameObjects, which will be our heat map and two variables for storing the number of rows and columns in the environment. There is nothing exciting going on here, but it is important to know where the data is coming from that we are using.

HEATMAPCELL.CS

This file is how we store the heat value at each element of the grid. Beyond this it has a bit of code to change the colour of the cell in the demo, but as this is largely Unity Engine specific code, we will not be looking at it. An important function to look at though is the `DecayValue()` function, which reduces the heat value stored in a cell every frame until it reaches zero.

Right, let us get that alien moving. Locate and open the following file: Alien.cs.

ALIEN.CS

This file is where all the alien code is located. It is the alien that affects the environment, so this is where the more interesting code in the application is found. We will be coding the `MakeMove()` function. Go ahead and scroll down the file until you find this function.

MakeMove()

To begin with we set up a few variables we need and get the heat values for neighbouring cells. The movement is split into the two types described above – searching for food and searching for the nest. We will look at these separately.

SEARCH FOR FOOD MOVEMENT

First, we will tackle movement when we are searching for food. Find the following line of code:

```
if (bHaveFood == false)
{
```

Everything we discuss below can be added below the following comment:

```
//Search for Food.
```

We are going to search through the neighbouring cells to determine which move is valid. And to do this iteration we will be using a do loop. So, go ahead and add the following:

```
do
{
```

Within the loop we are going to need a couple of variables to keep track of what our lowest scoring cell is and at what index this cell is stored.

```
float fLowestValue = 1.0f;
int bestIndex = -1;
```

We can only move up, right, down and left, which means there are four moves maximum. Open a for loop to allow us repeat our code in these four directions.

```
for (int index = 0; index <= 3; index++)
{
```

At the very start of the `MakeMove()` function, we got the heat values from the four neighbours. In the event of something being returned that is invalid, the element in the array will be set to NaN, which means 'Not a Number'. We need to ensure that the value we are working with is a legitimate number, so add the following code to do the check.

```
if (!float.IsNaN(values[index]))
{
```

On our first pass through this loop, the variable bestIndex will still be set to its initial value of −1. If this is the case on this pass through the loop, we have not recorded a value yet, so should just take this one.

```
if (bestIndex == -1)
{
    fLowestValue = values[index];
    bestIndex = index;
}
```

However, if this is not our first pass through the loop, we may have a value already stored. So let us check if the current value is lower than the one we have stored, and if this is the case, we want to override the stored data with the data for this direction.

```
else
{
    if (values[index] < fLowestValue)
    {
        fLowestValue = values[index];
        bestIndex = index;
    }
}
```

At this point we need to close off the remaining brackets. We have now checked all four directions.

We need to know what the row and column indexes are for this desired direction, so we need to call the following function that will set everything for us.

```
SetDesiredPositions((eAlienMovementDirection)bestIndex, ref
desiredRow, ref desiredCol);
```

And we should retain the direction we were previously moving in.

```
previousDirection = (eAlienMovementDirection)bestIndex;
```

To exit the do loop, we need to know if the direction we chose was a valid move. We have a handy function for this.

```
bFoundAValidMove = IsAValidMove(desiredRow, desiredCol);
```

Now we just need to close off the do loop with the while condition. This is where our bFoundAValidMove Boolean variable is useful.

```
} while (bFoundAValidMove == false);
```

If we exited the do loop, we have a valid position. So, we next need to heat up the current position. It is this heat that will influence our movements when returning to the nest. We do not simply want to add a value, instead we want to add a value based upon how many moves we have made away from the nest. This will result in applying more heat the closer to the nest the alien is.

```
float fHeat = ((float)(numberOfMovesUntilDeath -
currentMoveCount)) / (float)numberOfMovesUntilDeath;
```

With this new value we need to influence the environment. We do this by calling the following function and passing through the required heat value.

```
AdjustHeat(fHeat);
```

Remember, we are currently searching for food. So, it is crucial that with each move we check to see if we have located a food source.

```
CheckForFood();
```

Finally, we need to close off all remaining brackets. This will complete the movement for an alien searching for food. If at this point you have any problems, have a quick check with the Alien_Solution.cs file to ensure we stay on track.

SEARCH FOR NEST MOVEMENT

Next, we will tackle movement when we are looking to take our food back to the nest. Move to the else bracket of code below where we have just been working. There should be the following comment:

```
//Follow heat of the grid to get home.
```

We will add the following code below this. As with the previous section of code, we need some variables to keep track of what our highest scoring cell is and at what index this cell is stored. We also have an additional Boolean variable to track whether all neighbours scored zero. More on this later.

```
bool bAllDirectionsScoredZero = true;
float fHighestValue = -1.0f;
int bestIndex = -1;
```

As before, we can only move up, right, down and left. This gives us a maximum of four moves. Open a for loop to allow us to repeat our code in these four directions.

```
for(int index = 0; index <= 3; index++)
{
```

We need to ensure the heat value stored at the current index is a legitimate number, so add the following code to do the check.

```
if (!float.IsNaN(values[index]))
```

On our first pass through this loop the variable `bestIndex` will still be set to its initial value of −1. If this is the case on this pass through the loop, we have not recorded a value yet, so should just take this one.

```
if (bestIndex == -1)
{
   fHighestValue = values[index];
   bestIndex = index;
}
```

However, if this is not our first pass through the loop, we may have a value already stored. So let us check if the current value is higher than the one we have stored, and if this is the case, we want to override the stored data with the data for this direction.

```
else
{
   if (values[index] > fHighestValue)
   {
      fHighestValue = values[index];
      bestIndex = index;
   }
}
```

Add a bracket to close off the `if(!float.IsNaN(values[index]))` section of code.

Remember that `bAllDirectionsScoredZero` Boolean we set up? Well, it is here that we set whether it is false. We will loop through four times to check the four different directions and we only require one direction to return a value greater than zero to be able to set this Boolean to false. What we are saying is that we definitely have at least one direction with heat that we can move in.

```
if(values[index] > 0.0f)
{
    bAllDirectionsScoredZero = false;
}
```

Add a bracket to close off the for loop section of code.

We have now checked all four directions. Using the `bAllDirectionsScoredZero` Boolean we can quickly know if we found a direction that was hot. And if we did, then we can get the row and column indexes for the `bestIndex` we stored.

```
if(bAllDirectionsScoredZero == false)
{
    SetDesiredPositions((eAlienMovementDirection)bestIndex,
ref desiredRow, ref desiredCol);
}
```

If `bAllDirectionsScoredZero` is still true, it means all neighbours are equally bad. So we should keep moving in the same direction until we hit an obstacle.

```
else
{
   do
   {
      SetDesiredPositions(previousDirection, ref desiredRow,
ref desiredCol);
```

But is a movement in the direction we were previously heading a valid move? We should check this.

```
bFoundAValidMove = IsAValidMove(desiredRow, desiredCol);
if (bFoundAValidMove == false)
{
```

If it was not a valid move, we need to iterate through the available moves. `previousDirection` is an enum, so we can simply add 1 to the current value, although we do need to check if we have not gone beyond the enumerated options. In which case we should loop back to the starting enum.

```
if (previousDirection + 1 == eAlienMovementDirection.MaxMoves)
{
   previousDirection = eAlienMovementDirection.Right;
}
else
{
   previousDirection++;
}
```

Add a bracket to close off the `if(bFoundValidMove == false)` section of code and then close off the do loop using the `bFoundAValidMove` Boolean in the conditional check.

```
} while (bFoundAValidMove == false);
```

Add a final bracket to close off the `if(bFoundAValidMove == false)` segment of code.

Remember, the point of this section of the movement code is to move back to the nest. So, we should always check if we got home with food.

```
CheckForHome();
```

Finally, we need to cool down the current position just a little to ensure we do not keep moving back on ourselves.

```
AdjustHeat(fCoolDownAmount);
```

This completes the movement for an alien searching for the nest. Hopefully you have no errors and can return to the Unity project and click run. If not, check with the Alien_Solution.cs file to see a complete solution for this function.

FUTURE WORK

This project has plenty of room for expansion. You make it as simple or complicated as you wish, and following are a couple of suggestions.

- Try coding a quantity for the food. When the food source has run out, randomly position a new food source somewhere else.
- If you are feeling particularly ambitious, consider adding a rival swarm of aliens to compete for the food source that has a nest at the bottom right-hand corner of the environment. Maybe when two aliens from rival nests enter the same cell, the alien with the greater move count kills the other.

    Hint: You will need a separate heat map for the other nest of aliens.

5 Pathfinding

Over the years a lot of different approaches have been developed that can generate a path that will get your character from point A to point B, but none is more widely known or used than the A* algorithm. Now this approach is not perfect, it has a lot of shortcomings, but over the years, modifications have been made that improve upon the original. Before we delve into the algorithm itself and see how it works, let us first take a look at what pathfinding actually is.

In a game world, there can be many obstacles sprinkled throughout an environment; these can range from fully destroyed buildings right down to trash cans in an alleyway. It would be so much easier if we could just walk in a straight line to get to where we wanted, but that would no doubt be a very dull game. So given our environment will be strewn with obstacles, we need a way to navigate through it, and whatever solution we come up with needs to:

a. Calculate the path quickly.
b. Generate a path that is 'reasonable' to the player.

Getting both is not as easy as you might think. There is always a trade-off. We can easily get a rubbish path quickly, but then that is not 'reasonable' from the player's perspective and our characters look unintelligent. Alternatively, we could just wait for the 'best' path to be calculated, no matter how long it takes, but this creates other issues. The first is that whilst our pathfinding algorithm is running it will be stuck in a loop until it returns. This means no other game system can run whilst we are hogging all the resources. In other words, there will be no graphical updates, no physics updates and no updates of any kind. Our search for a path creates an unresponsive lagging game.

We could cater for this issue by splitting our algorithm in a manner that allows it to calculate over several frames. This would allow other systems to run their processes. This fixes our previous issue but does make our code a little more complicated. It also means our characters would look unintelligent whilst they stood in place waiting for a path to be returned. Again, we can fix this by returning partial paths to get the characters on their way, or we could allow them to randomly wander around the environment until we have a path, but would it not be great if we could just get the right path quickly?

As with most things in life nothing comes without compromise. Let us take a look at an area that can have a major impact upon performance but is something outside of the pathfinding algorithm itself: spatial representations.

SPATIAL REPRESENTATION

There are many ways in which we can represent the environment in code and the approach chosen can have a direct impact upon the speed of the search and the quality of the resulting path. For this section, we are going to be using the simple game world depicted in Image 5.1. It consists of four buildings that represent our obstacles.

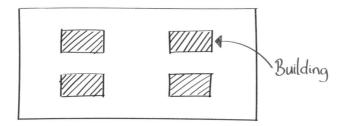

IMAGE 5.1   Simple game world.

The simplest approach to building a code representation the game can understand is to grid out the environment and store a value in each cell to indicate whether this area is accessible or not. Take a look at Image 5.2. The greyed-out areas are blocked and therefore not accessible. The empty cells can be walked through. This approach does not work well for nonrectangular shaped environments and can require a lot of nodes to represent the environment. Imagine an environment with 100*100 grid. This would give us 10,000 cells to explore.

Another limitation of such an approach is the resultant path can be angular. Given we are working with square sections of the environment this is to be expected, but it can look a little robotic. It is possible to smooth out an angular path to make it look more natural, but that is an additional process applied after the pathfinding algorithm has finished and incurs an additional cost in terms of processing time.

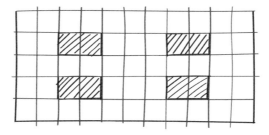

IMAGE 5.2   Grid-based approach.

Another approach is to use a collection of nodes to describe the world. This approach is commonly known as a waypoint map. Such an approach will dramatically reduce the number of calculations required when compared to the grid-based approach. The same environment that required 10,000 cells with the grid-based approach could be represented by a handful of nodes; around 500 would be reasonable, possibly less. Simply reducing the nodes in the search space will increase the speed of the search. Creating this type of representation is more challenging than the grid-based approach though. We need some way to place each node so that it can see at least one other node. This ensures that every node is accessible to the character. This can be achieved by hand placing them throughout the game world, but this is a tedious task that also allows for the introduction of human error.

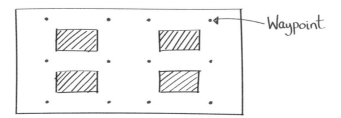

IMAGE 5.3   Waypoint approach.

Using a graph of nodes to represent the world adds an additional layer of complexity. If you take a look at Image 5.3 you can see that we have reduced the nodes dramatically from the number of cells we required for the grid-based approach seen in Image 5.2. But, in code we need some way of knowing which nodes are connected. Our game world internally is a graph, but at the moment there are no connections between the nodes. If we want our agent to go from the node at the top left of the world to the node at the bottom right, we need to know how the internal graph is structured so we can traverse the graph, node to node – around obstacles, until we get to the target node. However, a graph without connections would just calculate a direction vector using these two positions, which would give you a diagonal direction that would have the agent walk straight into the nearest building. Without knowing what the connections between nodes are, there is little point having the nodes.

In Image 5.4, we have connected the dots. You can now see which nodes are linked. So, using the previous example, the agent at the top-left node (node A) would have two options. She could move right or down. When she reaches the next node she will need to make another decision. In actuality the pathfinding algorithm will do this and return the entire path before the agent sets off on her journey, so you do not see the agent making these decisions in real time, but under the hood that is what the pathfinding algorithm will be doing.

It makes most sense to store these connections as a graph. That way we can traverse it like we could any other graph, from parent to child. When searching though, and we will cover this in the second part of this chapter, we need to make sure we do not end up going around in circles. We are not using a tree here, where each node has a single parent. Instead, we have nodes that can be both the parent and child. To demonstrate this let us use our previous example again. Our agent has moved right from the top-left node (node A) and is now at the connected node (node B). This node has four connections. One of these connections is the node she just came from (node A). We know we do not want to go back there, and it would be unwise to remove the connections throughout the search. Pathfinding algorithms cater for this problem by retaining information as to where they have already searched. They do not stop you from looking at a node you have previously passed through, but the cost of a path that repeats movements will be higher than those that go directly to the target node. Higher costing paths will remain unexplored whilst there are cheaper options available.

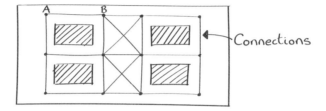

IMAGE 5.4   Waypoints with connections.

Let us get back to spatial representations. If we do not want to go down the route of hand placing the nodes, and the game uses a navigation mesh, we could generate our navigation nodes from this. Image 5.5 shows us our environment split into travers-able polygons. We need to generate the graph of nodes from which we can navigate the game world from this information.

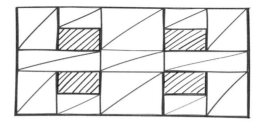

IMAGE 5.5   Navmesh approach.

The first step is to generate a single node for each polygon on the mesh. Take a look at Image 5.6. This approach describes the environment well but will need to run an additional process to remove nodes that are unnecessary and to create the links between them.

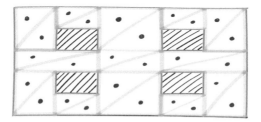

IMAGE 5.6   Nodes generated at centre of Navmesh polygons.

The nodes removed will be replaced with a node at an averaged position located somewhere between the two, and visible to its nearest neighbour. Image 5.7 shows the same environment seen in Image 5.6 but with the nodes in their post-process positions.

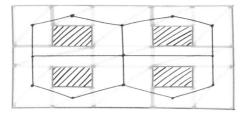

IMAGE 5.7   Repositioned Navmesh nodes.

Another approach generating our graph of traversable nodes could be to add nodes
to the corners of the objects that we place in the environment, and then run an additional process to join them up. This approach works well for designer created levels
and allows for the environment to be modified without worrying about the effect
upon the AI. Using our simple environment, we can see that we have four buildings.
If we were to add nodes to the corner of a building object, as seen in Image 5.8, when
we then place them in the world, we would have what can be seen in Image 5.9.

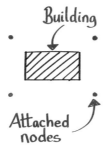

IMAGE 5.8   Object with attached nodes.

Now this is not exactly what we are after, but it does allow for guards to patrol the
area by following the contours of the buildings. But what we really want is what we
saw in Image 5.3. This can be achieved by running a process to remove nodes that
are not needed and to create the connections. In this case, it is better to only remove
nodes that come within some small range of another node.

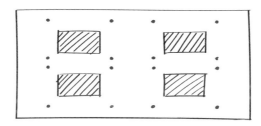

IMAGE 5.9   Game world built with objects.

From this point on, we will be using the grid-based approach for all our examples. It makes depicting the problems so much easier, which helps in the explanations. Just bear in mind that if you were to use a waypoint approach, the search speed would undoubtedly be faster and the resultant path less angular.

PATHFINDING

So, we have our internal representation of the environment, but we still have no way of finding a path around the obstacles that block our way to the target position. This is where pathfinding algorithms come in. There are many to choose from, all of which offer their own pros and cons. You could use A*, Theta*, HPA*, Jump-Point Search, D*, Directed Recursion Search; the list goes on. If you were to delve deeper into this area of research, you will quickly realise that a lot of the algorithms that have been developed simply improve upon the A* algorithm in some small way. So, for someone new to the area, there is merit to learning how to code the original A* algorithm and that is what we are about to focus on. But first it is worth mentioning the traditional algorithms Depth-first search and Breadth-first search. Both approaches will find the route between two nodes if one exists, but they are both undirected searches, meaning they will blindly search the entire tree until they either find the target or run out of nodes to search. The resulting path will also consist of all the nodes it visited to reach the target. Not really what we want. Our agent would appear as though it was meandering through the game world and visiting a lot of irrelevant places.

TERMINOLOGY: UNDIRECTED SEARCH

A search that makes no decision as to which next node will get it to the target faster. It can search the entire tree, which can take a long time.

A* Algorithm

The A* algorithm is an evolution of an older search approach. It is the obvious successor to the Dijkstra algorithm. The similarities between the two approaches can be seen in the way that the A* algorithm chooses which path to investigate next. Dijkstra's algorithm uses a cost so far approach, meaning that all decisions are made on the accumulated cost of the path to the current node. The A* algorithm however does not only use the cost so far but incorporates an estimation as to which route will result in the shortest path to the target node, making it a directed search algorithm. It is more efficient than Dijkstra's algorithm and will always find a path if one exists, but the A* algorithm will consume more time and memory than Dijkstra's algorithm if there is no possible path available as all routes need to be searched. However, when a path does exist, the A* algorithm will find the shortest route relatively quickly, but in the context of video games, it is still a time-consuming process and one that also performs poorly in large-scale environments.

TERMINOLOGY: DIRECTED SEARCH

An approach that uses information gained throughout the search to help guide which next node will get to the target faster.

The estimated cost from a starting position to a target position is calculated using a heuristic function. The type of heuristic used can have an effect on the paths returned, so choosing the correct one for your game is important. The most popular heuristic functions used are the Manhattan Distance and the Euclidean Distance. There are others, but for games these are the ones you will most commonly find.

TERMINOLOGY: HEURISTIC

This simply means to guess at the distance to the target node. It will probably be wrong, but it is a guess, nonetheless.

The Manhattan Distance approach takes its name from how Manhattan in New York is laid out in blocks and calculates its guess based upon a simple grid structure. It counts from the current cell, how many cells across the target is and how many cells up the target is. These values are then added together to give us our estimated cost. Image 5.10 shows the Manhattan Distance from the top-left cell to the bottom-right cell in our example environment. As you can see there are 10 cells across and 4 cells down, resulting in a Manhattan Distance of 14.

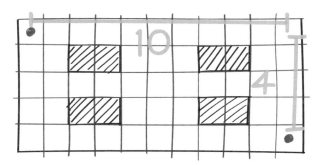

IMAGE 5.10   Manhattan Distance.

The Euclidean Distance is simply the length of the hypotenuse on a right-angle triangle, with each node's position forming the ends of the hypotenuse. Using Pythagoras' Theorem, it is just a matter of calculating the distance between two points. This value becomes the estimate from the next node to the target node.

Take a look at Image 5.11, which shows this being applied to our example game world. As you can see, this approach will consistently underestimate the distance to the destination. When using this approach, it has the effect of searching fewer nodes than the Manhattan approach does. Following the path of the hypotenuse (marked

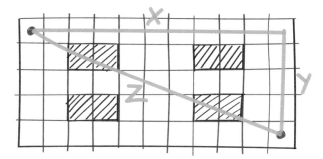

IMAGE 5.11 Euclidean Distance.

as Z in the image) you can see that we cannot actually get to our target node along it. Remember, it is just a guess. Remove the guess and you have Dijkstra's algorithm. Both approaches work, but each offers a slightly different result. For the explanation below, and for the tutorial section we will be using the Manhattan approach as it works well with the grid-based structure we are using and simplifies the explanation.

The formula for calculating the overall cost of a node in the A* algorithm is as follows:

$$f(x) = g(x) + h(x)$$

The *f* represents the final cost of the node, which is calculated by the cost so far $g(x)$ added to the estimate from this node to the target node $h(x)$. Each node must contain these three values when using the A* algorithm.

The A* algorithm also makes use of lists for storing the nodes it has encountered. An *OPEN* list is used for storing the nodes generated in the search, but yet to be expanded, and a *CLOSED* list containing the nodes that have been both generated and expanded to produce connected nodes. This is how we ensure we do not continually loop back on ourselves. Manipulation of these lists is where a lot of the processing time for the A* algorithm is consumed.

To explain how the A* algorithm works, we will be working through an actual example, where I can take you through the process step by step, but before that take a look at Image 5.12. This is the A* algorithm. It is written in pseudocode as you should be able to code this in any language. If you do not understand every step, do not worry. In the example below, we will be stepping through it visually, but it is worth taking a look at a few key stages in the pseudocode first. Note the fifth line: we only continue to search whilst there are nodes on the *OPEN* list. These are nodes that we have not yet explored. However, if we find the target node, we end the search early (lines seven to nine) regardless of whether there are still unexplored nodes on the *OPEN* list. Line twelve checks whether we are already aware of a node we have just encountered. If we know about it, we then check if it was cheaper for us to get to this node via our current route. If so, we update the node values. Finally, note lines 16 and 21 where we calculate the *f*, *g* and *h* values.

Let *n* = the starting node.
Assign *g*,*h* and *f* values to *n*.
Set the parent of *n* to be **NULL**.
Add *n* to the **Open** list

While the **Open** list is not empty:
    Let *b* be the best node from the **Open** list.
    Check if *b* is the target node.
        If so, unwind nodes via parent pointers to generate a path.
        End search.

    While *b* has unexplored connected nodes,
        Let *c* equal an unexplored node connected to *b*.
        Check whether *c* is on the **Open** or **Closed** list
        If so,
            Check whether the new route has a lower *f* value.
            If so,
                Set the parent of *c* to be *b* and set new *g*,*h* and *f* values.
            Otherwise,
                Discard this information
        Else,
            Set the parent of *c* to be *b*, and set new *g*, *h* and *f* values.
            Add *c* to the **Open** list.
    End while.
    Add *b* to the **Closed** list.
End While.

IMAGE 5.12   A* algorithm pseudocode.

STEP-BY-STEP GUIDE

Right, so now we have an overview of what the A* algorithm is doing, let us put this into action. The A* algorithm can be quite lengthy to explain, so we will look at the first couple of iterations in detail, but from then on, we will be summarising all subsequent loops. Graphical images of the search have been supplied throughout, along with the complete *OPEN* list for each stage.

Column

	0	1	2	3	4	5	6	7	8	9	10
0	(0,0)	(0,1)	(0,2)	(0,3)	(0,4)	(0,5)	(0,6)	(0,7)	(0,8)	(0,9)	(0,10)
1	(1,0)	(1,1)	(1,2)	(1,3)	(1,4)	(1,5)	(1,6)	(1,7)	(1,8)	(1,9)	(1,10)
2	(2,0)	(2,1)	(2,2)	(2,3)	(2,4)	(2,5)	(2,6)	(2,7)	(2,8)	(2,9)	(2,10)
3	(3,0)	(3,1)	(3,2)	(3,3)	(3,4)	(3,5)	(3,6)	(3,7)	(3,8)	(3,9)	(3,10)
4	(4,0)	(4,1)	(4,2)	(4,3)	(4,4)	(4,5)	(4,6)	(4,7)	(4,8)	(4,9)	(4,10)

(Row)

IMAGE 5.13   Cell identifiers.

Take a look at Image 5.13; this shows the naming convention that will be used throughout this example. We will be using the notation of (row × column). The terms cell and node will be used interchangeably throughout the explanation – they both refer to an element in the grid. The moves allowed for this example are in eight directions – Up, UpRight, Right, DownRight, Down, DownLeft, Left and UpLeft. This is the order in which they get added to our *OPEN* list, which is important to note, as adding them in a different order could produce a slightly different result. A horizontal or vertical move will cost 1, and a diagonal move will cost the square root of 2 (approximately 1.41). We do not need to worry about connections in a gridded environment, as in such a structure the neighbouring cells can be considered connected.

Image 5.14 is our gridded environment. Note that the cells filled with hashes are inaccessible. We want to get from the start node S to the target node T. These are located in cells (0, 0) and (4, 10), respectively. Throughout this example, the cells have been colour coded. Green is the cell we are currently examining, blue are cells on the *OPEN* list and red are cells on the *CLOSED* list. You need to decide how each new node we encounter gets added to these lists. In the example below, we are adding them to the bottom of the list to highlight how the *OPEN* list grows, but there is no reason why they could not be added to the top. This can influence the search if, when searching for the next cheapest node to explore we find multiple with the same cost. Personally, I would take the first one encountered in the list, which means the order in which the list is stored can have an impact. Remember that multiple paths can be found and the A* algorithm will find the cheapest. If there are multiple paths that cost the same value, then the order of the search will influence the direction the search takes.

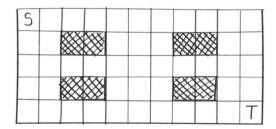

IMAGE 5.14 Start and target positions.

Iteration #1

To begin our search, we simply have our starting node, which is cell (0, 0). This is not the target node, so we expand that by adding all the nodes that we can reach from (0, 0) to the *OPEN* list. We cannot go Up or UpRight, so we skip those positions. We can go Right, DownRight and Down, so these get added to the *OPEN* list, but only if they are not already stored in our *CLOSED* list. They are not, so all three get added.

When adding a new node, we need to set the g value to be the cost of getting here, in this case (0, 1) and (1, 0) are horizontal moves, so g equals 1. (1, 1) is a diagonal move, so in this case g equals the square root of 2.

Our heuristic is the h value. Remember we are using the Manhattan Distance, so count how many horizontal and vertical moves it will take to reach the target node. At this stage we are not interested in obstacles. It is simply a guess. So, cell (0, 1) takes 13 moves, cell (1, 1) takes 12 moves and cell (1, 0) takes 13 moves to get to our target node. These are our estimates.

The *f* value is set to be the result of adding *g* and *h* together. This is the value that we will use to determine which node should be searched next.

The final step when processing a connected node is to set its parent. This is important as when we finally reach the target node, we need a way to wind back the search to generate the path. We do this by looking at the target node's parent, which shows how we got there. We then look at that node's parent to see how we got there and so on. This process continues until we find a parent set to null. Only the starting node will have a parent set in this way as it has no parent. Assuming we have stored each node throughout our backtracking, we now have a route. We are a long way away from that stage of the search at the moment, but it is worth remembering that storing the parent is a key part of our search process.

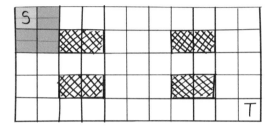

IMAGE 5.15 First iteration of A*.

We still have a few moves to assess. However, we cannot move DownLeft, Left or UpLeft from the starting cell so those get ignored. We are now finished with cell (0, 0), it can be removed from the *OPEN* list and added to the *CLOSED* list. The internal values for the starting node (0, 0) will be as follows, *g* is 0 because it took 0 moves to get there (remember, we start here), *h* is 14 as it would take 14 moves to get to the target cell from here, and *f* is equal to *g* and *h* added together giving a value of 14. Image 5.15 visually shows where we are after our first iteration of the A* algorithm and Image 5.16 shows the current state of our *OPEN* list. The last column on the right is the ID of the cell that got us to this position. Also, note the red arrow of the left of the table. This is to indicate which node has the cheapest *f* value and will be selected next for expansion.

OPEN LIST				
ID	g	h	f	Parent
(0,1)	1	13	14	(0,0)
(1,1)	$\sqrt{2}$	12	13.41	(0,0)
(1,0)	1	13	14	(0,0)

IMAGE 5.16 *OPEN* List after Iteration 1.

ITERATION #2

Our *OPEN* list still has nodes to explore, so the search continues. It is only when this list has been exhausted that the A* algorithm returns a result of no path possible. So, looking through our list we find that node (1, 1) has the lowest *f* value. This means that node (1, 1) is next to be expanded.

Cell (1, 1) can move in seven of the available eight directions. We will now look at each in turn in the order described above. Moving Up is valid from (1, 1), but we already have the node (0, 1) in our *OPEN* list. This does not mean we ignore it though. What we need to do is to calculate the cost of getting to cell (0, 1) via the current cell being expanded – that is cell (1, 1). So, it cost us 1.41 to get to cell (1, 1) and a move Up will cost us another 1. This gives us a *g* value of 2.14. The *h* value from (0, 1) is still 13, so our *f* value is 2.14 + 13 giving us an overall value of 15.14. If you take a look back at Image 5.16 and find the entry for cell (0, 1), you will see that it has an *f* value of 14. This means that whatever route to get to cell (0, 1), we have already stored is cheaper than going via our current cell (1, 1). So, we leave cell (0, 1) as it is and look at the next possible move. It is important to note here that if our *f* value had been lower than the *f* value stored for cell (0, 1), we would have modified its *g*, *h* and *f* values with those calculated to get there via the current cell (1, 1) and set its parent node to be cell (1, 1).

The next possible move is UpRight to cell (0, 2). This is a diagonal move, so it costs an additional 1.41 on top of whatever it cost us to get to our current cell (1, 1). Our current cell has a *g* cost of 1.41, so we add our movement cost to this giving cell (0, 2) a *g* value of 2.82. The *h* value from (0, 2) is 12, giving us an *f* value of 14.82.

A Right move steps into an inaccessible cell, so we ignore this move and look to DownRight. As we know a diagonal movement costs us 1.41 and this gets added to the cost of the current cell's movement cost. Our current cell (1, 1) has a *g* cost of 1.41, so we add our movement cost to this, giving cell (2, 2) a *g* value of 2.82. The *h* value from (2, 2) is 10, giving us an *f* value of 12.82.

We can also move Down from our current cell (1, 1) to cell (2, 1). So, let us go ahead and calculate the *g* cost. A horizontal or vertical move costs us 1, and cell (1, 1) has a *g* cost of 1.41. We add these together giving cell (2, 1) a *g* value of 2.41. It takes 11 steps to get to the target cell from cell (2, 1), so our *h* is 11. Adding *g* and *h* together gives us an *f* value of 13.41.

We can also move DownLeft to cell (2, 0). This is a diagonal move from the current cell (1, 1) so will cost us 1.41 on top of whatever the current cell's *g* value is. This results in cell (2, 0) having a *g* value of 2.82. The Manhattan Distance from this cell is 12, so that is our *h*, giving us an *f* value of 14.82.

We can also move Left to cell (1, 0). To our human eyes we can see that this is not the right direction to be heading in, but the A* algorithm needs to add all encountered nodes to the *OPEN* list in case the path it takes results in a dead-end. It appears that cell (1, 0) is already on our *OPEN* list. So, let us calculate our *g*, *h* and *f* values and see if this route is a better option.

As this is a horizontal move it costs us 1, which gets added to the *g* value of the current cell (1, 1), giving us a *g* of 2.41. We can see from Image 5.16 that the stored *g* value for node (1, 0) is 1, so we are already considering a more costly route. The *h* value does not change as the guess from this cell (1, 0) to the target node is the same result as the last time we calculated the Manhattan Distance, which is 13. If we add the new g and the h values together (2.41 + 13), we get an f value of 15.41. This is greater than the stored f value of 14, so we ignore this route.

The final move available to us is an UpLeft movement back to cell (0, 0) – our starting position. As can be seen in Image 5.17, this node is red signifying that it is currently residing in the *CLOSED* list.

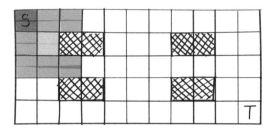

IMAGE 5.17   Second iteration of A*.

A move back to our starting position is never going to result in a change. Think about it. How can moving away from the starting position and then back to the starting position ever be cheaper than just not moving from the starting position in the first place? Let us go through the process anyway, just to be sure.

This movement is a diagonal move, costing us 1.41. The current cell (1, 1) has a g value of 1.41, so adding these together to get our new g cost gives us 2.82. If we look at what the g value was for cell (0, 0), we see it was 0. Remember we started there, so it costs us nothing to get there. The h value remains the same. It is a Manhattan Distance of 14. If we add our new g value and the h value together (2.82 + 14), we get an f value of 16.82, which is greater than our stored f value of 14. So, we ignore this move.

We have no more directions to try, so our current node, cell (1, 1) is fully expanded, and we now remove it from the *OPEN* list. It is then added to the *CLOSED* list. At this point it is worth taking a look at Image 5.18, which shows the current state of the *OPEN* list. Notice how the list is growing, and each time we need to search for the next node to expand, the process gets longer.

ID	g	h	f	Parent
(0,1)	1	13	14	(0,0)
(1,0)	1	13	14	(0,0)
(0,2)	2.82	12	14.82	(1,1)
(2,2)	2.82	10	12.82	(1,1)
(2,1)	2.41	11	13.41	(1,1)
(2,0)	2.82	12	14.82	(1,1)

OPEN LIST

(→ pointing to row (2,2))

IMAGE 5.18   *OPEN* List after Iteration 2.

As we have not yet found the target cell, and there are still entries in the *OPEN* list, we repeat the process with the next cheapest cell found in the *OPEN* list. As can be seen from the *OPEN* list in Image 5.18, node (2, 2) is the next cheapest option.

ITERATION #3

Node (2, 2) is not the target, so we must examine it to see which cells it connects to. We can only move in four directions from this cell – Right, DownLeft, Left and UpLeft. All other positions are inaccessible.

Right

This direction is a horizontal move to cell (2, 3) and incurs a cost of 1. The *g* value of the current cell (2, 2) is 2.82, so our *g* will be 3.82. The Manhattan Distance is 9, so that is our *h*, and the *f* value is as always *g* + *h* (3.82 + 9) giving an overall cost of 12.82. This cell is now added to the *OPEN* list.

DownLeft

Movement in a DownLeft direction is a diagonal move and puts us at cell (3, 1), so the incurred cost is 1.41. We add this to the current cell's *g* value (2.82) giving us a *g* value of 4.24. The Manhattan Distance is 10 giving us an *f* value of 12.82 (2.82 + 10). This cell is then added to the *OPEN* list.

Left

A Left move puts us at cell (2, 1). This is already on our *OPEN* list and the calculated *f* value via cell (2, 2) is more expensive, so no changes are required.

UpLeft

An UpLeft move puts us at cell (1, 1). This is also already on our *OPEN* list and the calculated *f* value via cell (2, 2) is more expensive, so again no changes are required.

Take a look at Image 5.19 to see the current state of the search. Notice we currently have two cells on the *CLOSED* list – indicated by their red colouring. Our current cell (highlighted in green) will soon be joining them as we have no further neighbours to expand.

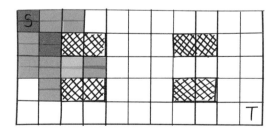

IMAGE 5.19   Third iteration of A*.

Our current node, node (2, 2) is now removed from the *OPEN* list and added to the *CLOSED* list. Image 5.20 shows the state of the *OPEN* list after three iterations of the main loop in the A* algorithm. The next cheapest option is pointed to by the red arrow and is cell (2, 3). It has an *f* value of 12.82, which is lower than all other cells in the list.

OPEN LIST				
ID	g	h	f	Parent
(0,1)	1	13	14	(0,0)
(1,0)	1	13	14	(0,0)
(0,2)	2.82	12	14.82	(1,1)
(2,1)	2.41	11	13.41	(1,1)
(2,0)	2.82	12	14.82	(1,1)
→ (2,3)	3.82	9	12.82	(2,2)
(3,1)	4.24	10	14.24	(2,2)

IMAGE 5.20   *OPEN* List after Iteration 3.

ITERATION #4

Cell (2, 3) is not the target, so we need to repeat the process and expand it to see what cells it is connected to. We can move in four directions from this cell – UpRight, Right, DownRight and Left. All other moves result in inaccessible cells. It has cost us 3.82 to get this far, a value that is stored as our *g* value. This will be used to calculate all connected cells' *g* values.

UpRight

This move positions us at cell (1, 4). It is a cell we have not encountered before, so it gets added to the *OPEN* list. Its *g* value is our current cell's *g* value plus the cost of a diagonal move. So, *g* is 5.23. The Manhattan Distance (*h* value) is 9. This gives us an *f* value of 14.23 (5.23 + 9).

Right

This move positions us at cell (2, 4). This is also a cell we have not encountered before, so it too gets added to the *OPEN* list. Its *g* value is our current cell's *g* value plus the cost of a horizontal move. So, *g* is 4.82. The Manhattan Distance (*h* value) is 8. This gives us an *f* value of 12.82 (4.82 + 8).

DownRight

A diagonal move down and to the right reaches node (3, 4). This is yet again another node we have not encountered, so it will be added to our *OPEN* list. A diagonal move costs 1.41, so adding this to our current node's *g* value we get a value of 5.23. The *h* value is sct to 7 as there are seven steps from node (3, 4) to the target node. Adding the *g* and the *h* together gives us an *f* value of 12.23 (5.23 + 7).

Left

With a Left move we encounter a cell that is on our *CLOSED* list. As we previously discussed a backwards move is never going to improve our path cost, but the A* algorithm does not know that this is a backwards step, so we need to calculate the *g, h* and *f* values to be sure.

A horizontal move incurs a cost of 1, giving us a *g* value of 4.82 (1 + 3.82) for cell (2,3) via this route. The heuristic is 10, and our *f* is 14.82 (4.82 + 10). This is more costly than the *f* value we have for cell (2, 3), which has an *f* of 12.82. Therefore, we ignore this route and no changes are applied.

I realise I have not supplied images of the *CLOSED* list, but you can take a look back at Image 5.20 to see what values cell (2, 3) had when it was selected as the current cell. These values were not changed when we removed it from the *OPEN* list and placed it onto the *CLOSED* list.

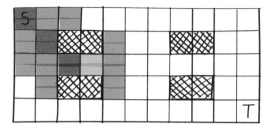

IMAGE 5.21   Fourth iteration of A*.

Image 5.21 shows us where we are in our search. Visually you can see we are slowly making our way toward the target, and as we do so, the *f* values are tightening. These can be seen in the *f* column of our *OPEN* list shown in Image 5.22. Meaning we are moving toward the actual cost rather than a heuristic cost. Our current cell, node (2, 3) can now be moved from the *OPEN* list and placed into the *CLOSED* list.

ID	g	h	f	Parent
(0,1)	1	13	14	(0,0)
(1,0)	1	13	14	(0,0)
(0,2)	2.82	12	14.82	(1,1)
(2,1)	2.41	11	13.41	(1,1)
(2,0)	2.82	12	14.82	(1,1)
(3,1)	4.24	10	14.24	(2,2)
(1,4)	5.23	9	14.23	(2,3)
(2,4)	4.82	8	12.82	(2,3)
→ (3,4)	5.23	7	12.23	(2,3)

IMAGE 5.22   *OPEN* List after Iteration 4.

Cell (3, 4) has the lowest cost on the *OPEN* list, so we take this as the next node to expand.

Iteration #5

Our current cell (3, 4) is not the target, so we begin another iteration of the search. There are seven possible moves from here. The move not allowed is to the Left which results in us stepping onto an inaccessible cell.

Up

A move directly above lands us in a cell already explored (2, 4). We can see it in the *OPEN* list in Image 5.22. The current cell's g value is 5.23, to which we add the cost of a vertical move. So our new g value is 6.23 if we get to node (2, 4) via the current cell. The g value stored in the *OPEN* list for cell (2, 4) is only 4.82, so we know this route is more expensive and no values need to be changed. At this stage, we will not even be calculating the h and f values as we know the Manhattan Distance from a specific cell will always be the same, so adding this to the new, higher g value will only result in a higher f value.

UpRight

This move results in an unexplored cell. To get to cell (2, 5), it will cost us 1.41 (diagonal cost) on top of our current cell's g value. This gives us a g value of 6.64 (1.41 + 5.23). The Manhattan Distance is 7 and our f is 13.64.

Right

Another unexplored node is found when we move to the right. It costs us 1 (horizontal cost) to make this move, which gives node (3, 5) a g value of 6.23 (1 + 5.23). Our heuristic calculates it will take 6 moves to get us to the target, resulting in an f value of 12.23 (6.23 + 6).

DownRight

Again, we have made a move that finds us at a cell not on the *OPEN* or *CLOSED* lists. To get to cell (4, 5) it will cost us an additional 1.41 (diagonal cost) on top of our current cell's g value. This gives us a g value of 6.64 (1.41 + 5.23). The Manhattan Distance is only 5, our lowest h yet. This results in an f value of 11.64 (6.64 + 5).

Down

A Down move gets us to cell (4, 4) and incurs a cost of 1 (vertical move). So, the g value is set at 6.23 (1 + 5.23). The h value is 6 as that is how many steps it takes to reach the target, resulting in an f of 12.63 (6.23 + 6).

DownLeft

This movement sees us reaching cell (4, 3). Any diagonal move from the current node is going to cost the same. So, as we saw with the UpRight and DownRight moves, we get a g value of 6.64 (1.41 + 5.23). It is the heuristic that makes the overall cost difference and what makes the A* algorithm differ from Dijkstra's algorithm. From cell (4, 3) the Manhattan Distance is 7, giving us an f value of 13.64 (6.64 + 7).

UpLeft

A move Up to the Left finds a cell already stored on the *CLOSED* list. As I've explained before a backwards step is never going to cost us less, but the A* algorithm still needs to go through the process of checking the values. This move gets ignored and no changes are required.

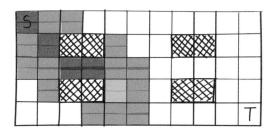

IMAGE 5.23   Fifth iteration of A*.

We are making our way across the environment now quite nicely now, and as you can see from both Image 5.23 and Image 5.24 our *OPEN* list is starting to grow. From Image 5.23 you can really start to see the power of the A* algorithm, as the red cells on the *CLOSED* list are starting to present the actual path we will eventually find, and the green cell is always pushing closer to the goal.

OPEN LIST				
ID	g	h	f	Parent
(0,1)	1	13	14	(0,0)
(1,0)	1	13	14	(0,0)
(0,2)	2.82	12	14.82	(1,1)
(2,1)	2.41	11	13.41	(1,1)
(2,0)	2.82	12	14.82	(1,1)
(3,1)	4.24	10	14.24	(2,2)
(1,4)	5.23	9	14.23	(2,3)
(2,4)	4.82	8	12.82	(2,3)
(2,5)	6.64	7	13.64	(3,4)
(3,5)	6.23	6	12.23	(3,4)
→ (4,5)	6.64	5	11.64	(3,4)
(4,4)	6.23	6	12.23	(3,4)
(4,3)	6.64	7	13.64	(3,4)

IMAGE 5.24   *OPEN* List after Iteration 5.

Looking at the options available to our *OPEN* list in Image 5.24, you can see that cell (4, 5) has the lowest *f* value. As it is not the target node the search goes on.

ITERATION #6

Cell (4, 5) is now our current node and from here there are only five valid moves. The invalid moves are all in a downward direction, which result in us stepping off the grid. Also, to speed things along a little I will not be exploring moves that get discarded as the cost of moving in that particular direction is more expensive than the values already stored. Moves already stored on the *OPEN* or *CLOSED* list that result in no change to the values already stored are Up, Left and LeftUp. This leaves us with two cells that need exploring – UpRight and Right.

UpRight

An UpRight movement from cell (4, 5) finds us at cell (3, 6). The *g* cost of getting to cell (4, 5) was 6.64 and a diagonalt cost is always 1.41. This gives us a *g* value of 8.05 (6.64 + 1.41) for cell (3, 6). The Manhattan Distance is 5, so we set our *h* to this. The *f* value becomes 13.05 (8.05 + 5).

Right

Moving to the Right sees us enter cell (4, 6). The *g* value is our parent cell's *g* cost, which is 6.64, added to the cost of a horizontal move, which is 1. So, our calculated *g* is 7.64 (6.64 + 1). The heuristic from this position is 4 as there are only 4 steps required to reach the target. With the *g* and *h* values set, we can now calculate the *f*, which is *g* and *h* added together. *f* becomes 11.64 (7.64 + 4).

As you can see from Image 5.25, we are continually pushing toward the target. The cell we are currently exploring is marked in green and located at (4, 5). It is somewhat clear how things are going to progress from this stage in the process, so if you have the hang of it, feel free to jump to Image 5.35 to see how things worked out. However, we will continue to progress through this environment step by step.

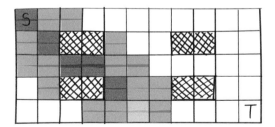

IMAGE 5.25   Sixth iteration of A*.

After the sixth iteration of the A* algorithm we have the *OPEN* list seen in Image 5.26. As we have not found the target cell yet and we still have cells to explore in the *OPEN* list, we will select the option with the lowest *f* value. This is cell (4, 6), which has an *f* value of 11.64.

OPEN LIST				
ID	g	h	f	Parent
(0,1)	1	13	14	(0,0)
(1,0)	1	13	14	(0,0)
(0,2)	2.82	12	14.82	(1,1)
(2,1)	2.41	11	13.41	(1,1)
(2,0)	2.82	12	14.82	(1,1)
(3,1)	4.24	10	14.24	(2,2)
(1,4)	5.23	9	14.23	(2,3)
(2,4)	4.82	8	12.82	(2,3)
(2,5)	6.64	7	13.64	(3,4)
(3,5)	6.23	6	12.23	(3,4)
(4,4)	6.23	6	12.23	(3,4)
(4,3)	6.64	7	13.64	(3,4)
(3,6)	8.05	5	13.05	(4,5)
→ (4,6)	7.64	4	11.64	(4,5)

IMAGE 5.26 *OPEN* List after Iteration 6.

ITERATION #7

At cell (4, 6) we only have one real option. All down movements are off the grid, so these can be ignored. Movements to cells already in the *OPEN* or *CLOSED* list will result in more expensive g values, so these too can be ignored for this explanation. This leaves us with a Right move.

It is important to note here that in a different environment, encountering a cell already on the *OPEN* or *CLOSED* list does not necessarily mean it will cost more. As the tendrils of a search reach dead ends, we can find that when we encounter the same cells from a different direction, this new route is less expensive. So do not assume because we are skipping this stage in this example it is for anything other than brevity. I have checked these moves and do not wish to take up more space than is needed, or to bore you with the same explanations.

Right

A horizontal move to the right results in cell (4, 7) and in terms of our g value costs us 1 more than what our current cell's g value is. So our g cost is 8.64 (7.64 + 1). The Manhattan Distance is getting quick to count now, and we only need 3 steps to reach the target. The f value for cell (4, 7) is 11.64. That is our g (8.64) added to our h (3).

As always, let us take a look at our environment at this stage of the search. This can be seen in Image 5.27.

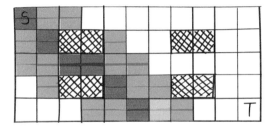

IMAGE 5.27   Seventh iteration of A*.

Our *OPEN* list does not appear to have grown through this iteration. Cell (4, 7) was added, but cell (4, 6) was also removed and placed into the *CLOSED* list. As can be seen in Image 5.28, cell (4, 7) may have just been added, but it is already the cheapest option available.

		OPEN LIST		
ID	g	h	f	Parent
(0,1)	1	13	14	(0,0)
(1,0)	1	13	14	(0,0)
(0,2)	2.82	12	14.82	(1,1)
(2,1)	2.41	11	13.41	(1,1)
(2,0)	2.82	12	14.82	(1,1)
(3,1)	4.24	10	14.24	(2,2)
(1,4)	5.23	9	14.23	(2,3)
(2,4)	4.82	8	12.82	(2,3)
(2,5)	6.64	7	13.64	(3,4)
(3,5)	6.23	6	12.23	(3,4)
(4,4)	6.23	6	12.23	(3,4)
(4,3)	6.64	7	13.64	(3,4)
(3,6)	8.05	5	13.05	(4,5)
→ (4,7)	8.64	3	11.64	(4,6)

IMAGE 5.28   *OPEN* List after Iteration 7.

ITERATION #8

This iteration of the A* algorithm is very similar to the previous iteration, in that there is only one real option from the current cell (4, 7). This option is a Right movement, all other moves are either off the grid or are to cells already explored.

Right

A horizontal move to the right sees us enter cell (4, 8). Given our current cell's (4, 7) *g* cost of 8.64 and a horizontal cost of 1, our new *g* value is 9.64 (8.64 + 1). The heuristic is the lowest value we have seen so far with a cost of 2, resulting in an *f* value of 11.64 (9.64 + 2).

Have you noticed how we are starting to get a lot of f values with a cost of 11.64? As we start to home in on the target, the g cost is offsetting to our h cost. This simply means our heuristics were accurate. Take a look at Image 5.29 to see what our environment looked like during the eighth iteration of the search.

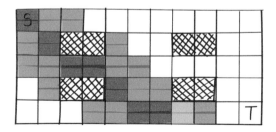

IMAGE 5.29   Eighth iteration of A*

After this iteration through the A* algorithm we have an *OPEN* list that looks like Image 5.30. We are yet to reach the target, and with an *OPEN* list with this many options, we again look for the lowest costing cell. At this point the lowest costing cell is (4, 8).

OPEN LIST				
ID	g	h	f	Parent
(0,1)	1	13	14	(0,0)
(1,0)	1	13	14	(0,0)
(0,2)	2.82	12	14.82	(1,1)
(2,1)	2.41	11	13.41	(1,1)
(2,0)	2.82	12	14.82	(1,1)
(3,1)	4.24	10	14.24	(2,2)
(1,4)	5.23	9	14.23	(2,3)
(2,4)	4.82	8	12.82	(2,3)
(2,5)	6.64	7	13.64	(3,4)
(3,5)	6.23	6	12.23	(3,4)
(4,4)	6.23	6	12.23	(3,4)
(4,3)	6.64	7	13.64	(3,4)
(3,6)	8.05	5	13.05	(4,5)
→ (4,8)	9.64	2	11.64	(4,7)

IMAGE 5.30   *OPEN* List *OPEN* List after Iteration 8.

ITERATION #9

Cell (4, 8) is essentially restricted in movement options in this environment. Up, DownRight, Down, DownLeft and UpLeft are all either off the grid or inaccessible. A Left move results in a cell already on the *OPEN* list. This leaves us with RightUp and Right.

RightUp

As always, a diagonal move carries a cost of 1.41. If we add this to the g value stored by cell (4, 8) we get a g value for cell (3, 9) of 11.05 (1.41 + 9.64). The Manhattan Distance to the target is 2 giving us an f value of 13.05 (11.05 + 2).

Right

Moving to the right results in us entering the cell at (4, 9). Adding the cost of a horizontal move to the g value already stored in the current cell (4, 8) results in a value of 10.64 (1 + 9.64). The target is in the very next cell, so the Manhattan Distance is 1. Our f value is simply 11.64 (10.64 + 1). There is that number again!

If you take a quick look at Image 5.31 you can see the environment just before the current cell (3, 9) gets added to the *CLOSED* list.

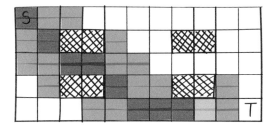

IMAGE 5.31   Ninth iteration of A*.

To the human eye it is obvious that the target cell is right next to us. The A* algorithm however must continue until it selects the target as the current cell to explore. Looking at Image 5.32, you can see that the lowest scoring cell is (4, 9) with our consistently low scoring 11.64. We choose this cell to explore next.

ID	g	h	f	Parent
(0,1)	1	13	14	(0,0)
(1,0)	1	13	14	(0,0)
(0,2)	2.82	12	14.82	(1,1)
(2,1)	2.41	11	13.41	(1,1)
(2,0)	2.82	12	14.82	(1,1)
(3,1)	4.24	10	14.24	(2,2)
(1,4)	5.23	9	14.23	(2,3)
(2,4)	4.82	8	12.82	(2,3)
(2,5)	6.64	7	13.64	(3,4)
(3,5)	6.23	6	12.23	(3,4)
(4,4)	6.23	6	12.23	(3,4)
(4,3)	6.64	7	13.64	(3,4)
(3,6)	8.05	5	13.05	(4,5)
(3,9)	11.05	2	13.05	(4,8)
→ (4,9)	10.64	1	11.64	(4,8)

OPEN LIST

IMAGE 5.32   *OPEN* List after Iteration 9.

Iteration #10

This iteration of the A* algorithm is very similar to the previous iteration, in that there are only two options from the current cell (4, 9). These are RightUp and Right. All other moves are either off the grid or are to cells already explored.

RightUp

Moving diagonally from the current cell (4, 9) to cell (3, 10) adds an additional cost of 1.41 to the g value stored by cell (4, 9) resulting in a new g value for cell (3, 10) of 12.05 (1.41 + 10.64). The Manhattan Distance to the target is 1 giving us an f value of 13.05 (12.05 + 1).

Right

Moving to the right is a horizontal move, which incurs a cost of 1. Adding this to the g cost stored in the current cell (4, 9) results in a g value of 11.64 for the cell at (4, 10). This cell is the target node, so the Manhattan Distance is 0, meaning that our f value is exactly the same as our g value 11.64 (11.64 + 0).

For the last time, take a look at the environment as it stands before the current cell gets added to the *CLOSED* list. Image 5.33 shows the target cell is blue, indicating that it has been added to the *OPEN* list.

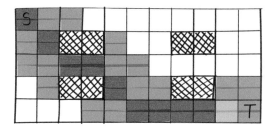

IMAGE 5.33   Tenth iteration of A*.

Looking now at the *OPEN* list in Image 5.34, we can see that the lowest scoring cell is (4, 10). The A* algorithm requires one more iteration to return a path. As with all previous iterations, it starts with us taking the lowest scoring cell from the list for expansion.

OPEN LIST				
ID	g	h	f	Parent
(0,1)	1	13	14	(0,0)
(1,0)	1	13	14	(0,0)
(0,2)	2.82	12	14.82	(1,1)
(2,1)	2.41	11	13.41	(1,1)
(2,0)	2.82	12	14.82	(1,1)
(3,1)	4.24	10	14.24	(2,2)
(1,4)	5.23	9	14.23	(2,3)
(2,4)	4.82	8	12.82	(2,3)
(2,5)	6.64	7	13.64	(3,4)
(3,5)	6.23	6	12.23	(3,4)
(4,4)	6.23	6	12.23	(3,4)
(4,3)	6.64	7	13.64	(3,4)
(3,6)	8.05	5	13.05	(4,5)
(3,9)	11.05	2	13.05	(4,8)
(3,10)	12.05	1	13.05	(4,9)
→ (4,10)	11.64	0	11.64	(4,9)

IMAGE 5.34 *OPEN* List *OPEN* List after Iteration 10.

ITERATION #11

When we take the lowest costing cell from the *OPEN* list for this iteration, we have found the target cell we were looking for. The A* algorithm can exit at this point. To calculate the path, we start with the target cell (4, 10) and work backwards from cell to cell using the stored parent value for each cell. When we reach the starting cell (0, 0) we will find that it has no parent. We can then use this list of parents to use as our path.

Take a look at Image 5.35 to see the *CLOSED* list as it stands when the A* algorithm completes. If you start with our target cell (4, 10), which is located at the

CLOSED LIST				
ID	g	h	f	Parent
(0,0)	0	14	14	NULL
(1,1)	1.41	12	13.41	(0,0)
(2,2)	2.82	10	12.82	(1,1)
(2,3)	3.82	9	12.82	(2,2)
(3,4)	5.23	7	12.23	(2,3)
(4,5)	6.64	5	11.64	(3,4)
(4,6)	7.64	4	11.64	(4,5)
(4,7)	8.64	3	11.64	(4,6)
(4,8)	9.64	2	11.64	(4,7)
(4,9)	10.64	1	11.64	(4,8)
(4,10)	11.64	0	11.64	(4,9)

IMAGE 5.35 *CLOSED* List.

bottom of the list, and look which cell was stored as its parent, and then repeat the process – parent to parent, you will do exactly what was described above to generate the path.

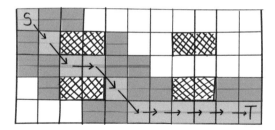

IMAGE 5.36   Final path.

In this scenario, we do find the target cell. The final path is depicted in Image 5.36. Notice how the cells that move away from the target have not been explored. If it had turned out that our route to the target cell had been blocked, let us say cell (4, 8) was inaccessible, these more expensive cells would have been explored in an attempt to find a path.

This step-by-step guide to the A* algorithm has been quite lengthy, but it is important to see exactly what is happening throughout the process. Having this understanding will make coding the search algorithm in the next section a lot easier, especially when it comes to debugging any potential problems.

FINAL THOUGHTS

Pathfinding is an area of game AI that you will always have to know. I have read books that claim it is not AI at all, but simply algorithmics. Although this statement is true, as a game AI programmer, pathfinding is something you are expected to know and be able to code. If an agent in your game goes in a direction that the player thinks stupid, guess which area of the game gets blamed. If an agent cannot find a path to a desired position, guess which area of the game is responsible. That is correct – the AI. So, make sure you have a good grasp of this topic, because as an AI programmer, pathfinding is something you most definitely should understand. And if you need any more convincing, just take a look online at any game AI programmer job advert.

PATHFINDING – PRACTICAL

PROJECT OVERVIEW

This project demonstrates pathfinding in a variety of ways. We will be focusing on the A* algorithm, but full implementations of Dijkstra's algorithm, Depth-first search (DFS) and Breadth-first search (BFS) are included. It also gives you the option to step through a search one iteration at a time (similar to the step-by-step guide described in the theory portion of this chapter).

The first part of the project allows you to create any environment you like, before moving on to the search part of the project. Screenshot 5.1 shows the search part of the project.

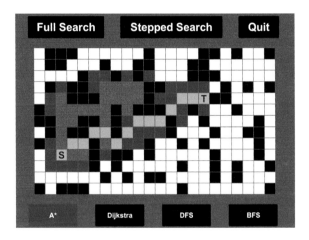

SCREENSHOT 5.1 Pathfinding project.

The options at the top of the screen allow you to search in two different manners. The options at the bottom of the screen allow you to change the algorithm that will be used for the search. A 'Full Search' runs the search using the currently selected algorithm until it returns a path or fails. A 'Full Search' using the A* algorithm will not work until we have gone through the tutorial below. A 'Stepped Search' runs a single iteration of the current algorithm and displays its current progress. This mode will work for the A* algorithm upon initial load so feel free to take a sneak peek at the path the A* algorithm generates.

Each cell is coloured to signify their current state. These are as follows:

- Black – Inaccessible cell.
- White – Accessible cell yet to be explored.
- Green – Current cell being expanded.
- Blue – A cell that resides on the *OPEN* list.
- Red – A cell that resides on the *CLOSED* list.

There are two cells marked with a character. These are as follows:

- S – Starting node.
- T – Target node.

When a search has completed, the cells that are part of the calculated path are coloured green. This is what is shown in Screenshot 5.1.

Be sure to have a play with Dijkstra, DFS and BFS. They all find paths in a different way, and it can be interesting to not only see the path they find, but how they found it. You may be surprised just how many nodes are assessed in the different approaches. When you have coded the A* algorithm using the guide below, you will be able to compare the results.

STEP-BY-STEP GUIDE

Open the Unity project named GameAi supplied with this book. Navigate through the folder system to the Chapter5_Pathfinding folder. It is located in the Assets folder. Click on the Chapter5_PathFinding scene. Run the application.

You can play around with generating different environments and then move on to the pathfinding part of the project. All algorithmic options work as expected apart from the 'Full Search' for the A* algorithm. We will be writing the code for this below.

Open the Scripts folder and locate the Algorithms folder. Within you will find a collection of pathfinding algorithm files, but we are only interested in the AStarAlgorithm.cs file. Click on this and locate the `Search()` function. As always, you will find an accompanying solution file with the complete code solution commented out. This is named AStarAlgorithm_Solution.cs.

AStarAlgorithm.cs

This file inherits from the BaseAlgorithm.cs file that all of the algorithmic options inherit from. This allows us to share common functionality. Do take the time to look at the base class and the other algorithm files.

Due to this application being written in the Unity game engine, there are some steps required to accessing nodes that you would not need to do if you were to write this in a different environment. I mention this purely to make you aware that some of the code supplied below should not be necessary, for example getting the gameobject from the grid, followed by calling the `GetComponent<Node>()` function, to access the Node details.

Let us get on with coding the A* algorithm. Locate the `Search()` function.

Search()
Locate the following line. Delete it and add the code described below at this location.

```
//Todo: Add code here.
```

The first thing we need to do is create variables to store the *g*, *h* and *f* values.

```
float g, h, f;
```

All algorithms return a path, so the path list is stored in the BaseAlgorithm.cs file. Take a look yourself. Before we start a new search, we need to clear out any game objects stored from a previous path.

```
Path.Clear();
```

If you look at the top of this file, you will see the creation of the *OPEN* list and the *CLOSED* list. We need to remove any data stored from a previous search.

```
OpenList.Clear();
ClosedList.Clear();
```

As every search starts with the start node, we need to add this to the *OPEN* list.

```
OpenList.Add(Grid.grid[Grid.StartX, Grid.StartY]);
```

We also need to know where the target is. So, get the target object so we can compare against it later.

```
GameObject targetObject = Grid.grid[Grid.TargetX, Grid.
TargetY];
Node targetNode = targetObject.GetComponent<Node>();
```

To start the actual A* algorithm, we need to check that our *OPEN* list has options. We know it does at this stage because we just added the start node. However, on subsequent iterations, we will have moved the starting node from the *OPEN* list to the *CLOSED* list and we do not know if we have run out of options.

```
while (OpenList.Count > 0)
{
```

We are now inside the A* algorithm. The first thing to do is to get the cheapest node from the *OPEN* list.

```
int indexOfCheapestNode = FindCheapestNodeInOpenList();
GameObject currentObject = OpenList[indexOfCheapestNode];
if (currentObject != null)
{
```

Now that we have a node, let us check if this is the target because if it is we can construct the path from the parent pointers and exit.

```
if (currentObject == targetObject)
```

```
{
    ConstructPath();
    UpdateVisuals();
    return;
}
```

At this stage in the algorithm, we have not found the target, so let us get the current node's details.

```
Node currentNode = currentObject.GetComponent<Node>();
Cell currentCell = currentObject.GetComponent<Cell>();
if (currentNode != null && currentCell != null)
{
```

Using the current node, we need to get all the connected nodes. In this example, we are going with four directions.

```
List<GameObject> childObjects = GetChildObjects(currentCell);
```

We need to calculate the costs for each connecting node. So we need a loop to iterate through them.

```
for (int i = 0; i < childObjects.Count; i++)
{
```

As described in the theory section, we need to set the *g*, *h* and *f* values. In this example, we are going with the Euclidean Distance for the *g*. This is the actual distance travelled, and we are using the Manhattan Distance for the heuristic. This is a guess. The *f* is simply the *g* and the *h* added together.

```
g = currentNode.g + GetEuclideanDistance(childObjects[i],
currentObject);
h = GetManhattanDistance(childObjects[i], targetObject);
f = g + h;
```

To access the required data in our project, we need to have access to the Node object. So let us get that now.

```
Node childNode = childObjects[i].GetComponent<Node>();
if (childNode != null)
{
```

If we already have this node stored on a list, we only want to change the details if this route is cheaper. So, add a Boolean to retain whether or not we need to set the values on this Node.

```
bool setValues = false;
```

Now check if this node is on either the *OPEN* list or the *CLOSED* list.

```
if (IsInList(ClosedList, childObjects[i]) ||
IsInList(OpenList, childObjects[i]))
{
```

Within this bracketed code segment, we are dealing with a node already stored on a list. So, check if it is cheaper to get to this node from here, and if so we can set that Boolean we created to true.

```
if (f < childNode.f)
    setValues = true;
```

We can close off the list check now with a bracket, but we are also going to add an else bracket to deal with nodes that were not in either list.

```
}
else
{
```

As our node is not on a list, we should add it to our *OPEN* list.

```
OpenList.Add(childObjects[i]);
```

And as it is a new node, we need to store the calculated g, *h* and *f* values. Set the `setValues` Boolean to true and close off this else code bracket.

```
setValues = true;
}
```

Using the `setValues` Boolean, we can now change the values stored for this node. If it was a new node, the values it currently has stored will be the default starting values. If it is a node stored on a list, we will be overwriting the values it has.

```
if(setValues)
{
    childNode.g = g;
    childNode.h = h;
    childNode.f = f;
    childNode.ParentX = currentCell.xPos;
    childNode.ParentY = currentCell.yPos;
}
```

Now we can close off the brackets. There should be three of them.

At this stage in the algorithm, we have chosen the cheapest node, checked if it was the target and iterated through its connections – setting each connected node's g, *h* and *f* values and adding it to the *OPEN* list. The next step is to move the current node from the *OPEN* list to the *CLOSED* list.

```
OpenList.Remove(currentObject);
ClosedList.Add(currentObject);
```

All that remains for us to do is to close off the brackets for this function – there should be two of them. When processing this function, we will loop back up to the while loop statement and find the next cheapest node and repeat the process until we find the target or run out of options.

You will notice that there are two additional lines of code.

```
UpdateVisuals();
firstPass = true;
```

Leave these where they are. They simply update the visuals and set a Boolean to true. This Boolean is used by the stepped approach. Without setting that here the stepped version of the A* algorithm would not work.

ConstructPath()

We are not going to code this function, but I would like us to take a look at how a path is generated from the results of the A* search. We start with the current node set to be the target node and then enter a do loop.

```
do
{
    if (currentObject != null)
    {
```

Within this loop we add the current node to the path. The `Add()` function adds elements to the end of the list, so this will result in a path from the target node to the starting node. Essentially, it is the path in reverse. We will address this issue after we have the complete path.

```
Path.Add(currentObject);
```

We then set the next node to be the node that the current node has stored as its parent node.

```
Node currentNode = currentObject.GetComponent<Node>();
if (currentNode != null)
{
  currentObject = Grid.grid[currentNode.ParentX, currentNode.
ParentY];
}
```

This process continues until we have found the starting node.

```
} while (currentObject != startObject);
```

Outside of this loop we need to add the starting node to our path list.

```
Path.Add(startObject);
```

And then simply reverse the list, so that the first element in the list will be the start node and the final element will be the target node.

```
Path.Reverse();
```

FUTURE WORK

At this stage through the book, you know how to move agents around, and you now know how to find a path in an environment. Try combining these approaches to have an agent search for a path and then move along that path from the starting position to the target position. When you are through with that, here are a couple more suggestions.

- If you are comfortable with the Unity game engine, try changing the size of the cells and increase the size of the grid to create more complex environments.
- You could also modify the code to allow movement in eight directions. How does this change the paths that are found?

6 Decision-Making

When you think about coding AI for a game character, you think about what you want them to do. Getting them to go here, or shoot that, or collect this for example. All those things describe single actions but knowing what an agent should do is only part of the problem. The other side of this problem is how to get them to make the correct decision between these options. Even back in the early days of arcade games, there were games where the AI-controlled characters did more than simply move across the screen from the right edge to the left edge – I'm looking at you Goomba. The ghosts in the game Pac-Man by Bandai Namco had different approaches to chasing down their yellow nemesis but also had a range of actions they could do. This chapter is going to look at how we handle all the different possible actions we want our character to handle. For example, how we control whether a ghost is chasing Pac-Man, or running away, or even returning to their home.

Before we begin, let us get some terminology out of the way. Actions, behaviours, states and tasks all amount to the same thing. They all describe what the agent is trying to achieve. Behaviour Trees obviously use the term 'behaviour', but these 'behaviours' could be described as 'states' if you so choose. It makes no difference. The same goes for a state machine. The "states" could be said to be an agent's current 'behaviour'. So let us not get bogged down in terminology. I will be using different terminology for different approaches, but just remember they amount to the same thing.

FINITE STATE MACHINE

The first solution to managing the different 'things' a character can do, which has been used since the early days of arcade games, is an approach called Finite State Machine, or FSM for short. There are various ways of implementing an FSM and we will discuss some of them as we progress through this chapter, but at its root it is an approach that describes the high-level actions available to an agent. It takes its name simply from the fact that there are a finite number of states from which to transition between. To explain what is meant by high level, let us take the ghosts in Pac-Man as an example. The high-level state of a ghost is to CHASE Pac-Man, but the low level is how the ghost actually does this. In Pac-Man each ghost has their own way in which they hunt the player down, but they are all in the same high-level state of CHASE.

It is important to note at this point that a state should only ever really do one thing – RUN, JUMP, SWIM and so on. Not RUN_AND_JUMP. Keeping it simple will allow your states to be reusable.

FSMs are great for drawing out as a sort of flow chart. Each state is a box or a circle and the transitions between them are arrows. The arrows show which states can transition into which states. If there is no arrow, then there is no transition. Imagine a game character that can be in the states RUN, JUMP, and CRAWL, depicted in Image 6.1. You may want the JUMP state to go into the RUN state, but not the CRAWL state. This is easily depicted as an FSM. Note how there is no arrow between JUMP and CRAWL. This also signifies that the character cannot JUMP from a CRAWL.

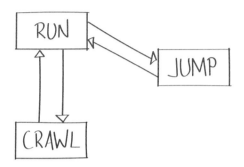

IMAGE 6.1 Generic character FSM.

Looking at Image 6.2, you can see how the overall behaviour of a Pac-Man ghost can be depicted extremely easily but look a little deeper and there is a lot of hidden complexity. We can see which states can transition to which states and what the conditions are for changing states. With this diagram, we can turn it into an FSM in code relatively easily.

To demonstrate the benefits of depicting your FSM in this manner, take a look at the transition from AT_HOME to EVADE. It states that when the ghost exits its home, if the power pill is still active it goes into an evade state. We could simply remove that transition and have the ghost stay in its home until the power pill expires, which means when the ghost exits its home, it would return to the CHASE state. Alternatively, we could remove the condition on the transition from AT_HOME to CHASE and have the ghost always chase when exiting the home, regardless of whether the power pill is still active.

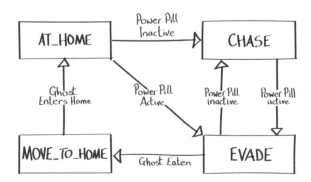

IMAGE 6.2 Ghost FSM.

On the code side of things, an individual state is expected to have certain functionality. An enter function, an update function and an exit function are all required. It is sensible to include a function to check for transitions too, as each state needs to handle whether it can make a transition, and to which state it transitions to. If a transition is required, the exit function is called on the current state, before calling the enter function on the new state. This is done to ensure that any clean-up from the previous state is done before any setup is done for the next state. Using the ghost again as an example, having the ghost exit whilst a power pill is active would mean the ghost itself needs to go into its blue version. This could be set in the enter function of the EVADE state.

After exiting and entering has completed, the update function is called on whatever the current state is. The update function is where the low-level code for completing the state is processed. For a project as simple as Pac-Man, this only involves setting a different position for the ghost to move to.

Now, FSMs are a relatively simple approach to undertake, but there are issues with this approach, which we will discuss momentarily. There are also different forms an FSM can take, again we will look at these shortly, but the simplest way to extend the basic approach is to allow a state to call multiple other states from within. This approach then becomes something called a Hierarchical Finite State Machine, or HFSM for short. A HFSM should only call other states that aid it in completing the task set for the parent state. An example here would be an agent within Call of Duty: Strike Team being instructed to FIND_COVER. This is not a straightforward task to achieve. Within this state the agent needs to exit the dumpster he is currently hiding in, find a safe location, calculate a safe path to that location, then repeatedly move between points on that path until he reaches the target position. Each of these elements can be self-contained in their own respective states. For example, EXIT_DUMPSTER could be used alone, or as part of the FIND_COVER state.

TERMINOLOGY: HIERARCHICAL FINITE STATE MACHINE

A finite state machine that allows for multiple substates to be called from within a single state.

LIMITATIONS

FSMs can appear somewhat predictable as the agent will always transition into the same state given the same conditions. If a player spots this, they can quickly lose their immersion in the experience. We can accommodate for this by having multiple options that achieve the same goal. For example, say we had a game where the player is trapped in a building and the enemies have to get into the building to detain him. Why not let them use windows as well as doors and maybe have them climb up a ladder and onto the roof. This would certainly keep the player on their toes and be more believable than allowing the player to stand in a corner and target the door. Having the bad guys spawn outside the door and keep running into the player's bullets is a sure fire way to lose that immersion.

Another limitation of the FSM approach is that you can only ever be in a single state at a particular time. Imagine a tank battle game where multiple enemies can be engaged. Image 6.3 shows a tank within range of two enemy tanks. Simply being in the RETREAT state does not look smart if you are about to run into the sights of another enemy. The worst-case scenario would be for our tank to transition between ATTACK and RETREAT states on each frame; an issue known as state thrashing. The tank would become stuck and appear to be confused about what to do in this situation.

TERMINOLOGY: STATE THRASHING

When an agent switches from one state to the next and back again on subsequent frames. The agent can appear stuck as it achieves neither of the states aims.

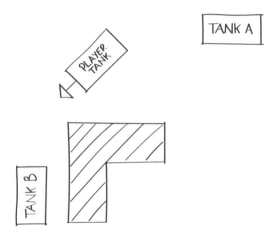

IMAGE 6.3   Tank battle.

Another potential issue with FSM is that the agent has no concept of memory. It does not know what it was previously doing. Granted this may not be important in the examples given. The ghosts in Pac-Man do not care about what they *were* doing, they only care about what they *are* doing, but in other games, this can prove to be extremely important. Imagine instructing a character to gather wood in a game like Age of Empires, and then the character gets into a fight. It would be extremely frustrating if the characters just stood around with nothing to do after the fight had concluded and for the player to have to go back through all the characters and re-instruct them after the fight is over. It would be much better for the characters to return to their previous duties.

FUZZY STATE MACHINE

What we need for our tank problem is some way for it to be in multiple states at the same time, ideally retreating from tank A, whilst attacking tank B. This is where Fuzzy State Machines, or FuSM for short, can come in handy. This approach allows you to have lots of available states, but to only be in a particular state to a certain degree. Image 6.4 provides a depiction for the tank example. Our tank could be 80% committed to the RETREAT state (avoid tank A) and 40% committed to the ATTACK state (attack tank B). This would allow it to both RETREAT and ATTACK at the same time. To achieve this, on each update your agent needs to check each possible state to determine its degree of commitment and then call each of the active state's update functions. This differs from a standard FSM, where you can only ever be in a single state. FuSMs can be in none, one, two or however many states you like at a particular time. This approach can prove tricky to balance and achieve the desired behaviours though, but it does offer an alternative to the standard approach.

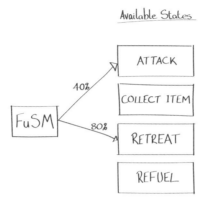

IMAGE 6.4   Tank FuSM.

STACK-BASED FSM

We can incorporate the idea of memory quite easily by using the stack data structure. The stack will hold AI states, with only the top-most element receiving the update call. This in effect means that when a state has completed, it is removed from the stack and the previous state is then processed.

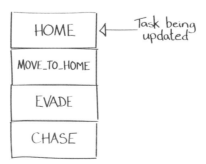

IMAGE 6.5   Stack-based FSM for a ghost.

Looking at Image 6.5, it shows how this could be achieved for a ghost in Pac-Man. Working from the bottom up you can see that the ghost was chasing the player, then the player collected a power pill, which resulted in the AI adding an EVADE state to the stack – this now gets the update call, not the CHASE state. The ghost did a poor job of evading the player and was eaten. At this point the ghost needs to return home, so the appropriate state was added. When it gets home, the ghost needs to know what to do whilst in this area, so the HOME state is added. This state resets the player and directs them back into the maze. At the point the ghost has exited home, the HOME task will be removed, which drops processing back to MOVE_TO_HOME. This is no longer required, so it will also get removed. We are now back in the EVADE task, which means the ghost 'remembers' what it was doing before it was eaten and ran off to home to be respawned. If, at this point, the power pill is still active the ghost will return to avoiding the player, however if the power pill has worn off, the EVADE state will get removed, putting the ghost back into its default state of CHASE. With only one state remaining on the stack, this will get the update calls until something else changes in the world.

BEHAVIOUR TREES

In 2002, Damian Isla expanded on the idea of HFSM in a way that made it more scalable and modular for the AI he developed for the game Halo 2 by Bungie. This became known as the Behaviour Tree approach. This has been used in many games since that point and has become a staple in AI game development. The general idea is that the Behaviour Tree is made up of nodes. These nodes can be one of three types: composite nodes, instructional nodes and leaf nodes. Image 6.6 depicts these most basic elements of a Behaviour Tree. Each type of node has a different function and affects the flow through the tree. All nodes have a common functionality in that they return their status to their parent node. This could be either SUCCESS, RUNNING or FAILURE.

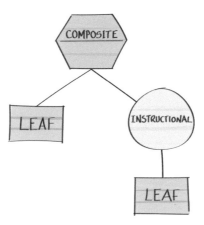

IMAGE 6.6   Basic Behaviour Tree nodes.

Each update the AI starts at the root node and works its way down the tree until it reaches a leaf node. Traversal down a tree every frame can take a lot of processing, so it makes sense to store the current node. That way on the next frame you have no need to work down the tree to find where you were, you can jump right to it. Image 6.7 shows a larger example of how this approach could be set up for a ghost in Pac-Man. The nodes in all images will be colour coded to help you identify their type. Leaf nodes are blue, composite nodes are green and instructional nodes are yellow.

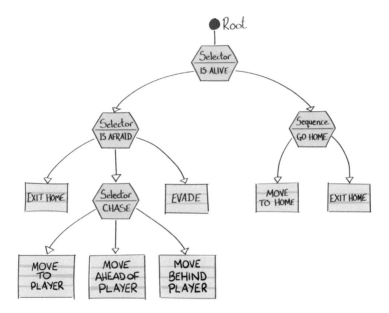

IMAGE 6.7   Behaviour Tree for a ghost.

A huge benefit to using a Behaviour Tree approach is to reduce code replication. Behaviour trees can be built from smaller Behaviour Trees, and passage down the tree can be passed to other parts of the tree. You can even make parts of the tree inaccessible, unlocking them during gameplay, making agents appear to be learning behaviours throughout the game. Alien Isolation by Creative Assembly did exactly this for the AI of the Xenomorph.

Let us now take a more detailed look at each of the different node types available to the Behaviour Tree approach.

LEAF NODES

An FSM state would be classified as a leaf node. Leaf nodes end a particular branch of the tree and do not have any child nodes. These are where the actual AI behaviours are located. They are easily spotted, as Leaf nodes always end a particular branch of the tree. For example, EXIT HOME, EVADE and MOVE AHEAD OF PLAYER are all Leaf nodes. These all instruct the ghost as to what it actually needs to do.

INSTRUCTIONAL NODES

Instructional nodes control the flow back up the tree and can only have a single child. The purpose of this node could affect the flow through the tree in a variety of ways. For example, it could repeatedly call the child regardless of the status returned for a set period of time, or indefinitely if required, or possibly until some condition is met. The instruction could even modify the status returned, say inverting the status – so a SUCCESS becomes a FAILURE and vice versa. From what first appears to be a collection of simple concepts, complex behaviours will develop.

TERMINOLOGY: DECORATOR

In other texts, instructional nodes are called decorators. The terms are interchangeable. I just feel the term 'instructional' describes what they do better.

COMPOSITE NODES

Composite nodes can have multiple child nodes and are used to determine the order and the requirements for which the children are called. Let us look at this a little more in depth. There are two main forms of composite nodes known as sequence and selector. A composite node returns its status differently depending upon its function.

Selector composite nodes will work through all of its child nodes in some order until one returns SUCCESS, which allows the Selector node to return a status of SUCCESS. It only returns FAILURE when all options have been exhausted. Image 6.8 depicts a simple branch of a Behaviour Tree that starts with a Selector composite node. This node could first try Leaf1 and if that returns SUCCESS, the Selector node will also return SUCCESS. If Leaf1 returned FAILURE, the Selector would then try another child, let us say Leaf2, to see if that option fares any better. Only when all three options have failed does the Selector itself return a status of FAILURE. It is important to note that the order in which the Selector composite node iterates through its children is dependent upon the criteria for the specific composite node. All children may try to achieve the same goal, meaning any child could be randomly selected. Alternatively, the composite could have a condition for selecting children. Take a look back at Image 6.7. Find the IS AFRAID Selector. The child chosen here depends upon a condition of the ghost's internal state.

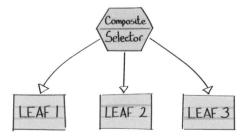

IMAGE 6.8   Selector composite node.

A Sequence composite node differs from the Selector version of a composite node in the way it processes its child nodes. It will run through all of its child nodes in order and will return a status of FAILURE on the first child that returned a FAILURE status. All child nodes after the failing node do not get processed. So, looking at Image 6.9, which looks suspiciously similar to Image 6.8, the Sequence compost node will first flow through the Leaf1 node. Whilst it is running, we return a RUNNING status. If Leaf1 returns SUCCESS, the Sequence composite node still returns a status of RUNNING, but it now flows through Leaf2. It is only when Leaf1, Leaf2 and Leaf3 all return a status of SUCCESS does the Sequence composite node return a status of SUCCESS.

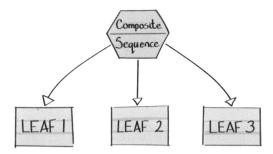

IMAGE 6.9   Sequence composite node.

For both composite node types, the order the child nodes are called is important. It could be simply in the order in which they are described by the tree, or a specified order or even randomly. Looking again at Image 6.7, The CHASE Selector allows the ghost to select a single path down the tree by choosing a random option, whereas the GO HOME Sequence has to complete all child paths to complete its behaviour. It is worth noting that GO HOME Sequence would not work if the child nodes were in a different order.

Behaviour trees can take a lot of time to set up and problems cannot always present themselves. You can be left wondering why an agent did this or that. My advice would be to use a lot of debug output so you can track the behaviours as they change.

FINAL THOUGHTS

Whatever the choice for your game, keep it simple. If an FSM can do what is required, then do not feel the need to implement a Behaviour Tree. Understand the reasons for choosing an approach and select the most suitable option. If a Behaviour Tree gives you the functionality you need, go for that. Game development is hard enough as it is without making it more difficult because you just wanted to try some cool approach you have never used before.

DECISION-MAKING – PRACTICAL

PROJECT OVERVIEW

This project is a version of the arcade classic Pac-Man. The player takes control of the main character and must collect all the dots in the environment before getting eaten by the ghosts. The large yellow dots located in each corner give the player the ability to eat the ghosts, but this only lasts a short time.

There are two AI modes of play available. The first is with the ghost AI handled by an FSM. This is the default option when you begin the game. The second approach is the ghost AI being handled by a Behaviour Tree. You can switch between each approach by pressing the spacebar. Screenshot 6.1 shows the game in action using the Behaviour Tree depicted in Image 6.7.

When you open the project, you will find that the ghost AI for Behaviour Trees has not been coded. The game plays fine using the FSM approach, but if you press the spacebar to switch to the Behaviour Tree approach, all the ghosts just stand still. This approach will not work until we have followed the step-by-step guide below.

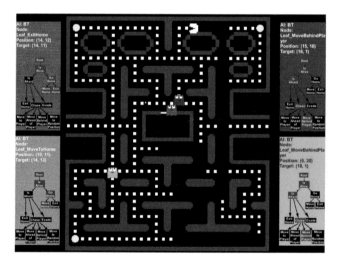

SCREENSHOT 6.1   Classic Pac-Man style game.

As can be seen in the screenshot, each ghost has a corresponding panel at the side of the screen. This shows us what state or behaviour a ghost is currently in. For the Behaviour Tree approach, it also shows how the tree is navigated.

STEP-BY-STEP GUIDE

Open the Unity project named GameAi supplied with this book. Navigate through the folder system to the Chapter6_DecisionMaking folder. It is located in the Assets folder. Click on the Chapter6_DecisionMaking scene. Run the application. Press the spacebar to switch the AI approach from FSM to Behaviour Tree. It is not much fun when the ghosts do nothing.

To be able to code the Behaviour Tree AI for a ghost, we first need to implement a collection of functions specific to this problem. If you take a look back at Image 6.7, you will see all of the Behaviour Tree nodes that we will be coding. We will work through all of these even though some are very similar. Open the BehaviourTree folder. All the files of interest are located within.

To begin, we need to look at a couple of files but will not be changing any of the code within.

BEHAVIOURTREE.CS

The Behaviour Tree class is where the AI gets updated every frame. We start at the root node and work our way down the tree until we get to the desired leaf node. If you take a look at the top of this file, you will see that we have member variables for the ghost being controlled and the player. Both of these must be set up for the game to run.

We also have a `TreeNode _ Base` object called `rootNode` that is being set to the `Selector _ IsAlive` node. This is where all the action starts. We will look at `Selector _ IsAlive` shortly, but it will come as no surprise that it checks to see if the ghost is alive or not and directs the flow of the tree from there.

If you take a look at the `Update()` function. You will see a call to `OnUpdate()` on the root node. This happens every frame and we start from the root of the tree. We need to do this as circumstances beyond a ghost's control can affect things, for example the player collecting a power dot.

TREENODE _ BASE.CS

All nodes in the Behaviour Tree inherit from this node. In order to build the desired tree structure, we will be allocating children nodes in the constructor for each of the behaviours. The constructor for the base node should therefore be overridden. The `OnUpdate()` function should also be overridden by the behaviours that inherit from `TreeNode _ Base`.

SELECTOR _ ISALIVE.CS

Our Behaviour Tree starts here. This is our root. We need to determine if the ghost is alive or not and depending on the result of this check we will navigate different branches of the tree.

Selector_IsAlive()

Locate the constructor and delete the following line:

```
//Delete me.
```

Now we can add the desired children for this node. Feel free to check back with Image 6.7 as we go to ensure we are building the tree we wanted. Add the following lines of code to add the required child nodes:

```
childrenNodes.Add(new Selector_IsAfraid());
childrenNodes.Add(new Sequence_GoHome());
```

OnUpdate()

As described above, we simply need to know if the ghost is alive or not. We do this by checking if the ghost has been eaten – ghosts never really die. Delete the following and add the code snippets below:

```
//Delete me.
return Status.FAILURE;
```

If the ghost has not been eaten, then we send the flow of the tree down the left branch of the tree to the `Selector _ IsAfraid` node. This is not to say the ghost should be afraid, but to select what action to take.

```
if (!ghost.HasBeenEaten())
{
    return childrenNodes[0].OnUpdate(ghost, player);
}
```

Otherwise, the ghost has been eaten so must return to its home to regenerate. This is the right-hand branch of the tree and we flow to the `Sequence _ GoHome` node.

```
else
{
    return childrenNodes[1].OnUpdate(ghost, player);
}
```

SELECTOR _ ISAFRAID.CS

The purpose of this behaviour is to determine the next action for a ghost if the ghost has not been eaten. This includes being in the ghost home and acts like a respawn for the ghost. This node is a selector and there are three choices, ExitHome, Evade and Chase.

Selector_IsAfraid()

Locate the constructor and delete the following line:

```
//Delete me.
```

We can now add the different behaviours that this selector will choose between. Add the following lines of code to add the required child nodes:

```
childrenNodes.Add(new Leaf_ExitHome());
```

```
childrenNodes.Add(new Leaf_Evade());
childrenNodes.Add(new Selector_Chase());
```

OnUpdate()

The decision here is whether we are currently in the ghost home, if a power dot is active or none of these. If the ghost is at home, then it needs to leave. If the player is now powered up, the ghost needs to run away. If neither of these conditions are met, the ghost should chase the player.

So, to begin, remove the following lines:

```
//Delete me.
return Status.FAILURE;
```

And add an if statement to check the home condition. As we saw in the constructor, the behaviour at Index 0 is `Leaf _ ExitHome`, so let us call that as the next node.

```
if (ghost.IsInHome())
{
    return childrenNodes[0].OnUpdate(ghost, player);
}
```

It is possible that the player is powered up, so check that. If so, call the `OnUpdate()` function on the behaviour at Index 1, which we know is `Leaf _ Evade`.

```
if (ghost.IsPowerPillActive())
{
    return childrenNodes[1].OnUpdate(ghost, player);
}
```

Otherwise, we should give chase. This is the behaviour located at Index 2.

```
else
{
    return childrenNodes[2].OnUpdate(ghost, player);
}
```

Leaf _ ExitHome.cs

This is the first leaf node we have encountered thus far. The constructor is empty as a leaf has no children. This is where the tree ends. The purpose of this behaviour is to get the ghost out of the home.

OnUpdate()

The update for a leaf is an action. It is the place where we direct the ghost to do what is required. There is no decision required.

Locate the following and delete it.

```
//Delete me.
return Status.FAILURE;
```

First, we want to change the visuals of the ghost to ensure the relevant sprites are used.

```
ghost.ghostVisuals.SetSpriteSet(SpriteSet.Chasing);
```

Then set the desired position. This is set at the top of this class and will never change.

```
ghost.SetTargetBoardPosition(exitPos);
```

We now need to navigate our way out of the home. There are two movement functions available: `Move()` and `MoveHome()` that use the target board position we have just set. `MoveHome()` allows for movement into and out of the home, `Move()` does not. So let us call the relevant movement function.

```
ghost.MoveHome();
```

A leaf should return its current status. Failure is not an option for this behaviour. We are either in the home or not. If the ghost is at the exit position, then we can assume we are outside of the home and can return a status of SUCCESS.

```
if (ghost.GetBoardPosition() == exitPos)
{
    return Status.SUCCESS;
}
```

If we are not at the exit position, we are yet to exit the home and should continue to run this node until we are successful.

```
else
{
    return Status.RUNNING;
}
```

Selector _ Chase.cs

There are a variety of ways to chase the player. At the top of the file, we have a member variable to keep track of which node was running the last time we were in this composite node.

```
private int previousRunningNode = 0;
```

Selector_Chase()
Locate the following and delete it:

```
//Delete me.
```

We can now add the different behaviours that this selector will choose between. Add the following lines of code to add the required child nodes. Take a look back at Image 6.7 to see this visually.

```
childrenNodes.Add(new Leaf_MoveToPlayer());
childrenNodes.Add(new Leaf_MoveAheadOfPlayer());
childrenNodes.Add(new Leaf_MoveBehindPlayer());
childrenNodes.Add(new Leaf_MoveToRandomPosition());
```

To ensure each ghost has a different approach to chasing when first running the game, we need to generate a random index to use as the child for the tree to flow through.

```
System.Random rnd = new System.Random();
previousRunningNode = rnd.Next(0, childrenNodes.Count);
```

OnUpdate()

As always, locate the following lines of code and delete them:

```
//Delete me.
return Status.FAILURE;
```

We need to call the `OnUpdate()` function on the selected child behaviour. This will return a status that we can use to determine if we should select a different child behaviour to run on the next frame.

```
Status ghostStatus = childrenNodes[previousRunningNode].
OnUpdate(ghost, player);
```

Check the status returned. If it was a SUCCESS, we can select a random index in the same manner as we did in the constructor.

```
if (ghostStatus == Status.SUCCESS)
{
    System.Random rnd = new System.Random();
    previousRunningNode = rnd.Next(0, childrenNodes.Count);
}
```

And finally, return the status we have.

```
return ghostStatus;
```

Leaf _ MoveToPlayer.cs

This node is a leaf, so ends this branch of the tree. We are going to move toward the player for a set time duration. We set this duration at the top of the class. Feel free to modify this value to give different results.

```
private const float kMaxDuration = 10.0f;
private float duration = kMaxDuration;
```

OnUpdate()

Locate the following lines of code and delete them:

```
//Delete me.
return Status.FAILURE;
```

As we are only doing this behaviour for a duration, we need to deduct delta time from the current value stored.

```
duration -= Time.deltaTime;
```

Set the relevant visuals for a ghost who is currently in a chase leaf behaviour.

```
ghost.ghostVisuals.SetSpriteSet(SpriteSet.Chasing);
```

Set the desired position to be the position of the player.

```
ghost.SetTargetBoardPosition(player.GetBoardPosition());
```

Move the ghost to the desired position.

```
ghost.Move();
```

Now we have enacted the movement, we need to check if the duration for this behaviour has expired. When the time reaches zero, we will return the status SUCCESS to allow our parent node to select another way to chase the player. We should also reset the duration of this behaviour in case we run this leaf again.

```
if (duration <= 0.0f)
{
    duration = kMaxDuration;
    return Status.SUCCESS;
}
```

If the duration still has time to run, we should return a status of RUNNING to the calling parent node.

```
else
{
    return Status.RUNNING;
}
```

LEAF _ MOVEAHEADOFPLAYER.CS

This node is another leaf so also ends this branch of the tree. This leaf looks to cut off the player by moving to a position ahead of the player. At the top of the file, we set the duration for this in exactly the same manner as we did for the `Leaf _ MoveToPlayer` node.

OnUpdate()

In the usual way, delete the following lines of code:

```
//Delete me.
return Status.FAILURE;
```

Next, deduct delta time from the current duration value stored.

```
duration -= Time.deltaTime;
```

Set the correct visuals for the ghost.

```
ghost.ghostVisuals.SetSpriteSet(SpriteSet.Chasing);
```

This is the point that this behaviour differs from `Leaf _ MoveToPlayer`. We need to calculate a position ahead of the player, which depends upon the direction the player is currently moving. This position will either be a change in the row or column of the player's current direction.

```
Vector2Int positionAheadOfPlayer = new Vector2Int();
switch (player.GetDirection())
{
case Direction.Left:
    positionAheadOfPlayer = player.GetBoardPosition() + new
Vector2Int(-1, 0);
break;

case Direction.Right:
    positionAheadOfPlayer = player.GetBoardPosition() + new
Vector2Int(1, 0);
break;

case Direction.Up:
    positionAheadOfPlayer = player.GetBoardPosition() + new
Vector2Int(0, -1);
break;

case Direction.Down:
    positionAheadOfPlayer = player.GetBoardPosition() + new
Vector2Int(0, 1);
break;
}
```

At this point, we do not know if the selected position is valid. Call the `IsCellAccessible()` function from the GameWorld class to determine this. If this check returns true, then we set this position as the target board position.

```
if (GameWorld.IsCellAccessible(positionAheadOfPlayer))
{
    ghost.SetTargetBoardPosition(positionAheadOfPlayer);
}
```

If the position is not valid, let the ghost just head for the player's current position. This could happen at the edge of the environment.

```
else
{
    ghost.SetTargetBoardPosition(player.GetBoardPosition());
}
```

Now we have a position stored, we can call the relevant movement function.

```
ghost.Move();
```

With movement handled, we need to check if the duration for this behaviour has expired. When the time reaches zero, we will return the status SUCCESS to allow our parent node to select another way to chase the player. At this point, we should reset the duration variable to allow this behaviour to be run again for the full duration.

```
if (duration <= 0.0f)
{
    duration = kMaxDuration;
    return Status.SUCCESS;
}
```

If the duration still has time to run, we should return a status of RUNNING to the calling parent node.

```
else
{
    return Status.RUNNING;
}
```

LEAF _ MOVEBEHINDPLAYER.CS

This node is another leaf so ends this branch of the tree. It has a simple task to achieve, and that is to move to a position behind the player. At the top of the file, we set the duration for this in exactly the same manner as we did for the `Leaf _ MoveToPlayer` node.

OnUpdate()

Start as usual by deleting the following lines of code:

```
//Delete me.
return Status.FAILURE;
```

Deduct the time that has passed since the last update from the current duration value stored.

```
duration -= Time.deltaTime;
```

Set the correct visuals for the ghost.

```
ghost.ghostVisuals.SetSpriteSet(SpriteSet.Chasing);
```

Next, we need to calculate the position behind the player, which again depends upon the direction the player is currently moving. This position will either be a change in the row or column of the player's current direction.

```
Vector2Int positionBehindPlayer = new Vector2Int();
switch (player.GetDirection())
{
case Direction.Left:
    positionBehindPlayer = player.GetBoardPosition() + new
Vector2Int(1, 0);
break;

case Direction.Right:
    positionBehindPlayer = player.GetBoardPosition() + new
Vector2Int(-1, 0);
break;

case Direction.Up:
    positionBehindPlayer = player.GetBoardPosition() + new
Vector2Int(0, 1);
break;

case Direction.Down:
    positionBehindPlayer = player.GetBoardPosition() + new
Vector2Int(0, -1);
break;
}
```

We still need to check if the selected position is valid by calling the IsCellAccessible() function from the GameWorld class. If this check returns true, then we set this position as the target board position.

```
if (GameWorld.IsCellAccessible(positionAheadOfPlayer))
{
    ghost.SetTargetBoardPosition(positionAheadOfPlayer);
}
```

If the position was not valid, the ghost should just head for the player's current position.

```
else
{
    ghost.SetTargetBoardPosition(player.GetBoardPosition());
}
```

Now that we have a position stored, we can call the relevant movement function.

```
ghost.Move();
```

Next, we need to check if the duration for this behaviour has expired. When the duration reaches zero, we should return a status of SUCCESS and reset the duration of this behaviour in the event that we run this leaf again.

```
if (duration <= 0.0f)
{
    duration = kMaxDuration;
    return Status.SUCCESS;
}
```

If there is still time to run, we should return a status of RUNNING to the calling parent node.

```
else
{
    return Status.RUNNING;
}
```

Leaf _ MoveToRandomPosition.cs

This node is another leaf, so as always the branch of the tree ends here. This behaviour moves a ghost to a random position. At the top of the file, we set the duration for this in exactly the same manner as we did for all previous leaf behaviours and create a member Vector2Int variable to store a random board position.

```
Vector2Int randomPosition = new Vector2Int();
```

This is set in the constructor by calling the `ResetRandomPosition()` function.

OnUpdate()

Locate the following lines of code and delete them:

```
//Delete me.
return Status.FAILURE;
```

Deduct the current duration value by delta time.

```
duration -= Time.deltaTime;
```

And then set the correct visuals for the ghost.

```
ghost.ghostVisuals.SetSpriteSet(SpriteSet.Chasing);
```

We have already selected a random position to move to, so set that as the desired position to move to.

```
ghost.SetTargetBoardPosition(randomPosition);
```

Move the ghost to the desired position.

```
ghost.Move();
```

After the desired duration, we will return a status of SUCCESS to allow our parent node to select another way to chase the player. We should also call the `ResetRandomPosition()` function to choose a different random position to move to the next time we use this leaf node. The duration needs to be reset at this point too.

```
if (duration <= 0.0f)
{
    duration = kMaxDuration;
    ResetRandomPosition();

    return Status.SUCCESS;
}
```

Otherwise, we need to keep running this leaf node; so by returning a status of RUNNING, we can ensure we get the update on the next frame.

```
else
{
    return Status.RUNNING;
}
```

Leaf _ Evade.cs

Although we will not be changing any code in the constructor, it is worth taking a look to see that we generate a random position **not** in the environment for the ghost to evade to. This position is used whenever the ghost is in this node and processing the `OnUpdate()` function.

OnUpdate()

Start as usual by deleting the following lines of code:

```
//Delete me.
Return Status.FAILURE;
```

Change the visuals of the ghost to show they are evading the player.

```
ghost.ghostVisuals.SetSpriteSet(SpriteSet.Evading);
```

Set the desired position to the randomly generated position that is located outside of the environment.

```
ghost.SetTargetBoardPosition(randomEvadePosition);
```

Move the ghost using the appropriate movement function. In this scenario, we want movement that does not access the ghost home.

```
ghost.Move();
```

As we do not expect the ghost to actually reach this position (remember it is off the board), we should return a status of RUNNING. This leaf needs to keep processing until the player's power has worn off. The response to the power dot expiring will be handled further up the tree. It is not the responsibility of this leaf to handle that change in circumstances.

```
return Status.RUNNING;
```

SEQUENCE _ GOHOME.CS

There are a specific number of steps required for a ghost to go home. First it must move to the home location so that it can regenerate, then it needs to exit the home. Only when both of these have returned a status of SUCCESS can this composite node return a status of SUCCESS.

Sequence_GoHome()

Scroll down to the constructor and delete the following line of code:

```
//Delete me.
```

Now we can add the relevant steps to this sequence. These are the leaf to `MoveToHome` and the leaf for `ExitHome`. Feel free to take a look at Image 6.7 to see this depicted.

```
childrenNodes.Add(new Leaf_MoveToHome());
childrenNodes.Add(new Leaf_ExitHome());
```

OnUpdate()

Locate the following lines of code and delete them:

```
//Delete me.
return Status.FAILURE;
```

We need to keep track of whether a child node is running or not. Even one child node running will return a status of RUNNING to the calling parent node.

```
bool childIsRunning = false;
```

We are going to loop through all of the children nodes until all have returned successfully or one of them has failed.

```
for(int i =0; i < childrenNodes.Count; i++)
{
```

For each child node, we will call the `OnUpdate()` function. This loop will work through all the children until it reaches one that returns a status of RUNNING or FAILURE. In the event of the child at Index 0 returning a status of RUNNING, the child at Index 1 will not get processed.

```
switch (childrenNodes[i].OnUpdate(ghost, player))
{
```

The child returned a status of FAILURE, so we should return this information immediately to the calling node in the Behaviour Tree.

```
case Status.FAILURE:
    return Status.FAILURE;
break;
```

The child returned a status of SUCCESS, so exit the switch statement at this point and iterate around the loop again. This allows us to test each child behaviour until we reach one that returns a status of FAILURE or RUNNING.

```
case Status.SUCCESS:
    continue;
break;
```

If the current child in the loop is still running, set the appropriate flag and exit the for loop with a continue.

```
case Status.RUNNING:
    i = childrenNodes.Count;
    childIsRunning = true;
    continue;
break;
```

We are going to assume that in any other scenario the child returns a status of SUCCESS. This should never happen but has been added for the sake of completing the switch statement correctly.

```
default:
break;
```

Close off the switch statement and the for loop with two brackets.

```
    }
}
```

Determine if one of the child nodes is still running, and if so set the current status to RUNNING. If not, we can assume that it was a SUCCESS. Return this to the calling parent node. If the child had returned FAILURE, we would have returned from this function before reaching this point.

```
return childIsRunning?  Status.RUNNING : Status.SUCCESS;
```

Leaf _ MoveToHome.cs

This leaf node will actually move us to the ghost home and is called from `Sequence _ GoHome`. The constructor is empty as a leaf has no children. This is where the tree ends. The purpose of this behaviour is to get the ghost into the ghost home.

OnUpdate()

Start as usual by deleting the following lines of code:

```
//Delete me.
return Status.FAILURE;
```

Change the visuals of the ghost to show they are only eyes.

```
ghost.ghostVisuals.SetSpriteSet(SpriteSet.Eyes);
```

Set the desired position to the home position. This is set at the top of this class and will never change.

```
ghost.SetTargetBoardPosition(homePos);
```

Move the ghost using the `MoveHome()` function, which allows movement within the home as well as the rest of the environment.

```
ghost.MoveHome();
```

For this leaf, failure is not an option. It should continue to run until the ghost is located at the home position. So, let us check if we are in position, and if so, return a status of SUCCESS. We are also going to set the ghost's internal variable, so it knows it has no longer been eaten.

```
if (ghost.GetBoardPosition() == homePos || !ghost.
HasBeenEaten())
{
    ghost.SetEaten(false);
    return Status.SUCCESS;
}
```

Otherwise, we must still be trying to get home, so return a status of RUNNING.

```
else
{
    return Status.RUNNING;
}
```

That's it. Go back across to the Unity engine and click run. If all has gone well, you should be able to press the spacebar and the ghosts now play using the Behaviour Tree approach. As ever, if you have errors, refer to the solution files that are located in the same folder. It is easy to miss something.

FUTURE WORK

There is so much more you can do with Behaviour Trees. A couple of suggestions for additions could be:

- Modify the duration a ghost is in a particular leaf, so different behaviours are enacted for different amounts of times.
- Why not sketch out your own Behaviour Tree that acts differently for each ghost. You could have one ghost that always tries to cut off the player, whilst another always tries to attack from the rear.

7 Fuzzy Logic

Decision-making can be very binary. We either do a thing or we do not do a thing. Let us say our agent is deciding whether to attack an opponent with her water pistol. What criteria are required? Distance to the opponent seems an obvious choice. In this fictional game, we do not want to get ourselves wet, so let us say if they are 2 metres away – a distance that can soak them but not us, we attack, but if they are further away than 5 metres we do not attack. Seems logical … How about if they are 1 metre and 99 centimeters away? Or 5 metres and 1 centimeter away? Hopefully, you can see how ridiculous that would be. The opponent at a distance of 5 metres can take one step backwards and be safe.

It would be great if there was some way to remove those boundaries. Some way to stipulate – if the opponent is near or far then do not attack, but if they are in the middle then fire away, whilst at the same time blurring the boundaries between these ranges. In other words, we need a different way to determine our actions that are not binary in nature, and that my friends is where Fuzzy Logic comes to save the day.

So, tell me more about this Fuzzy Logic thing I hear you say. Well lucky you as that is exactly what this chapter is about. Fuzzy Logic is a method by which we can take crisp values and use something more akin to language to assess them – the near, middle and far terms used in the example.

TERMINOLOGY: CRISP VALUE

A crisp value is the actual numbers we use in game – 20, 4, 3.5 etc.

Computers process numbers, so do games, but humans not so much. Consider the terms: hot and cold, tall and small, near and far etc. For a computer these terms mean absolutely nothing, yet as humans we tend to say things like, 'I hope the weather is warm today'. We do not say, 'I hope the weather is 20 degrees Celsius today'. Do we? Fuzzy Logic bridges the gap. That is not to say we do not need the numbers, we do, but we need to convert them into our linguistic terms, process them and return to a single number again.

TERMINOLOGY: LINGUISTIC TERM

A term in our vocabulary that describes a set of values. Easily understood by humans, not so much by computers. For example, Near and Far, Safe and Dangerous.

As a visual overview, Image 7.1 shows how Fuzzy Logic takes our crisp values, processes them and returns another crisp value.

DOI: 10.1201/9781003305835-7

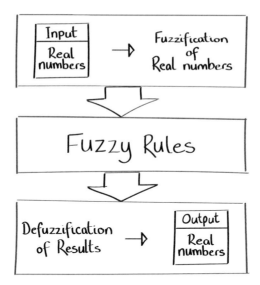

IMAGE 7.1   Fuzzy Logic process.

We are going to tackle each of these stages in turn, but as usual we will use a game example to do this.

Imagine our agent is a player in the game Speedball 2 by The Bitmap Brothers. Any game will do where the agent needs to assess options and throw the ball. When developing this sort of a game it would be great if we could get some expert advice, but in reality, we tend to decide these things for ourselves. For this example, let us pretend the sport of Speedball is real and we could talk to an actual player and get their insight on how they make their decisions about the riskiness of a throw. It is quite possible that we would get something like this:

If I'm under lots of pressure and the receiver has limited coverage and the distance of the throw is far, then that is a safe throw.

However, if I'm under a minimum of pressure and the receiver has lots of coverage and the distance of the throw is short, then that is a risky throw.

Just from these two statements we have learned a lot. We now know there are three different inputs a player uses to assess the current situation to enable them to make a decision. And the output of these statements is the riskiness of a throw. The words highlighted in red are the inputs, and the words highlighted in blue are the linguistic terms these inputs will use.

The inputs we will use are:

- Distance
- Pressure
- Coverage

The output is:
- Riskiness

SETS

Using the distance input, we need to create some linguistic terms to accommodate all the player's expertise. Looking again at the statements, the player used the terms short and far to describe the distance of the throw. What distance do we classify as a far throw? What about a short throw? We should ask our fictitious Speedball player friend these questions, but for now let us make up some numbers.

- Less than 5 yards is a short throw.
- Greater than or equal to 20 yards is a far throw.
- Anywhere in-between is a medium throw.

So given these values as a starting point, let us group together distances in yards from 0 to 100 into these categories.

$$Short = (0, 1, ..., 5)$$

$$Medium = (6, 7, ..., 19)$$

$$Far = (20, 21, ..., 100)$$

If we graph each of these out, we get the graphs seen in Images 7.2–7.4. The horizontal axis is the distance in yards, and the vertical axis describes whether a distance is in the specified set or not. Select a distance and see where the red line is at that position. A result of 1 means a distance is in the set, and a result of 0 means the distance is not in the set. It can only ever be one of these results.

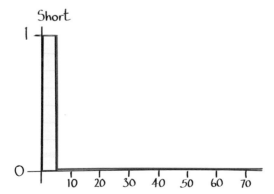

IMAGE 7.2   Short set.

If we were to select a distance, say 19 yards, and plug it into each of these graphs, you will find that it only returns 1 on the Medium graph. On the others, it lands outside

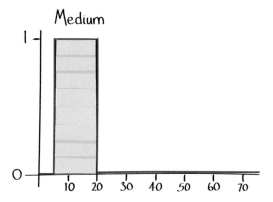

IMAGE 7.3   Medium set.

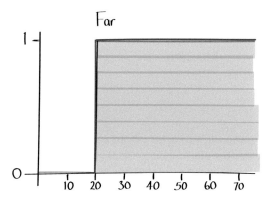

IMAGE 7.4   Far set.

of the coloured area. This is very binary. The value on the vertical axis can only ever be 1 or 0. In effect we are saying that a 19-yard throw:

- Is NOT a Short throw
- Is a Medium throw
- Is NOT a Far throw

We may very well agree but let us re-run our test but this time with a throw of 20 yards. What you will find is that 20 yards:

- Is NOT a short throw
- Is NOT a Medium throw
- Is a Far throw

So, are we really saying that with a 1-yard change we have gone from a Medium throw to a Far throw?

You could rightly say that there has to be a cut-off at some point, and I would agree. How about if we add 19 yards into the Far group as well as the Medium group?

We would now be considering 19 yards as a Medium throw and a Far throw. How is that possible? It cannot be equally both Medium and Far. Surely it is one or the other? You might be saying to yourself that in reality it is a bit of both – Medium and Far. And again, I would agree, however, changing the boundary in this way did not actually solve any problems, as we still have the original issue. What do we do about the 1-yard change we now see between an 18-yard throw and a 19-yard throw?

Would it not be better if there was some way to say that yes 19 yards is both Medium and Far? It is not 100% Medium or 100% Far, but it definitely features in both brackets to some degree. This is where membership functions in Fuzzy Sets prove useful.

FUZZY SETS

A Fuzzy Set is a linguistic term represented using a membership function. So, for our distance example we could have three Fuzzy Sets, each taken from a linguistic term – Short, Medium and Far. When all these terms are grouped together into a single graph it is called a Fuzzy Manifold.

TERMINOLOGY: FUZZY SET

A Fuzzy Set is a linguistic term represented using a membership function. A Fuzzy Set allows for a degree of membership rather than a binary (true or false) result.

A membership function is how a term is represented in the set. For Medium, we are going to use a triangle function. This can be seen in Image 7.5.

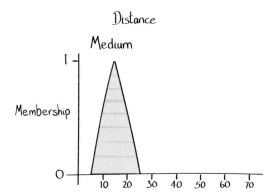

IMAGE 7.5   Medium set membership.

The points of the triangle can be set to wherever best describes your problem. Here we went for a midpoint of 15 yards as the central point, so the peak of a medium throw lies at this distance. The starting yard marker and ending yard marker can also be moved, I however selected 5 yards and 25 yards, respectively.

This allows for a distance to be contained within a linguistic term from 0 to 1. Not an absolute true or false, but a gradient from 0 to 1. Any values that fall outside of the triangle return a 0.

If we take our previous examples of a 19-yard throw and a 20-yard throw again and see where they land on our medium Fuzzy Set. We now have the membership values depicted in Image 7.6.

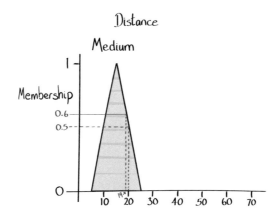

IMAGE 7.6   19- and 20-yards membership of the Medium set.

19 yards is:

• a member of the Medium Fuzzy Set to a degree of 0.6.

And 20 yards is:

• a member of the Medium Fuzzy Set to a degree of 0.5.

We still need to cater for the extremes – Short and Far. For these, we are going to do something a little bit different. We will still have a gradient away from the peak, but all distances at the extremes are firmly in the group. Take a look at the new Fuzzy Set for Short in Image 7.7.

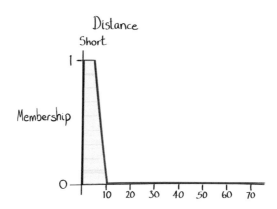

IMAGE 7.7   Short set membership.

We have retained 5 yards and below as full membership in Short, with a gradient towards greater distances. Meaning the Fuzzy Set for Short distances drops off at the 5-yard mark and ends at the 10-yard mark.

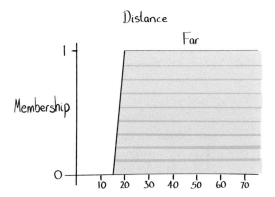

IMAGE 7.8   Far set membership.

Image 7.8 depicts the Fuzzy Set for Far. As you can see, the gradient starts at 15 yards and peaks at 20 yards. Full membership of this set continues for all distances greater than 20 yards.

Let us take another look at those previous examples of a 19-yard throw and a 20-yard throw, but this time focusing on the Far Fuzzy Set. Image 7.9 shows how these distances result in different membership values.

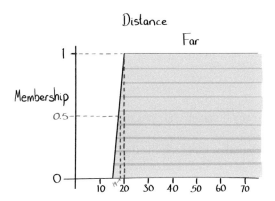

IMAGE 7.9   19- and 20-yards membership of far set.

19 yards is:

• a member of the Far Fuzzy Set to a degree of 0.5.

And 20 yards is:

- a member of the Far Fuzzy Set to a degree of 1.0.

This means that our example distances fall into both the Medium and Far Fuzzy Sets. It has no membership in the Short Fuzzy Set. Feel free to go back to our Short set and check for yourself. It will have a membership of 0.

Combining all our Fuzzy Sets into a single graph for Distance creates what is called a Fuzzy Manifold. This can be seen in Image 7.10.

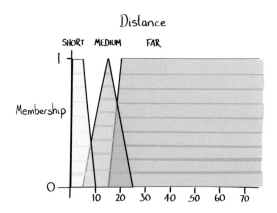

IMAGE 7.10   Distance Fuzzy Manifold.

TERMINOLOGY: FUZZY MANIFOLD

When all Fuzzy Sets are collected together to describe the range of possibilities, it is called a Fuzzy Manifold.

We can now plug in any distance and determine its membership to any of the Fuzzy Sets we created.

Hopefully, this all makes sense. As the distance increases from 0 yards across the range, it starts firmly in the Short Fuzzy Set, but the membership in Short decreases the greater the distance rises until it is no longer considered Short at all. As membership in Short decreases, the membership in the Medium Fuzzy Set increases.

When coding this, it produced better results with the Medium Fuzzy Set lasting a little longer at full membership. We can do this by chopping off the top of the triangle. Image 7.11 depicts the modified Distance Fuzzy Manifold.

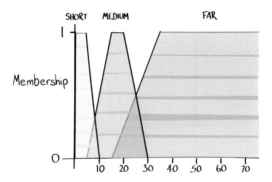

IMAGE 7.11   Modified distance Fuzzy Manifold.

Notice that the Medium Fuzzy Set has changed to a trapezoid. This allows for the peak of the Fuzzy Set to last longer than the triangle approach did. There are other membership formats that can come in useful. The choice of which to use is very much based upon the problem at hand. The common approaches are:

BINARY MEMBERSHIP

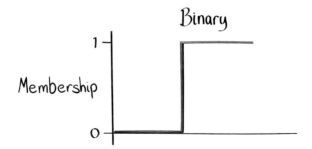

IMAGE 7.12   Binary step function.

The red line on Image 7.12 shows where the membership lies across the horizontal axis. A value is either full membership or no membership at all. This approach is very much what we were using before we started exploring Fuzzy Logic.

SIGMOID CURVE MEMBERSHIP

This approach gives a smoother transition from 0 to 1 than the binary step function described above. Take a look at Image 7.13 and notice how the angular edges of a set have been curved.

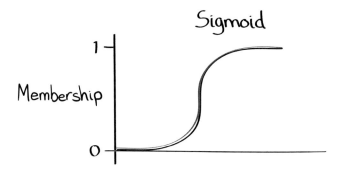

IMAGE 7.13   Sigmoid function.

GAUSSIAN MEMBERSHIP

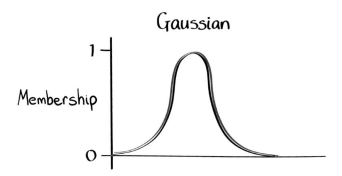

IMAGE 7.14   Gaussian function.

A Gaussian approach gives a smoother blend to that offered by the triangle approach. Image 7.14 is a rough sketch of how this looks. The triangle approach is acceptable for most problems.

HEDGES

There is one last area of fuzzy membership that is worth mentioning. In language, we often use terms like very, somewhat and extremely, amongst others. It is relatively easy to incorporate these, and in Fuzzy Logic terminology the idea is called 'hedges'.

It is simply a matter of modifying your membership result in an appropriate manner. Below are three examples:

- Very – Square the result.
- Somewhat – Get the square root of the result.
- Extremely – Cube the result.

As we are dealing with values between 0 and 1, these approaches will work to condense or expand the result. Image 7.15 depicts the effect on a triangular Fuzzy Set.

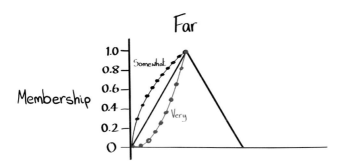

IMAGE 7.15   'Somewhat' and 'Very' hedges.

TERMINOLOGY: HEDGE

Hedges are the Fuzzy Logic way of incorporating linguistic modifiers to our terms, for example Very, Nearly etc. Hedges take the result of membership from a Fuzzy Set and refine them to return a more condensed or expanded result.

For fun let us take another look at our two distances and see what their membership in the Very Far Fuzzy Set they have.
19 yards

- Far membership of 0.5 becomes 0.25 membership of the Very Far Fuzzy Set.

20 yards

- Far membership of 1.0 remains 1.0 membership of the Very Far Fuzzy Set.

FUZZY RULES

For any of this to be of use to us, we need to return to what our fictitious player told us. This information will produce the rules that our fuzzy system will use to combine our inputs and produce our output. There are a couple of ways you can produce the rules.

The first approach is to create rules which fit the problem you are trying to solve. This method has fewer rules.

The second method is to combine all of your Fuzzy Sets to produce the rules. This method has a lot of rules but does cover every eventuality. We will be going with this second approach as it allows for a fuller explanation of the fuzzy process.

When planning a fuzzy system, it is useful to create a table with the columns representing the operators and terms used. We have three Fuzzy Manifolds (Distance,

Coverage and Pressure) each with three Fuzzy Sets. We also have a Fuzzy Manifold for our output (Riskiness). A table header for this would look something like Image 7.16.

IMAGE 7.16   Rule set headers.

The Fuzzy Sets for each Fuzzy Manifold are as follows:

- Distance (Short, Medium and Far)
- Coverage (Limited, Some and Lots)
- Pressure (Minimum, Some and Lots)
- Riskiness (Safe, OK and Dangerous)

Before we go through the process of generating all our rules, we need to consider how fuzzy operators work and how we combine results. So far, we have only dealt with individual results from a Fuzzy Set, but now we need to be able to combine it with the results from other Fuzzy Sets to be able to build our rules. We do this in much the same way as traditional set theory works. We have the following three options:

AND
This is the set theory equivalent of Union. It is a simple matter of taking the lowest of the two values or in coding terminology: MIN(x, y)

OR
This is the set theory equivalent of Intersection. Simply take the highest of the two values or in coding terminology: MAX(x, y)

NOT
This is the set theory equivalent of Complement. It takes a single value and returns the degree of membership not in the set. Again, this is not difficult. Just deduct the degree of membership of the Fuzzy Set from 1. In coding terminology: 1.0-Fuzzy Set(x)

TERMINOLOGY: FUZZY SET OPERATORS

Fuzzy Set Operators work pretty much the same way that traditional set operators work. We can use one of the following: AND, OR and NOT.

Now that we have operators covered, let us get back to creating those rules. We need to populate the table with every combination of our input Fuzzy Sets. That gives us 3*3*3 rows, which equals 27 rules. Take a look at Images 7.17–7.19. I have split the table into three and highlighted in the blue columns what makes each of these tables different. Also, take note that we are using both the AND operator and the OR operator for different rules. The OR operators all occur at the bottom of Image 7.19. This would all be based on the feedback we got from our fictional player.

We could expand this to include every combination of operators for every combination of Fuzzy Sets, but this is overkill for this explanation and, in reality, is never really needed. Remember, if this were a real sport, we would be basing our rules on expert advice.

Rule #	Distance Fuzzy Set	Operator	Coverage Fuzzy Set	Operator	Pressure Fuzzy Set	=	Riskiness Fuzzy Set
1	SHORT	AND	LIMITED	AND	MINIMUM	Then	Ok
2	MEDIUM	AND	LIMITED	AND	MINIMUM	Then	Ok
3	FAR	AND	LIMITED	AND	MINIMUM	Then	SAFE
4	SHORT	AND	SOME	AND	MINIMUM	Then	DANGEROUS
5	MEDIUM	AND	SOME	AND	MINIMUM	Then	DANGEROUS
6	FAR	AND	SOME	AND	MINIMUM	Then	DANGEROUS
7	SHORT	AND	LOTS	AND	MINIMUM	Then	DANGEROUS
8	MEDIUM	AND	LOTS	AND	MINIMUM	Then	DANGEROUS
9	FAR	AND	LOTS	AND	MINIMUM	Then	DANGEROUS

IMAGE 7.17   Fuzzy Rules (with pressure set to **Minimum**).

Rule #	Distance Fuzzy Set	Operator	Coverage Fuzzy Set	Operator	Pressure Fuzzy Set	=	Riskiness Fuzzy Set
10	SHORT	AND	LIMITED	AND	SOME	Then	Ok
11	MEDIUM	AND	LIMITED	AND	SOME	Then	SAFE
12	FAR	AND	LIMITED	AND	SOME	Then	SAFE
13	SHORT	AND	SOME	AND	SOME	Then	Ok
14	MEDIUM	AND	SOME	AND	SOME	Then	Ok
15	FAR	AND	SOME	AND	SOME	Then	DANGEROUS
16	SHORT	AND	LOTS	AND	SOME	Then	DANGEROUS
17	MEDIUM	AND	LOTS	AND	SOME	Then	DANGEROUS
18	FAR	AND	LOTS	AND	SOME	Then	DANGEROUS

IMAGE 7.18   Fuzzy Rules (with pressure set to **Some**).

Rule #	Distance Fuzzy Set	Operator	Coverage Fuzzy Set	Operator	Pressure Fuzzy Set	=	Riskiness Fuzzy Set
19	SHORT	AND	LIMITED	AND	LOTS	Then	Ok
20	MEDIUM	AND	LIMITED	AND	LOTS	Then	SAFE
21	FAR	AND	LIMITED	AND	LOTS	Then	SAFE
22	SHORT	AND	SOME	AND	LOTS	Then	Ok
23	MEDIUM	AND	SOME	AND	LOTS	Then	Ok
24	FAR	AND	SOME	AND	LOTS	Then	DANGEROUS
25	SHORT	AND	LOTS	OR	LOTS	Then	DANGEROUS
26	MEDIUM	AND	LOTS	OR	LOTS	Then	DANGEROUS
27	FAR	AND	LOTS	OR	LOTS	Then	DANGEROUS

IMAGE 7.19   Fuzzy Rules (with pressure set to **Lots**).

For each rule, we take the values in the game and plug them into the relevant Fuzzy Sets. The degree of membership for each Fuzzy Set is then entered into the table.

The input Fuzzy Manifolds used are depicted in Images 7.20–7.22. There is a Fuzzy Manifold for each of the inputs discussed – Distance, Coverage and Pressure.

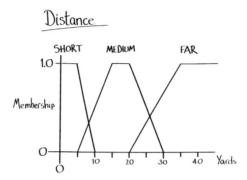

IMAGE 7.20   **Distance** Fuzzy Manifold.

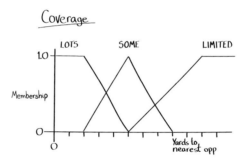

IMAGE 7.21   **Coverage** Fuzzy Manifold.

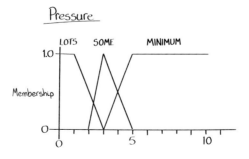

IMAGE 7.22   **Pressure** Fuzzy Manifold.

The output Fuzzy Manifold used will describe the Riskiness of the throw and can be seen in Image 7.23.

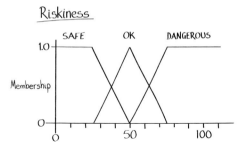

IMAGE 7.23   Riskiness Fuzzy Manifold.

In the Riskiness Fuzzy Manifold, the values along the horizontal axis are not that relevant. We could have chosen 0–10, or something else if we had wanted, but 0–100 seems like a sensible choice. The shape of the sets is also something that can be changed, but a simple shoulder/triangle/shoulder setup gives a good spread.

To give an example of this process we will step through rules 1, 13 and 27. These have been chosen as they offer some rule variety. The values plugged into each Fuzzy Set will be for the following game scenario:

The Speedball player with the ball has an opponent 4 yards away, the receiver is 22 yards downfield, and he also has an opponent 4 yards away from him.

Let us plot this information on our three Fuzzy Sets. Images 7.24–7.26 show a red line where the information described above falls along the horizontal axis in the manifold.

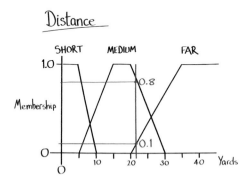

IMAGE 7.24   Determine a degree of membership for the throw in each distance set.

The Distance of the throw was 22 yards, so taking a look at Image 7.24, you can see the red line at the 22-yard mark. This falls into both the Medium Fuzzy Set and the Far Fuzzy Set.

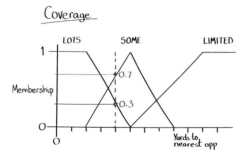

IMAGE 7.25   Determine a degree of membership for the distance of the nearest opponent to the receiver in each coverage set.

Coverage described how far away an opponent was to the potential receiver. Our example had this player with a 4-yard radius clear of opponents. Plotting this onto the Coverage Fuzzy Manifold, you find it is within the Lots Fuzzy Set and the Some Fuzzy Set. This is shown in Image 7.25.

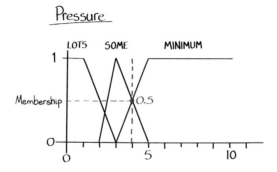

IMAGE 7.26   Determine a degree of membership for the distance of the nearest opponent to the ball carrier in each pressure set.

Pressure was based upon the distance the nearest opposing player was to the ball carrier. Our example stated the nearest opponent was 4 yards away, so looking at Image 7.26 you can see that this falls into the Some Fuzzy Set and the Minimum Fuzzy Set and that they have the same degree of membership.

   Note: the values in the diagrams are estimated. When calculated by a computer the values returned will be accurate.

So, for rule 1:

Rule 1	SHORT	AND	LIMITED	AND	MINIMUM	Then	OK

Replace the Fuzzy Set with the degree of membership value returned:

Rule 1	0.0	AND	0.0	AND	0.5	Then	OK

And rule 13:

Rule 13	SHORT	AND	SOME	AND	SOME	Then	OK

Becomes:

Rule 13	0.0	AND	0.7	AND	0.5	Then	OK

And rule 27:

Rule 27	FAR	AND	LOTS	OR	LOTS	Then	DANGEROUS

Becomes:

Rule 27	0.1	AND	0.3	OR	0.0	Then	DANGEROUS

Next, for each rule we need to combine the three Fuzzy Set degrees of membership to produce a single value to plug into our Riskiness Fuzzy Manifold. We will be using the operators to do this.

For rule 1, all the operators are AND, so we take the minimum value, which is 0.0. Our completed row for this rule now becomes:

	Distance		Coverage		Pressure		Riskiness
Rule 1	SHORT 0.0	AND	LIMITED 0.0	AND	MINIMUM 0.5	Then	OK 0.0

For rule 13, all the operators are again AND, so we take the minimum input value again:

	Distance		Coverage		Pressure		Riskiness
Rule 13	SHORT 0.0	AND	SOME 0.7	AND	SOME 0.5	Then	OK 0.0

For rule 27, we find a different operator. There is now an OR operator in play. We can go about this in two ways.

We could take the minimum value of the Distance and Coverage values, then use this result against the Pressure value, where we take the maximum value:

$$\text{Max}(\text{Min}(0.1, 0.3), 0.0) = 0.1$$

Or we could take the maximum value from Coverage OR Pressure, then take the maximum value of this and the Distance value:

$$\text{Min}(0.1, \text{Max}(0.3, 0.0)) = 0.1$$

Either way we get the same result to use as our DANGEROUS value. Rule 27 is now complete:

	Distance		Coverage		Pressure			Riskiness
Rule 27	FAR 0.1	AND	LOTS 0.3	OR	LOTS 0.0	Then		DANGEROUS 0.1

COMBINING RESULTS

Ideally, we want a single value from all these rules. Remember the diagram of how Fuzzy Logic works way back at the start in Image 7.1? We need to go through a defuzzification process and end with a single crisp value. For this we need to combine all the results for each Fuzzy Set within the output Fuzzy Manifold. That is, we need a single result for the SAFE Fuzzy Set, a single result for the OK Fuzzy Set and a single result for the DANGEROUS Fuzzy Set.

To accomplish this, it is simply a matter of ORing all the rules that apply to that Fuzzy Set. In other words, all rules that output to DANGEROUS get combined, all rules that output to SAFE get combined and all rules that output to OK get combined. Look at the last column of the tables (Images 7.17–7.19) to see which output Fuzzy Sets are used.

There are eight rules that have the output in the OK Fuzzy Set in the Riskiness Fuzzy Manifold. These are: Rule1, Rule2, Rule10, Rule13, Rule14, Rule19, Rule22 and Rule23.

The values that these rules produce are shown in Image 7.27, when the rules have been run through the process detailed above.

Rule:	1	2	10	13	14	19	22	23
Result:	0.0	0.0	0.0	0.0	0.5	0.0	0.0	0.0

IMAGE 7.27   Rules that output to the **OK** set in the Riskiness manifold.

If we now OR all these results (take the highest value), we get a value of 0.5 for the Fuzzy Set OK for the output Fuzzy Manifold Riskiness.

When you have done this for the remaining two output Fuzzy Sets within Riskiness you get the results shown in Image 7.28.

Term:	Combined Value
SAFE	0.0
Ok	0.5
DANGEROUS	0.5

IMAGE 7.28   Combined results for each Riskiness set.

At this point, we could just take the highest value and use that. In the example above, this would mean that DANGEROUS scored and OK scored joint highest. If a throw could be described as dangerous it probably should not be attempted. We would run through the process described for all receivers and the option with the highest SAFE value would be chosen.

DEFUZZIFICATION

Although taking the highest scoring set will work for some scenarios, it does not take into consideration the other Fuzzy Sets in the Riskiness Fuzzy Manifold. To incorporate the whole Fuzzy Manifold, we can go for a more sophisticated approach to combining the results, which take all output Fuzzy Sets into consideration. First, we need to modify our Riskiness Fuzzy Manifold to represent the degrees of memberships our rules have just calculated. This is achieved by cutting off our Fuzzy Sets at the degree of membership value.

SAFE returned a value of 0.0 (see Image 7.28), so we cut this Fuzzy Set off at 0.0. This results in what you see in Image 7.29.

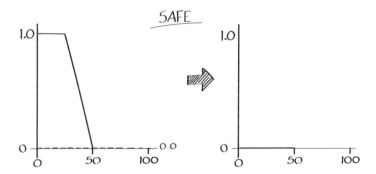

IMAGE 7.29   Cut off the **Safe** set at 0.0.

OK returned a value of 0.5, so we cut it off halfway up. Take a look at Image 7.30.

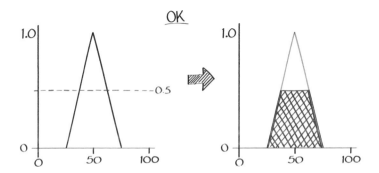

IMAGE 7.30   Cut off the **OK** set at 0.5.

As it turned out, DANGEROUS also returned a value of 0.5, so we cut that set off halfway up as well. This can be seen in Image 7.31. Of course, if it had resulted with 0.2, we would have chopped it off lower.

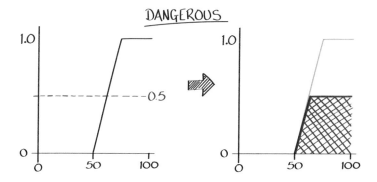

IMAGE 7.31   Cut off the **Dangerous** set at 0.5.

The combined result looks something like Image 7.32, where you can see the three individual Fuzzy Sets that make up the Riskiness Fuzzy Manifold.

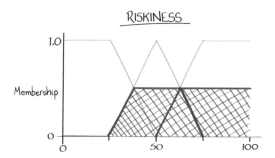

IMAGE 7.32   Resultant Fuzzy Manifold of combined cut-off sets.

Next we need to get a single crisp value from our modified output manifold. There are a couple of approaches that can be taken, and each is described below.

HIGHEST MEMBERSHIP MEAN VALUE

This approach works by using the highest scoring Fuzzy Set in the manifold – both OK and DANGEROUS were equally the highest in our example, so we will view this as one homogeneous set. We take the first value on the horizontal axis where the Fuzzy Set is at its highest degree of membership and add this to the value on the horizontal axis where this peak ends. We then divide the total by two, giving a single result for the manifold.

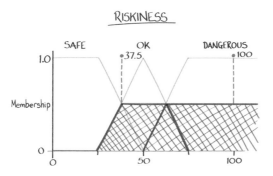

IMAGE 7.33   Calculating the highest membership mean value.

The start point is at 37.5, and the end point is at 100, which gives us the following:

$$\frac{37.5+100}{2}=68.75$$

GEOMETRIC CENTROID VALUE

The centroid approach works by calculating the centre of mass for the combined output manifold. This is achieved by splitting the horizontal axis of the graph into evenly spread segments, and then taking the degrees of membership for each Fuzzy Set at that point. Take a look at Image 7.34, an **X** has been drawn onto the graph to show these points. Notice on the 50 segments that the OK set returns a 0.5 degree of membership, whereas the DANGEROUS set returns 0.0.

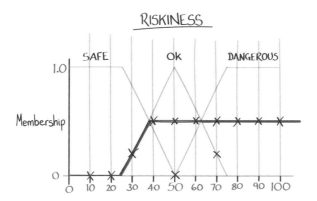

IMAGE 7.34   Splitting manifold into representative segments.

The results for each Fuzzy Set are added together and then multiplied by the value used on the horizontal axis. With the total for all segments added together, we then divide that by the summed total of all the degrees of membership.

This may sound complicated, but it's really not. We will step through the process below and before you know it, it will all make sense.

This approach has the effect of finding the centre of mass for the manifold. Imagine the horizontal line on the graph is a scale like that seen in Image 7.35. If we place a number of kilograms equal to the membership value at each of the equally spread segments, we can move the pivot to the point where we have balance. This would result in the centroid value. This can be expensive, computationally, especially if we are running this calculation multiple times per frame.

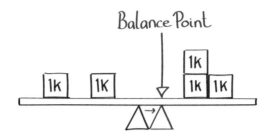

IMAGE 7.35   Balance point.

Let us work through our example step-by-step.

Looking at Image 7.34, we need to collate all the membership values for each Fuzzy Set at the segment. We have split the set into ten segments at intervals of 10, so those will be the values we use on the horizontal axis.

With all the degrees of membership values collated, we then add each segment's values together. Image 7.36 contains all the membership values for each set and totals them.

Segment value	SAFE Degree of Membership	OK Degree of Membership	DANGEROUS Degree of Membership	Total
10	0.0	0.0	0.0	0.0
20	0.0	0.0	0.0	0.0
30	0.0	0.2	0.0	0.2
40	0.0	0.5	0.0	0.5
50	0.0	0.5	0.0	0.5
60	0.0	0.5	0.5	1.0
70	0.0	0.2	0.5	0.7
80	0.0	0.0	0.5	0.5
90	0.0	0.0	0.5	0.5
100	0.0	0.0	0.5	0.5

IMAGE 7.36   Membership values at each representative segment.

We now have all the data we need to calculate our numerator and denominator.

The numerator is calculated by first multiplying the result in each row of the table by the segment value of the same row. Then sum all the results.

$$\underline{\text{Numerator}}$$
$$10 \times 0.0$$
$$20 \times 0.0^{+}$$
$$30 \times 0.2^{+}$$
$$40 \times 0.5^{+}$$
$$50 \times 0.5^{+}$$
$$60 \times 1.0^{+}$$
$$70 \times 0.7^{+}$$
$$80 \times 0.5^{+}$$
$$90 \times 0.5^{+}$$
$$\underline{100 \times 0.5^{+}}$$
$$295$$

The denominator is calculated by summing the result column from the table.

$$\underline{\text{Denominator}}$$
$$0.0$$
$$0.0^{+}$$
$$0.2^{+}$$
$$0.5^{+}$$
$$0.5^{+}$$
$$1.0^{+}$$
$$0.7^{+}$$
$$0.5^{+}$$
$$0.5^{+}$$
$$\underline{0.5^{+}}$$
$$4.4$$

With these two values we can now calculate a single crisp value. This is the output of our input crisp values being fuzzified, processed and defuzzified.

$$\frac{295}{4.4} = 67$$

Going back to the analogy of the weight scale, we can now stack up our weights equivalent to the total degree of membership at each segment and then move the pivot to the position of 67.0 on our horizontal axis, which is where the balance point is. It looks something like Image 7.37.

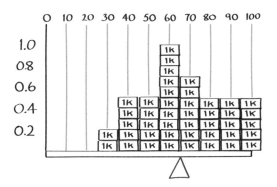

IMAGE 7.37 Balance point for **Riskiness** Fuzzy Manifold.

Averaged Degree of Membership

A less intensive approach to defuzzification is to calculate an average of the maximum values. For this we calculate the numerator in a less intensive manner, by choosing a representative value for each Fuzzy Set in the output Fuzzy Manifold. (This should be about the middle of the Fuzzy Set where it has a membership of 1.0. **Note:** This is done on the uncut Fuzzy Manifold.)

If we do this for our Riskiness Fuzzy Manifold, you can see from Image 7.38 that you get the following values:

- SAFE = 12.5
- OK = 50
- DANGEROUS = 87.5

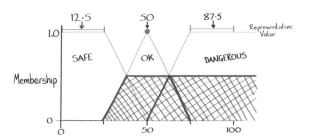

IMAGE 7.38 Average representative highest membership value.

Next, we take the degree of membership at the representative value. In our example, the OK Fuzzy Set has a degree of membership at 0.5 and the DANGEROUS Fuzzy Set has a degree of membership at 0.5 in the truncated output set.

From Image 7.38 you can see that the degree of membership of the SAFE Fuzzy Set has a value of zero so could be ignored, but for completion's sake we will include it in the example below.

To calculate the numerator, we simply multiply our representative value with the degree of membership, and sum all the results. For the denominator, we sum the three degrees of membership.

	Numerator	Denominator
SAFE	$12.5*0.0$	0.0
OK	$50*0.5^{+}$	0.5^{+}
DANGEROUS	$87.5*0.5^{+}$	0.5^{+}
	68.75	1.0

$$\frac{68.75}{1.0} = 68.75$$

So those are your three options. As you can see the Geometric Centroid approach gives the most precise result, but it performs a lot more calculations than the other two. Depending on your game, precision might not be that important, in which case you can go with one of the simpler options.

Now we have a single crisp value for this receiver. We should now repeat the process for all players that the ball carrier could potentially pass to. The one with the highest defuzzified value is the best option.

This whole explanation may seem restricted to my fictitious Speedball player, but it's really not. You could replace Speedball with Soccer player, or Quarterback. And remember, if you were making a game of a real sport, then you would be able to seek out an actual expert and get their insights.

FINAL THOUGHTS

Fuzzy logic is a great solution to the problems described at the beginning of this chapter, but it is not always the right choice. The key here is understanding the problem you are trying to solve. As has been said before, do not try to use an approach because it looks clever, or it is new. Use the approach that solves the problem and gives you the most bang for your buck.

FUZZY LOGIC – PRACTICAL

PROJECT OVERVIEW

This project is a version of a classic artillery game. Two tanks take up random positions at either side of the environment and take turns to fire rockets at each other. Each tank needs to decide what angle to fire at and how much power to apply. The wind changes every shot, so it is not quite as simple as it first appears.

There are two modes of play available. You can play a two-player game, or you can play a one-player game where the second tank is controlled by the AI. Screenshot 7.1 shows the game in action. As the project currently stands, the AI tank will just drop its missile. It will not take a proper turn until we have followed the step-by-step guide below.

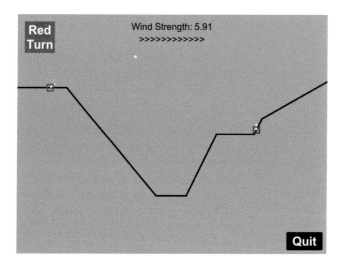

SCREENSHOT 7.1   Classic artillery game.

The AI will make its decisions using a fuzzy system. It does not need to defuzzify the results. As always in game development you only implement as much is required. There is no benefit in processing the defuzzification side of the Fuzzy Logic approach when we can get the result we are looking for without doing so.

STEP-BY-STEP GUIDE

Open the Unity project named GameAi supplied with this book. Navigate through the folder system to the Chapter7_FuzzyLogic folder. It is located in the Assets folder. Click on the Chapter7_FuzzyLogic scene. Run the application. It is not an enjoyable experience when the enemy AI tank does not fire back.

To be able to code fuzzy AI for a tank, we first need to implement a collection of functions specific to this problem. We will start with these functions before we move on to coding the aiming and power functions for firing rockets.

FuzzyFunctions.cs

This file is where all the specific fuzzy functionality is found. As you progress through the various examples below, if at any time you have any problems, please refer to the FuzzyFunctions_Solution.cs file located in the same folder as FuzzyFunctions.cs. This contains the complete solution, but all the code is commented out, so it does not cause any duplicate declaration issues for our project.

We will start with the fuzzy operators – AND, OR and NOT.

AND(float a, float b)

As described in the theory part of this chapter, the AND function simply returns the lower of two values. Locate the following:

```
//Delete me.
return 0.0f;
```

And replace it with this single line of code:

```
return Mathf.Min(a, b);
```

OR(float a, float b)

The OR function returns the higher of two values. Locate the following:

```
//Delete me.
return 0.0f;
```

And replace it with:

```
return Mathf.Max(a, b);
```

NOT(float a)

The NOT function returns the membership not in a set. Locate the following:

```
//Delete me.
return 0.0f;
```

And replace it with the following:

```
return 1.0f - a;
```

Next, we will move on to fuzzy membership functions – Gradient, ReverseGradient, Triangle, BinaryStep and Trapezoid.

Gradient(float fValue, float fLow, float fHigh)

An example of the gradient set can be seen in Image 7.39. The parameters passed into this function are depicted on the graph for clarity.

There are three parts to this function, the first is what membership value should be returned if the input value is less than the start of the gradient (`fLow`). The second is calculating the membership value beyond the end of the gradient (fHigh), and the final is calculating the membership on the gradient.

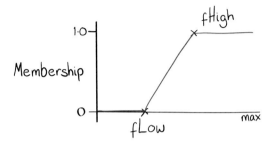

IMAGE 7.39   Gradient set with naming convention.

Locate the following lines of code and delete them:

```
//Delete me.
return 0.0f;
```

Let us first deal with returning zero membership if the input value is less than the start of the gradient:

```
if(fValue <= fLow)
{
    return 0.0f;
}
```

Next, we deal with returning full membership if the input value is beyond the end of the gradient:

```
else if(fValue >= fHigh)
{
    return 1.0f;
}
```

Finally, we handle calculating the membership value when the input value falls on the gradient line. We are also considering a scenario where the start and end points of the gradient are the same, meaning there is no line gradient.

```
else
{
    float fDifference = fHigh - fLow;
    if(fDifference == 0.0f)
    {
        return 0.0f;
    }
```

```
    else
    {
        return ((fValue - fLow) / fDifference);
    }
}
```

ReverseGradient(float fValue, float fLow, float fHigh)

An example of the reverse gradient set can be seen in Image 7.40. The parameters passed into this function are also depicted on the graph for clarity.

This is for gradients that are in the opposite direction as those seen in the Gradient() function. There are three parts to this function, the first is what membership value should be returned if the input value is less than the start of the gradient (fHigh). The second is calculating the membership value beyond the end of the gradient (fLow), and the final is calculating the membership on the gradient.

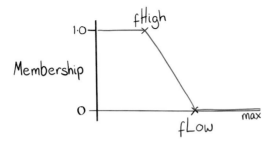

IMAGE 7.40   Reverse gradient set with naming convention.

Locate the following lines of code and delete them:

```
//Delete me.
return 0.0f;
```

Let us first deal with returning full membership if the input value is less than the start of the gradient:

```
if(fValue <= fHigh)
{
    return 1.0f;
}
```

Next, we deal with returning zero membership if the input value is beyond the end of the gradient:

```
else if(fValue >= fLow)
{
    return 0.0f;
}
```

Finally, we handle calculating the membership value when the input value falls on the gradient line. Again, we are going to consider the scenario where the start and end points of the gradient are the same, meaning there is no line gradient.

```
else
{
    float fDifference = fLow-fHigh;
    if (fDifference == 0.0f)
    {
        return 0.0f;
    }
    else
    {
        return 1.0f - ((fValue - fHigh) / fDifference);
    }
}
```

Triangle(float fValue, float fLowStart, float fHigh, float fLowEnd)

An example of the triangle set can be seen in Image 7.41. The parameters passed into this function are depicted on the graph for clarity.

There are four parts to this function, but where the triangle set differs greatly from the gradient functions is that there are two gradients to deal with. Looking at the four scenarios, we need to deal with input values less than the start (fLowStart), input values greater than the end point (fLowEnd), and then the two gradients.

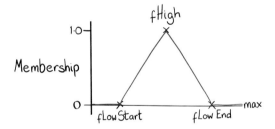

IMAGE 7.41   Triangle set with naming convention.

Locate the following lines of code and delete them:

```
//Delete me.
return 0.0f;
```

Let us first deal with returning zero membership if the input value is less than the start of the left gradient or greater than the end of the right gradient:

```
if (fValue <= fLowStart || fValue >= fLowEnd)
{
    return 0.0f;
}
```

Next, we need to handle the left gradient line:

```
else if ((fValue > fLowStart) && (fValue < fHigh))
{
   float fDifference = fHigh - fLowStart;
   if (fDifference == 0.0f)
   {
      return 0.0f;
   }
   else
   {
      return ((fValue - fLowStart) / fDifference);
   }
}
```

And finally, we deal with the right gradient line:

```
else
{
   float fDifference = fLowEnd - fHigh;
   if (fDifference == 0.0f)
   {
      return 0.0f;
   }
   else
   {
      return 1.0f - ((fValue - fHigh) / fDifference);
   }
}
```

BinaryStep(float fValue, float fCutoff, bool bPositiveIfGreaterThanCutoff)

An example of the binary set can be seen in Image 7.42. The parameters passed into this function are also depicted on the graph for clarity.

There is only really one scenario to handle for this function. This is the input value being greater than the cut-off or not. However, we are going to handle a reverse binary function at the same time. Therefore, we are passing in a Boolean value to determine whether we return full membership or zero membership if beyond the cut-off value.

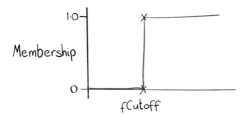

IMAGE 7.42   Binary set with naming convention.

Locate the following lines of code and delete them:

```
//Delete me.
return 0.0f;
```

As we are going to handle both a binary set and a reverse binary set, we need to branch based on the bool passed in:

```
if(bPositiveIfGreaterThanCutoff)
{
```

Now we can handle the returning of full membership, or zero membership based upon the cut-off:

```
if(fValue >= fCutoff)
{
    return 1.0f;
}
else
{
    return 0.0f;
}
```

To be able to handle the reverse binary set we need an else bracket, so add that next.

```
}
else
{
```

A reverse binary set returns membership opposite to that of a binary set. Add the following code, and as you have probably noticed the only real change is the if statement.

```
if(fValue < fCutoff)
{
    return 1.0f;
}
else
{
    return 0.0f;
}
```

All that remains is for us to close off the final bracket.

Trapezoid(float fValue, float fLowStart, float fHighStart, float fHighEnd, float fLowEnd)

An example of a trapezoid set can be seen in Image 7.43. The parameters passed into this function are depicted on the graph for clarity.

This set is very similar to the triangle set function, but it has an additional scenario to deal with. This is the chopped off part of the triangle (fHighStart to fHighEnd), during which we need to return full membership.

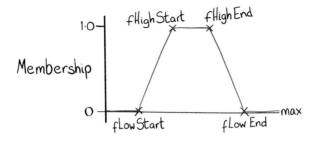

IMAGE 7.43   Trapezoid set with naming convention.

Locate the following lines of code and delete them:

```
//Delete me.
return 0.0f;
```

First deal with returning zero membership if the input value is less than the start of the left gradient:

```
if(fValue <= fLowStart)
{
    return 0.0f;
}
```

Next, we can deal with returning full membership if the input value is anywhere along the chopped off portion of the triangle:

```
else if((fValue >= fHighStart) && (fValue <= fHighEnd))
{
    return 1.0f;
}
```

Before we handle the gradients, we need to return zero membership if the input value is greater than the end of the right gradient:

```
else if(fValue >= fLowEnd)
{
    return 0.0f;
}
```

Now we can look at the gradients. The following code will handle the left gradient line. We are also going to deal with the scenario where the start and end points of the gradient are the same, meaning there is no line gradient.

```
else if((fValue > fLowStart) && (fValue < fHighStart))
{
   float fDifference = fHighStart - fLowStart;
   if (fDifference == 0.0f)
   {
      return 0.0f;
   }
   else
   {
      return ((fValue - fLowStart) / fDifference);
   }
}
```

Finally, we can look at the right line gradient, whilst also dealing with the scenario where the start and end points of the gradient are the same, meaning there is no line gradient.

```
else
{
   float fDifference = fLowEnd - fHighEnd;
   if (fDifference == 0.0f)
   {
       return 0.0f;
   }
   else
   {
       return 1.0f - ((fValue - fHighEnd) / fDifference);
   }
}
```

TankPlayerAi.cs

It is time to start using these functions and writing some Fuzzy Manifolds and Fuzzy Rules to handle the problem. Our tank needs to choose an angle to aim at the opponent and a power level for the shot. We are going to split these into two separate functions that have their own manifolds and rules. As you work through the following coding exercises, remember that if you get stuck there is a full solution in the same folder. Look for the file called TankPlayerAi_Solution.cs.

SetAim()

The purpose of this function is to calculate an angle with which to aim at the opponent. We will be dealing with the power of the shot separately. We are going to keep this simple. The two elements we will be dealing with are: the elevation of the opponent (i.e. are they higher than us, lower than us or about the same) and the wind speed.

So to kick things off, locate the following line of code in the `SetAim()` function and delete it.

```
//Todo: Add code here.
```

To keep things easy to read, we will be creating a variable to hold the current height difference to the opponent.

```
float fElevation = vecToOpp.y;
```

To ensure we are only working with positive values in our Fuzzy Sets, we need to shift the elevation by 75. We are using 75 as the maximum height of the environment is 150 units, and the centre of the environment is at 0. This means the bottom of the environment is at −75 and the top is at 75. What we need is a range from 0 to 150 and adding 75 to the current *y* position of the tank gives us this.

```
float fElevationShift = 75.0f;
fElevation += fElevationShift;
```

Now we are ready to calculate the membership for each of the three Fuzzy Sets we will be using for elevation: BELOW, SAME and ABOVE. This elevation Fuzzy Manifold looks something like Image 7.44.

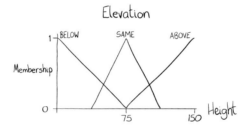

IMAGE 7.44   Elevation Fuzzy Manifold.

Using the functions we wrote in the FuzzyFunctions.cs file we can do this easily. It is important to make sure we are sending through the correct parameters. The first set we will look at is the BELOW set. This will use the reverse gradient set.

```
float fElevation_Below = FuzzyFunctions.
ReverseGradient(fElevation, fElevationShift, 0.0f);
```

Visually this looks like Image 7.45.

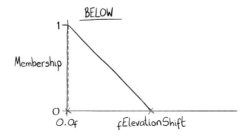

IMAGE 7.45   BELOW Fuzzy Set using function parameter names.

Next, we can get the membership for the SAME Fuzzy Set. This will use a triangle set.

```
float fElevation_Same = FuzzyFunctions.Triangle(fElevation,
fElevationShift - 32.5f, fElevationShift, fElevationShift +
32.5f);
```

Visually this looks like Image 7.46.

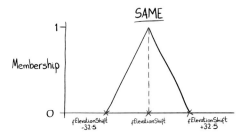

IMAGE 7.46 SAME Fuzzy Set using function parameter names.

The last set in this manifold is the ABOVE set. Let us do that using a gradient set.

```
float fElevation_Above = FuzzyFunctions.Gradient(fElevation,
fElevationShift, fElevationShift + 75.0f);
```

Visually this looks like Image 7.47.

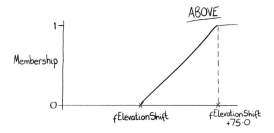

IMAGE 7.47 ABOVE Fuzzy Set using function parameter names.

Now that we have our membership values for the elevation Fuzzy Manifold, we can move on to the Wind Fuzzy Manifold. As ever, we look to simplify things where we can and in this game the AI tank is always to the right of the environment, so a negative wind toward the player and a positive wind is against the AI.

First, get the wind strength from the environment and store it in a local variable.

```
float fWindStrength = environment.fWindStrength;
```

As with the elevation calculations, it makes things easy if we are only dealing with positive numbers. This means we need to shift the wind strength to ensure it is positive. We do this by adding on the maximum wind strength allowed.

```
fWindStrength += Environment.kMaxWindStrength;
```

So let us look at the Fuzzy Manifold we will be using for wind strength. It contains four sets: FAST_WITH, SLOW_WITH, SLOW_AGAINST and FAST_AGAINST. The Fuzzy Manifold looks something like Image 7.48.

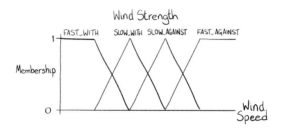

IMAGE 7.48   Elevation Fuzzy Manifold.

The four sets are calculated by adding the following function calls. If you are a little confused by any of these calls, take a look back at the code we wrote for each of the fuzzy functions (Triangle for example) and look at the order of the parameters we are passing through. It can help your understanding if you draw out the sets and label the points on the horizontal axis with the respective parameter as we did for the elevation sets.

```
float fWind_Fast_With = FuzzyFunctions.
ReverseGradient(fWindStrength, Environment.kMaxWindStrength
- 2.5f, Environment.kMaxWindStrength - 5.0f);
float fWind_Slow_With = FuzzyFunctions.Triangle(fWindStrength,
Environment.kMaxWindStrength - 5.0f, Environment.
kMaxWindStrength - 2.5f, Environment.kMaxWindStrength + 2.5f);
float fWind_Slow_Against = FuzzyFunctions.
Triangle(fWindStrength, Environment.kMaxWindStrength - 2.5f,
Environment.kMaxWindStrength + 2.5f, Environment.
kMaxWindStrength + 5.0f);
float fWind_Fast_Against = FuzzyFunctions.
Gradient(fWindStrength, Environment.kMaxWindStrength + 2.5f,
Environment.kMaxWindStrength + 5.0f);
```

We are making some good progress now. Using the fuzzy membership values we calculated above, we can now code some Fuzzy Rules. Before we do this, we need to put together a table of all the combinations we want to handle. For this example, we are using the table from Image 7.49. Feel free to change these however you want. For example, you may feel that the angle output sets should be different. That's great. Switch them around and see the different results you get.

Rule#	Elevation Fuzzy Set	Operator	Wind Strength Fuzzy Set	=	Angle Fuzzy Set
1	ABOVE	AND	FAST_AGAINST	Then	LOW
2	SAME	AND	FAST_AGAINST	Then	LOW
3	BELOW	AND	FAST_AGAINST	Then	LOW
4	ABOVE	AND	SLOW_AGAINST	Then	MEDIUM
5	SAME	AND	SLOW_AGAINST	Then	HIGH
6	BELOW	AND	SLOW_AGAINST	Then	MEDIUM
7	ABOVE	AND	SLOW_WITH	Then	HIGH
8	SAME	AND	SLOW_WITH	Then	MEDIUM
9	BELOW	AND	SLOW_WITH	Then	LOW
10	ABOVE	AND	FAST_WITH	Then	LOW
11	SAME	AND	FAST_WITH	Then	LOW
12	BELOW	AND	FAST_WITH	Then	LOW

IMAGE 7.49   Angle Fuzzy Rules.

Combining two different sets in the manner depicted in Image 7.49 requires use of the AND function we coded earlier. Work through the code below to calculate the values for each rule. We will deal with the output set next.

```
float fRule1 = FuzzyFunctions.AND(fElevation_Above,
fWind_Fast_Against);
float fRule2 = FuzzyFunctions.AND(fElevation_Same,
fWind_Fast_Against);
float fRule3 = FuzzyFunctions.AND(fElevation_Below,
fWind_Fast_Against);

float fRule4 = FuzzyFunctions.AND(fElevation_Above,
fWind_Slow_Against);
float fRule5 = FuzzyFunctions.AND(fElevation_Same,
fWind_Slow_Against);
float fRule6 = FuzzyFunctions.AND(fElevation_Below,
fWind_Slow_Against);

float fRule7 = FuzzyFunctions.AND(fElevation_Above,
fWind_Slow_With);
float fRule8 = FuzzyFunctions.AND(fElevation_Same,
fWind_Slow_With);
float fRule9 = FuzzyFunctions.AND(fElevation_Below,
fWind_Slow_With);

float fRule10 = FuzzyFunctions.AND(fElevation_Above,
fWind_Fast_With);
float fRule11 = FuzzyFunctions.AND(fElevation_Same,
fWind_Fast_With);
float fRule12 = FuzzyFunctions.AND(fElevation_Below,
fWind_Fast_With);
```

Now we have all the rule values, we need to combine all rules that output to the same angle set (HIGH, MEDIUM and LOW). Before we do this, we need to understand just what is meant by a LOW angle, a MEDIUM angle and a HIGH angle. Take a look at Image 7.50. The AI tank is always located to the right of the environment, so only needs to rotate the turret to the left. When we want to aim LOW, this is a rotation from upward, which means we need to rotate between 90° and 60°. A MEDIUM angle is between 60° and 30°, and a HIGH angle is between 30° and 0°.

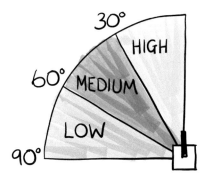

IMAGE 7.50   Angle aiming.

Add the following code to get the value for each angle. Notice we are using the OR function we wrote earlier to combine rules.

```
float fAngle_Low = FuzzyFunctions.OR(fRule1, FuzzyFunctions.
OR(fRule2, FuzzyFunctions.OR(fRule3, FuzzyFunctions.OR(fRule9,
FuzzyFunctions.OR(fRule10, FuzzyFunctions.OR(fRule11,
fRule12))))));

float fAngle_Medium = FuzzyFunctions.OR(fRule4,
FuzzyFunctions.OR(fRule6, fRule8));

float fAngle_High = FuzzyFunctions.OR(fRule5, fRule7);
```

For this example, we will not be defuzzifying the results. It is simply wasted processing for this particular scenario, so we will be handling how we choose an angle differently. Instead, we will just take the highest scoring angle. Add the following code to check for a LOW shot:

```
if (fAngle_Low > fAngle_Medium && fAngle_Low > fAngle_High)
{
```

We want a LOW shot, so let us randomly choose a low angle in the relevant range.

```
fDesiredAngle = Random.Range(kMediumAngleRange,
kLowAngleRange);
```

LOW was not the highest scoring angle, so let us check if MEDIUM has a greater value than HIGH.

```
}
else if (fAngle_Medium > fAngle_High)
{
```

We want a MEDIUM shot, so again we choose a random angle in the relevant range.

```
fDesiredAngle = Random.Range(kHighAngleRange,
kMediumAngleRange);
```

LOW and MEDIUM were not the highest. This means we want a HIGH angle shot.

```
}
else
{
```

Randomly choose a HIGH angle in the relevant range.

```
fDesiredAngle = Random.Range(0.0f, kHighAngleRange);
}
```

If you are still with me at this stage, well done. It can be quite tricky to visualise what we are doing, but after you have done this a few times, it starts to make sense. Next, we will be moving on to calculating the power of the shot.

SetPower()

Like the way we calculated the angle to aim at, we are going to come up with an appropriate power level. We are going to be using the wind strength again, so there is nothing new there, but this time we will be using the distance the opponent is from us. For this we will be using the magnitude of the vector between the two tanks. Right, to the code.

Find the following line of code in the `SetPower()` function and delete it. All subsequent code will go in place of this line.

```
//Todo: Add code here.
```

To keep things neat and tidy, we will be creating a local variable to hold the current distance to the opponent.

```
float fDistance = vecToOpp.magnitude;
```

Before we delve into the code to determine the membership of this distance in the Fuzzy Manifold for Distance, we first need to create it. Image 7.51 depicts the three Fuzzy Sets we will be using (NEAR, MEDIUM and FAR).

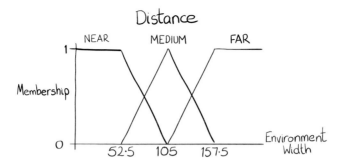

IMAGE 7.51   Distance Fuzzy Manifold.

Something to bear in mind is that the width of the environment is 210. So, when we are dealing with distances in our Fuzzy Sets, we can utilise this knowledge. For example, we know that 105 will be half the distance of the environment.

```
float fDistance_Near = FuzzyFunctions.
ReverseGradient(fDistance, 105.0f, 52.5f);
float fDistance_Medium = FuzzyFunctions.Triangle(fDistance,
52.5f, 105.0f, 157.5f);
float fDistance_Far = FuzzyFunctions.Gradient(fDistance,
105.0f, 157.5f);
```

We are going to calculate the wind strength in the same way as we did for the aiming, so will not be going through this in detail. The code is below for you to add at this stage of the tutorial without flipping between pages, but if you require an explanation I'm afraid you will have to go back and reread the `SetAim()` function explanation.

```
float fWindStrength = environment.fWindStrength;
fWindStrength += Environment.kMaxWindStrength;

float fWind_Fast_With = FuzzyFunctions.
ReverseGradient(fWindStrength, Environment.kMaxWindStrength
- 2.5f, Environment.kMaxWindStrength - 5.0f);
float fWind_Slow_With = FuzzyFunctions.Triangle(fWindStrength,
Environment.kMaxWindStrength - 5.0f, Environment.
kMaxWindStrength - 2.5f, Environment.kMaxWindStrength + 2.5f);
float fWind_Slow_Against = FuzzyFunctions.
Triangle(fWindStrength, Environment.kMaxWindStrength - 2.5f,
Environment.kMaxWindStrength + 2.5f, Environment.
kMaxWindStrength + 5.0f);
float fWind_Fast_Against = FuzzyFunctions.
Gradient(fWindStrength, Environment.kMaxWindStrength + 2.5f,
Environment.kMaxWindStrength + 5.0f);
```

Now that we have the wind strength implemented, we can move forward with the Fuzzy Rules for power. The rule sets chosen can be seen in Image 7.52, but feel free to change any of this to see how the results may change.

Rule #	Distance Fuzzy Set	Operator	Wind Strength Fuzzy Set	=	Power Fuzzy Set
1	NEAR	AND	FAST_AGAINST	Then	MEDIUM
2	MEDIUM	AND	FAST_AGAINST	Then	STRONG
3	FAR	AND	FAST_AGAINST	Then	STRONG
4	NEAR	AND	SLOW_AGAINST	Then	LIGHT
5	MEDIUM	AND	SLOW_AGAINST	Then	MEDIUM
6	FAR	AND	SLOW_AGAINST	Then	MEDIUM
7	NEAR	AND	SLOW_WITH	Then	LIGHT
8	MEDIUM	AND	SLOW_WITH	Then	MEDIUM
9	FAR	AND	SLOW_WITH	Then	MEDIUM
10	NEAR	AND	FAST_WITH	Then	LIGHT
11	MEDIUM	AND	FAST_WITH	Then	LIGHT
12	FAR	AND	FAST_WITH	Then	MEDIUIM

IMAGE 7.52   Power Fuzzy Rules.

Combining two different sets in the manner depicted in Image 7.52 again requires use of the AND function. Work through the code below to calculate the values for each rule. We will deal with the output set next.

```
float fRule1 = FuzzyFunctions.AND(fDistance_Near,
fWind_Fast_Against);
float fRule2 = FuzzyFunctions.AND(fDistance_Medium,
fWind_Fast_Against);
float fRule3 = FuzzyFunctions.AND(fDistance_Far,
fWind_Fast_Against);

float fRule4 = FuzzyFunctions.AND(fDistance_Near,
fWind_Slow_Against);
float fRule5 = FuzzyFunctions.AND(fDistance_Medium,
fWind_Slow_Against);
float fRule6 = FuzzyFunctions.AND(fDistance_Far,
fWind_Slow_Against);

float fRule7 = FuzzyFunctions.AND(fDistance_Near,
fWind_Slow_With);
float fRule8 = FuzzyFunctions.AND(fDistance_Medium,
fWind_Slow_With);
float fRule9 = FuzzyFunctions.AND(fDistance_Far,
fWind_Slow_With);

float fRule10 = FuzzyFunctions.AND(fDistance_Near,
fWind_Fast_With);
float fRule11 = FuzzyFunctions.AND(fDistance_Medium,
fWind_Fast_With);
float fRule12 = FuzzyFunctions.AND(fDistance_Far,
fWind_Fast_With);
```

Using the details from the rule set seen in Image 7.52, we can now combine rules using the OR function to give us a single crisp value for each of the output sets (LIGHT, MEDIUM and STRONG).

```
float fPower_Light = FuzzyFunctions.OR(fRule4, FuzzyFunctions.
OR(fRule7, FuzzyFunctions.OR(fRule10, fRule11)));
float fPower_Medium = FuzzyFunctions.OR(fRule1,FuzzyFunctions.
OR(fRule5, FuzzyFunctions.OR(fRule6, FuzzyFunctions.OR(fRule8,
FuzzyFunctions.OR(fRule9, fRule12)))));
float fPower_Strong = FuzzyFunctions.OR(fRule2, fRule3);
```

As we did for the aiming implementation, we are not going to be defuzzifying these results. Instead, we will simply take the highest scoring output set and then choose a power level within the required range.

First, we check if LIGHT power was the highest scoring option.

```
if(fPower_Light > fPower_Medium && fPower_Light >
fPower_Strong)
{
```

It was, so now randomly choose a light power in the relevant range.

```
fDesiredPower = Random.Range(kMinPowerRange, kLowPowerRange);
```

LIGHT was not the highest, so maybe MEDIUM is. Let us check.

```
}
else if(fPower_Medium > fPower_Strong)
{
```

We do want a MEDIUM shot, so again choose a random power level from the medium range.

```
fDesiredPower = Random.Range(kLowPowerRange,
kMediumPowerRange);
```

If neither LIGHT nor MEDIUM was the highest scoring options, that only leaves the STRONG option.

```
}
else
{
```

Set the power level to a random value from the strong power range.

```
fDesiredPower = Random.Range(kMediumPowerRange,
kStrongPowerRange);
}
```

And that's it. If all has gone well you should be able to save your files, switch back to the Unity project and click the play button. If for any reason your code does not compile, remember that there is a solution file located within the same folder. Take a look through and see what was missed.

FUTURE WORK

This example did not defuzzify the result. Try implementing the defuzzification process and compare the results to what we currently have. To do this, you are going to need to test different shots that include angle and power. It is going to need a little thought before you jump right into this. Good luck.

Did the result prove better? Were the results worth the extra code, processing and complexity in implementing that extra step?

8 Chess AI

When it comes to board game AI such as Chess, there are two things to consider. There is obviously figuring out which move we should take, but before that we need somehow to score the board to be able to determine how good the move was. This chapter will first cover the mechanics of an AI playing the game and once we have that covered, we will delve into Chess itself to see how we can score different board configurations to indicate more advantageous moves.

The approach we will be using in this chapter is called the Minimax algorithm, which was originally developed by Claude Shannon way back in 1949. There are alternative approaches which build upon the Minimax algorithm that can be used to solve this problem, such as Negamax or Expectimax, but we will be focusing on the original; however, if you feel like challenging yourself, feel free to look them up yourself after completing the tutorial.

The Minimax algorithm is a method of selecting the best choice of action in multiplayer games where each player is working towards a mutually exclusive goal and perfect information is known about the outcome of each move. It is applied to game trees, where each move is a branch on the tree and the resulting new board configuration is a node.

TERMINOLOGY: PERFECT INFORMATION

This is where all players know what effect their move will have upon the game board. There are no hidden details like in Poker where only the player knows what cards they hold.

The simplest game to depict this would be Tic-tac-toe. There are a limited number of moves available to each player, and that number reduces each turn. Image 8.1 depicts how from a starting board – with no moves made, the game can be described as a tree. Each descent down the tree illustrates the options available to the next player given the new configuration of the board resulting from the previous player's turn.

DOI: 10.1201/9781003305835-8

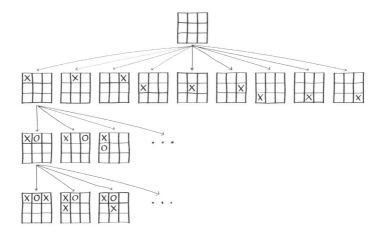

IMAGE 8.1   Tic-tac-toe game tree.

MINIMAX ALGORITHM

Let us take a look at Chess. Imagine we have the pieces set up in the standard starting configuration as in Image 8.2. However, we wish to delve deep into the game tree to determine which move will lead to the best outcome. This requires us to move every piece to every possible position that it can legitimately move to; without cheating, and then evaluate how good it is for the active player.

TERMINOLOGY: ACTIVE PLAYER

The player whose turn it is. This is not the same as the current player used when delving down the game tree.

Say we wish to look four moves ahead. We take a single piece and make its first valid move for the active player. This generates a new node (a game board in this new configuration). We cannot know how good this move will be until we have assessed what the opponent will do in response, so the current player becomes the opponent, and we then generate a node for every possible move that they can make in response. This is still only two moves ahead, so the current player becomes the active player again and we then generate every single move that they can make in reply. And yes, you guessed it, we then need to generate every single move the opponent can then make in response. Now that is a lot of nodes, and one big game tree.

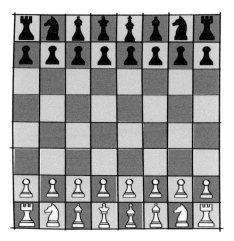

IMAGE 8.2   Starting configuration of a Chess board.

Once we are at the desired depth, we can then assess how good the board's current configuration is for the active player. There is no point assessing the nodes at depth 1, 2 or 3 because we need to know what the responses will be. So, it is only at a depth of 4 that we do this. The depth of the search is sometimes called the horizon, because you cannot see beyond the horizon.

TERMINOLOGY: HORIZON

This is the term used for how many moves ahead we are looking at, also known as the depth of a search.

With the game board scored, we can then work our way back up the tree. This is a recursive function, so when we get to the actual code side of things, there is not a great deal to it, but bear in mind that we are working backwards from a board configuration that occurs in four projected moves' time, and that only the nodes at the depth required are scored. As we move back up the tree, nodes at higher levels will take the score of their child node.

I just read all that back, and it is a lot to wrap your head around. So let us step through this process with some images. Image 8.3 is a game tree where we have delved four moves ahead. When we have reached the depth required, we score the node. As you can see there are scores for each of the nodes at a depth of four.

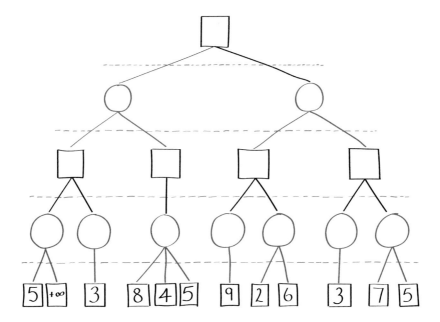

IMAGE 8.3   Game tree looking four moves ahead.

In reality, the recursive function would delve down to the node scoring 5 at the bottom left, then work back up to its parent, before going down to a depth of 4 again to score the +infinity node (+infinity would be a winning checkmate). However, it makes it easier to explain if you can see the scores for all the nodes at the required depth but remember that the values depicted are unknown until we have recursively delved down that branch of the tree.

Now we have the board we have scored (we are still looking at the bottom left node that scored a 5), we need to work back up the tree and determine what each parent node should be scored. The score will be the same value as one of its children, but the question is – which one?

Each step up the tree we will work on the principle that each player will take the best option available to them. Take a look at Image 8.4. To the left we have added the terms maximum and minimum. These represent what is best for the current player. Note that the current player may not be the same as the active player. So, at the bottom (depth 4), that is a move for the active player so we want the maximum score. One level up, the current player becomes our opponent and what is best for them is to choose the move that is worst for the active player (minimum). And so on.

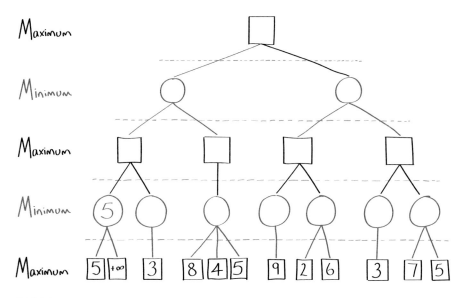

IMAGE 8.4   Scoring opponent's move (minimum).

So back to Image 8.4. At a depth of 3, we have taken the lowest scoring value from all the node's children. It has two children, one scoring a value of 5 and the other scoring a value of +infinity. Obviously 5 is less than +infinity, which is why the 5 is taken. Image 8.5 shows all the scores filled in for a depth of three.

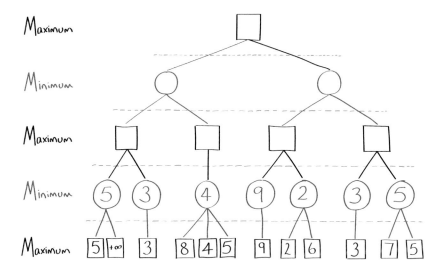

IMAGE 8.5   Minimum scores at a depth of 3.

At a depth of 2, the current player becomes the active player, and we need to take the highest scoring child. The first node has a choice of a 5 or a 3, so it will take the 5 as this is the greater value. Image 8.6 shows what our tree looks like with all the maximum values chosen at a depth of 2.

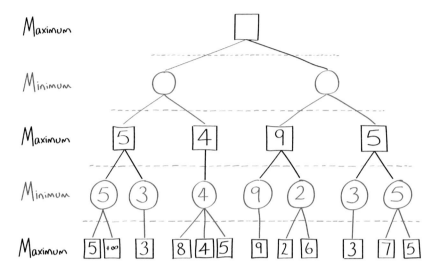

IMAGE 8.6   Maximum scores at a depth of 2.

By now I think you will be getting the hang of it, so Image 8.7 has the completed tree. At a depth of 1, we took the lowest scoring value from the children, and then at a depth of 0 we took the highest scoring child's value.

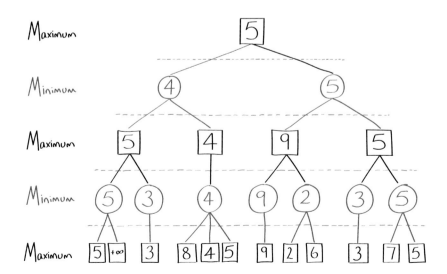

IMAGE 8.7   Complete tree scores.

Looking at Image 8.7, you can see that the move that went to the right of the tree resulted in the better outcome. There were higher scoring nodes sprinkled throughout the tree, but as we are working with the assumption that the opponent is not going to choose a move that is bad for them, those moves never saw the light of day. Now that is not to say an opponent will not make a mistake. They undoubtedly will, it is just that you cannot plan for it.

The algorithm itself is provided in Image 8.8 as pseudocode. Hopefully this makes it easy enough for everyone to follow, regardless of your preferred programming language. The image also includes notes on what is happening at each iteration of the call to the function. Remember, it is a recursive function, so this is all that you need. Apart from the evaluation function that is, but we will be dealing with that shortly.

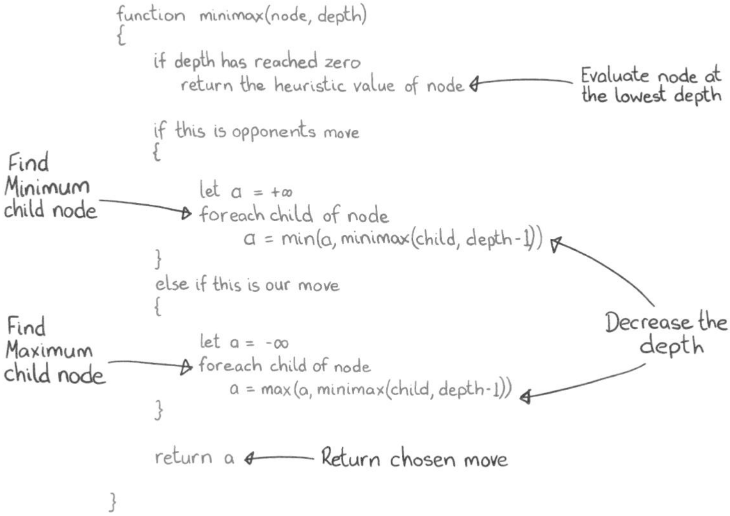

IMAGE 8.8 Minimax pseudocode.

It is impractical to completely analyse games such as Chess using the Minimax algorithm. We control just how much of the game we wish to assess with the depth value. In other words, we cannot look all the way down the game tree from start to finish, so we look *n* moves ahead. We can however optimise our search using a technique called AlphaBeta pruning.

ALPHABETA PRUNING

AlphaBeta pruning is an excellent optimisation to the Minimax algorithm. We end up with the exact same results but search less of the tree. This is achieved because we are recursively searching down the tree, and as we move back up the tree, we are retaining details; details that allow us to make choices about the viability of subsequent branches. How this is done will be explained shortly, but before that, take a look at Image 8.9, which shows a completed game tree that has been searched using the Minimax algorithm, but has been pruned with the AlphaBeta optimisation. The blue lines represent where branches have been pruned.

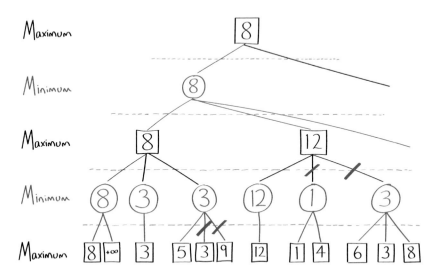

IMAGE 8.9   Game tree with branches pruned.

We can prune branches of the tree because we know at each depth what the cut-off value will be. For example, if we are on a row marked as maximum, we know we will be taking the highest value from our children. If a child has returned up the tree with a lower value, then all its other children can be ignored and not searched. Why? You ask. Well because we also know that that child will be taking the lowest values as it is on a minimum row. So, if it returns a lower number, searching subsequent children will only result in that number getting lower, and considering we will only be taking values higher than the one already stored, it is a pointless endeavour.

The processing time saved by not searching every branch allows us to search deeper down the tree on the branches that were not pruned. This results in AI that can look more moves ahead but gives us the same results as if we had not used AlphaBeta pruning. Take a look at Image 8.10. This is the pseudocode for the Minimax algorithm with AlphaBeta pruning incorporated. The changes are minimal. It is not very often in games programming that you come across an approach that provides benefits without compromises required elsewhere, so if using the Minimax algorithm, it makes no sense at all to not use AlphaBeta pruning.

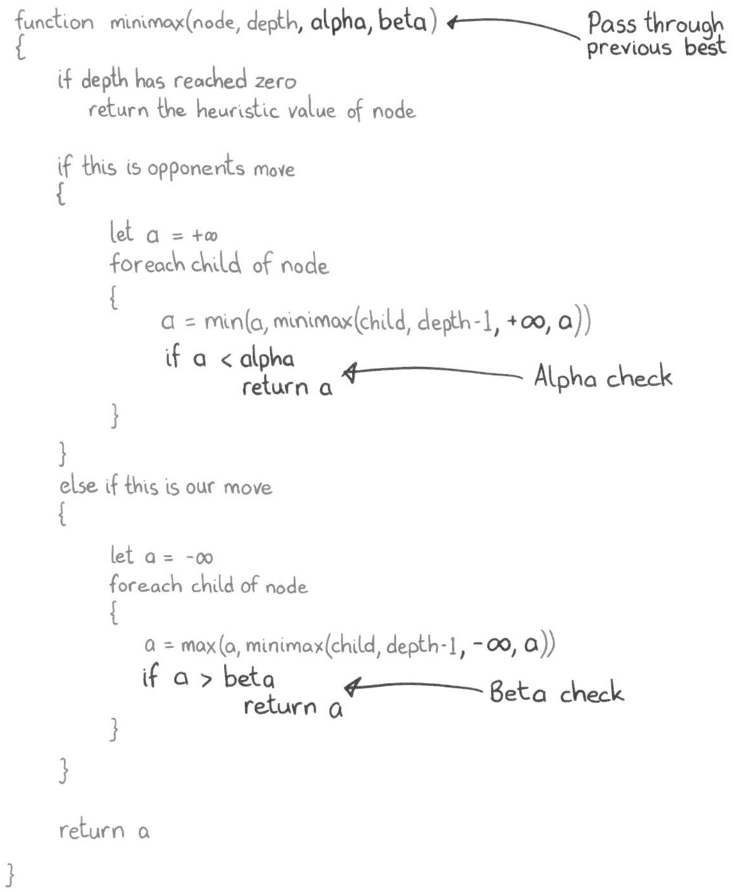

```
function minimax(node, depth, alpha, beta) ←————— Pass through
{                                                   previous best
    if depth has reached zero
        return the heuristic value of node

    if this is opponents move
    {
        let a = +∞
        foreach child of node
        {
            a = min(a, minimax(child, depth-1, +∞, a))
            if a < alpha
                return a ←————— Alpha check
        }
    }
    else if this is our move
    {
        let a = -∞
        foreach child of node
        {
            a = max(a, minimax(child, depth-1, -∞, a))
            if a > beta
                return a ←————— Beta check
        }
    }

    return a

}
```

IMAGE 8.10   Minimax pseudocode with AlphaBeta pruning.

I appreciate that the explanation above may have hurt your head a little. It hurt mine reading it back again. So, we are going to work through the modified approach and see what happens at each step. Unlike the original description of the Minimax algorithm where we filled in all the node values at the lowest search depth, with AlphaBeta pruning it is important that we only fill in the node values as they are encountered. This makes following the flow of the algorithm easier and as we never actually calculate some of the nodes, there is no point giving them a value.

To start, we delve down the tree to the required depth. Image 8.11 depicts this using blue arrows. Once we reach a depth of 4, the board is scored, and the value is stored in the tree node. We currently have a board that scored an 8.

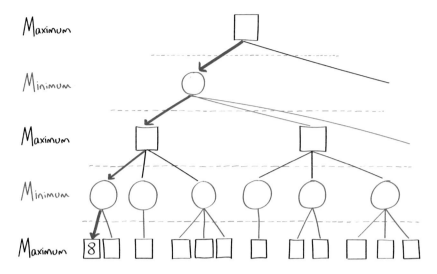

IMAGE 8.11   Delve to the required depth.

The parent node is looking to take the minimum values from its children. As we only have one node scored at this point, the value of 8 is stored in the parent node. The next child is then explored. This returns a value of +infinity, which the parent will not take as it is higher than the currently stored value. Image 8.12 shows our game tree as it currently stands. There is no difference from what the standard Minimax algorithm would have done at this point.

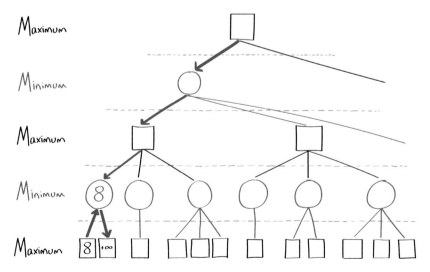

IMAGE 8.12   Minimum of child values stored.

With all children searched, processing returns to the parent node on the maximum row. The value of 8 is the only one available at this stage, so it retains this. The next child on the minimum row has one child, so we delve back down to a depth of 4 (see Image 8.13).

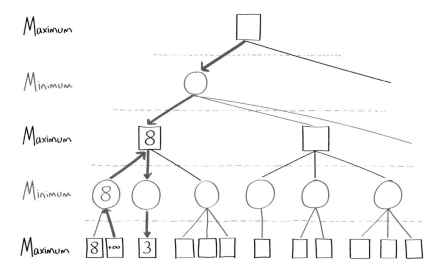

IMAGE 8.13   Delve to the required depth on the next child.

The board is scored a 3 and placed in the node. As it is the only child, the parent must also take this value. Take a look at Image 8.14. The search moves back to the parent that currently stores a value of 8 on the maximum row, the two values are compared (current value of 8 and next child value of 3), and as our current value is higher, we keep the 8.

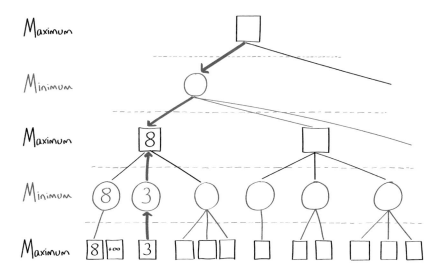

IMAGE 8.14   Return to the parent node on the maximum row.

We have one more child to search, so we descend down the tree again until we reach a depth of 4. The board here is scored and returns a value of 5, which is stored in the node. Image 8.15 shows this value being worked back up the tree to its parent, who must take the first value returned. After all, it has nothing to compare against.

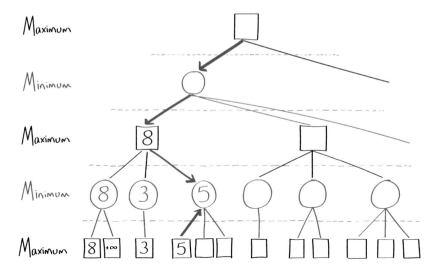

IMAGE 8.15   Store the first child's score in the parent.

It is at this point that AlphaBeta pruning makes an impression. We have just stored a value of 5 in the parent node. This node has two more children to search. As the parent in question is on the minimum row, the only way for the value stored to be changed is if a child returns a lower value. So, in effect, the 5 can only get lower.

We also know that its parent has an 8 stored (the node at search depth 2), and it is on a maximum row. So, the only way for the stored value of 8 to be changed is if a child returns with a value higher than 8. So, the 5 will only get lower, and a value of 5 is too low to change the value of the node on the maximum row that stores an 8. There is no point searching anymore of the children in this branch as they cannot be selected. Image 8.16 shows these subsequent branches pruned. We do not know what they scored, and it does not matter.

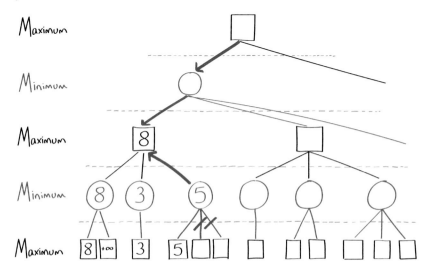

IMAGE 8.16   Pruned branches that do not need to be searched.

Hopefully you are with me at this point. If not, continue through the remaining steps so you have an overview and then go back to the start of this section and step through the images again. Trust me, it does make sense.

So, to continue, look at Image 8.17. We have worked our way back up to the node at a depth of 1 (on the minimum row), stored the value returned by the child and delved down the branch to the right. Remember if a node does not currently have a value stored. It does not matter if it is a minimum or a maximum, we have nothing to compare against so must take the child's value.

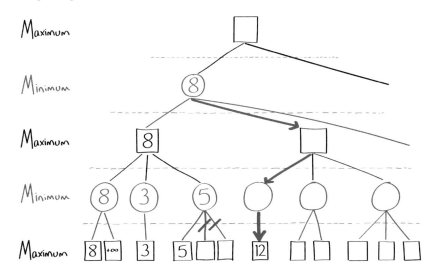

IMAGE 8.17   A further branch explored.

Without over-explaining, Image 8.18 has worked back through its parents and stored the value it has. We are now at another interesting point for AlphaBeta pruning.

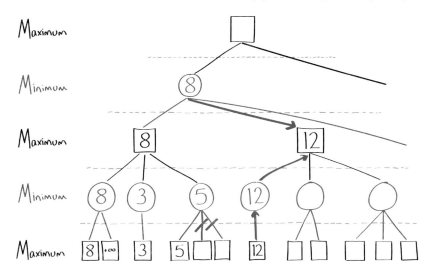

IMAGE 8.18   Only value from a child must be stored in parents.

We know that the highest node in the tree with an allocated score (the one at a depth of 1) has a value of 8 stored and it is on a minimum row. This means that the node will only change its value if a child returns a lower scoring board than 8. The child we are looking at already has a value of 12, which is higher. And that child is on a maximum row, so it will only get higher. There is no point delving down either of these two remaining branches, as they can only increase the value of 12, which is already going to be ignored. Therefore, we can prune these branches as shown in Image 8.19.

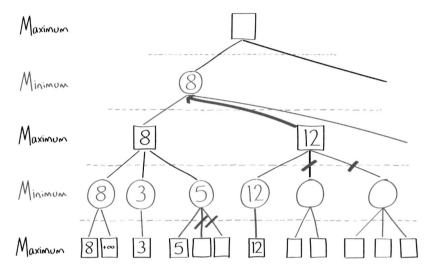

IMAGE 8.19   A value of 12 is too high and it will only get higher.

After Image 8.19, we do not know what the other child node values are, and we do not care. It would take too long to process them and then not use the information gained. In the complete tree depicted in Image 8.9, I have filled in some values. You can see that regardless of higher or lower scoring values at the nodes that were pruned, the result was the same.

EVALUATION FUNCTIONS

As stated at the start of this chapter, the Minimax algorithm can be used for any multiplayer games where the players are working towards mutually exclusive goals and perfect information is known. What makes each game different is the board representation and the evaluation function. This section will focus on evaluating the configuration of pieces on a Chess board, and we will look at its internal representation later.

An evaluation function is used to test how good the current board configuration is for the active player. We can use a single evaluation function for the current player (remember this switches between players as we delve down the tree) as Chess is a zero-sum game.

TERMINOLOGY: ZERO SUM

A game where a win for one player is equal to the loss from the opponent is termed zero sum.

To be able to score the board, we need to use a variety of techniques. Each piece needs a value, but this can change depending upon the current scenario. The location of a piece on a board is important, just as how many moves a piece has available, or possibly the number of attacking options available. How we implement these can have a huge impact upon the intelligence of your AI.

VALUING PIECES

We need to decide which pieces are more important than others. In Chess all pieces bring different abilities and options to the game unlike a game like Draughts where all pieces are the same unless kinged. Image 8.20 gives an example of piece values, but this can be modified to whatever values you deem appropriate.

IMAGE 8.20   Chess piece values.

If you decide to develop different AI opponents who favour different pieces, then changing these scores is a simple way to ensure they favour particular pieces over others. For example, if you want an AI to favour Knights over Bishops, just set the Knights to have a higher valuation than the Bishop. Using just this approach, at the start of a game, you will have the score of 73 for your army as seen in Image 8.21.

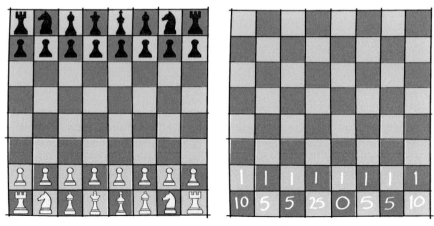

IMAGE 8.21   Starting valuation.

Now, this board valuation does not take into consideration the opponent pieces, but before we incorporate them let us step through a short example to demonstrate why we need both army valuations. Take a look at Image 8.22.

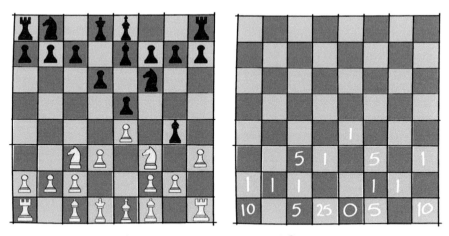

IMAGE 8.22   Piece valuations.

If it is our move (we are white), there is a Bishop at G4 who is threatening our Knight at F3. We however have a Pawn at H3 that can do something about it. Image 8.23 shows the board if the Pawn were to take the Bishop.

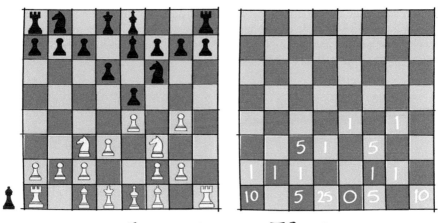

Evaluated score = 73 points

IMAGE 8.23   Score after taking the Bishop.

As you can see, we have taken a piece from the opponent, but the score for the board is still 73. Now what happens if we did not take that Bishop and just moved our Pawn forward. Take a look at Image 8.24.

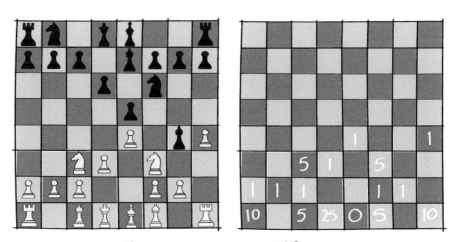

Evaluated score = 73 points

IMAGE 8.24   Score after not taking the Bishop.

In this board configuration, the opponent gets to keep their Bishop, and the board is still scored at 73. So, both these move options are equivalent. The Minimax algorithm would not prefer one board over the other, and it is obvious which one is better.

To incorporate the opponent's piece valuations is quite simple. We could deduct the opponent army valuation from our army valuation or divide our army valuation by the opponent army valuation. Image 8.25 replicates the move made in Image 8.24 where the Pawn did not take the Bishop.

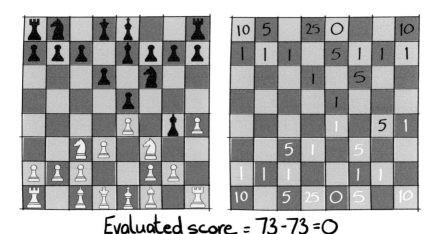

IMAGE 8.25   Score after not taking the Bishop.

Image 8.26 replicates the move to take the Bishop as previously made in Image 8.23, but this time you can see the score of the board configuration is positive for us.

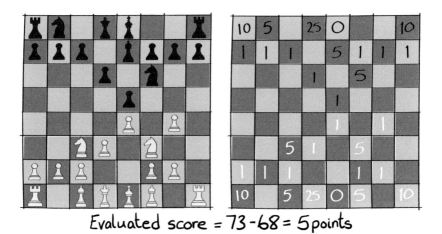

IMAGE 8.26   Score after taking the Bishop.

It is important to note that we are not taking into consideration where the pieces are on the board. So far we have only considered the values of the pieces on the board, which will lead to the Minimax algorithm selecting higher scoring boards – those where we have more pieces, or at the very least pieces whose accumulated value is greater than that of the opponent.

BOARD POSITIONING

Some positions on the gameboard offer advantages over other positions. As an example, we will be using positions at the centre of the board. These positions offer a wider range of attacks, whilst also reducing the opponent's ability to attack. Take a look at Image 8.27. For simplicity, we will award a board configuration, an additional score of 5, if a friendly piece is located at any of these positions. If an opponent occupies one of these spots, then the board would have 5 points deducted.

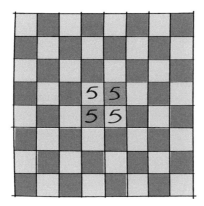

IMAGE 8.27   Bonus points for desirable positions.

The central positions are not the only positions that offer advantages, but positioning can depend upon the piece in question. This will be addressed in the following section.

MOVES AVAILABLE

The number of moves available is another evaluation that can have an impact upon the attacking intelligence. It is similar to positioning but takes into consideration each piece's ability rather than the physical location on the board. All pieces bring something different to the game, so all should be considered. For example, a Rook with an open channel is preferable to a constrained Rook. For this we are going to add one point for each valid move that each piece can make. That is one point for each space the piece can stop on.

Image 8.28 demonstrates this idea for a Knight located at one of the central positions described in Image 8.27. As you can see the Knight has a valuation of 5 points, it gets an additional 5 points for its location on the board, and then an additional 8 points for the eight available moves.

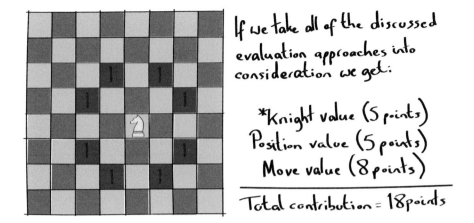

If we take all of the discussed evaluation approaches into consideration we get:

*Knight value (5 points)
Position value (5 points)
Move value (8 points)
_____
Total contribution = 18 points

IMAGE 8.28   Scoring a Knight using valuation, position and number of moves.

On an empty board the score is quite substantial, so let us take a look at a Knight in an actual board. Image 8.29 does just this. The valuation for a Knight is still 5 points, it is not located at a position with a score and has 5 possible moves.

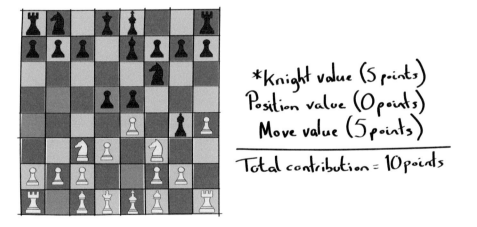

*Knight value (5 points)
Position value (0 points)
Move value (5 points)
_____
Total contribution = 10 points

IMAGE 8.29   Scoring a Knight in gameplay.

Let us take a look at a different type of piece. This example will focus on a Rook. Image 8.30 shows how differently a Rook moves to a Knight. With both channels available the Rook adds a huge 14 points to the board score. Although this is not that likely to happen very often in a real game, it does demonstrate how moving a Rook into a position where a channel is open will result in a higher scoring board. The Minimax algorithm would not know that this was a good option if we did not enhance the score to reflect the advantage.

IMAGE 8.30   Scoring a Rook using valuation, position and number of moves.

In a proper board layout as in Image 8.31, the Rook does not have both channels free to move in. Looking at the four available positions on row A that it could move to, it is only A2 that offers an open channel, which results in a higher scoring board. So, we can assume that given the choice, the AI would move here.

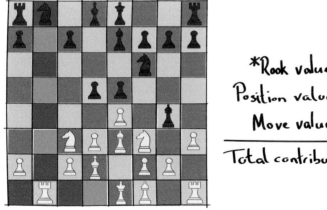

IMAGE 8.31   Scoring a Rook in gameplay.

ATTACKS AVAILABLE

Similar to the number of moves available is the number of attacks available. This should complement the moves available approach rather than replace it. An attack is where one of our pieces can take one of the opponent's pieces.

There are a couple of approaches we could take here. The first is to award an additional point to the score of the board for each attack. The second is to award the point value of the piece that could be taken. Take a look at Image 8.32 where we are looking at the Knight in C3. It could take a Pawn or an opposing Knight. If we go with the first approach, we get an additional 2 points. If we go with the second approach, this board configuration would get an additional 6 points – 5 points for the Knight and 1 point for the Pawn.

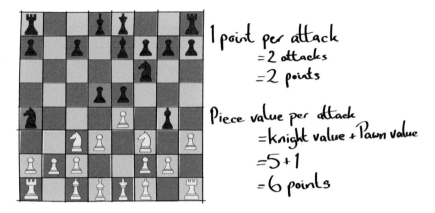

IMAGE 8.32 Calculating number of attacks for a Knight.

There is a valid argument that the second approach is unnecessary as when an opponent gets a piece taken, their total piece valuation is less than the amount of the piece taken. Although this is true, the attacks available approach is more of a look ahead, rather than what has happened. So, if the board in Image 8.32 were at the deepest depth we are searching, the score of the board would represent options going forward, and not just what occurred when the piece was moved.

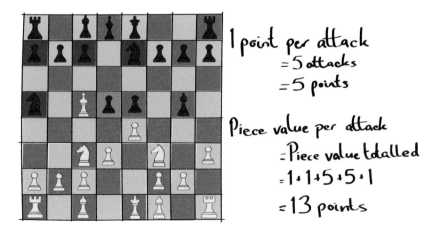

IMAGE 8.33 Calculating the number of attacks for the Queen.

Repeating the process again, but this time with the Queen, Image 8.33 demonstrates just how much of a difference in the scores there can be, 5 points and 13 points is quite a difference. Which will work better? Well, that depends upon the other scoring approaches used. As with many of the techniques discussed in this book, there is no *right* way. There are just a *myriad* of ways. Try out different combinations and see what works for you. The famous Deep Blue Chess computer uses around 8000 different approaches to calculating the score of a board, which goes to show just how complicated the game of Chess actually is.

FINAL THOUGHTS

This chapter has covered quite a lot, but you now have the foundations to code your own Chess AI. To finish this chapter, we will cover a few alternative approaches that could be considered.

PLAYBOOKS

There are stages of a game of Chess that are predictable. It is a game that has been played for centuries and there are well-defined openings to the game. What Chess player really thinks four moves ahead when moving that first Pawn? So, this brings us to the concept of Playbooks. It is a good idea for our AI to have access to a list of opening moves and their counters. This requires simply searching through a mini database (playbook) to find the move the opponent made and then return the suggested response.

ITERATIVE DEEPENING

When searching the game tree using the Minimax algorithm, we could search just one move ahead to see if we find a win condition, and if we do then we take that move. If we do not find a win condition, then we search a level deeper. Repeat this process until we hit a win condition, or we hit the maximum depth allowed.

   Searching iteratively in this manner will speed up processing if a win condition is higher up the tree as you are not searching as deep as the allowed search depth. However, if a win condition is not found, it will take longer as each iteration requires the search to begin again at the initial board, resulting in a lot of duplicate searches.

MOVE REDUCTION

The speed of processing the game tree is directly connected to the number of nodes searched. If we reduce this number, the speed of the search will increase. One way to do this is to limit the number of moves assessed for each piece type. This can lead to misleading results as you are only searching a partial game tree, but if you distribute the moves available for processing intelligently between the pieces you have, you can still get satisfactory results.

CHESS AI – PRACTICAL

PROJECT OVERVIEW

Early in the development of this book, it was decided to focus on the reader's understanding of the principles discussed. As such there are times where readable code comes at the expense of processing speed. This Chess project is a prime example of that. The AI is extremely slow when making a decision. Yes, this makes the game a little dull to play, but this project is about understanding the decision-making. When you understand this, you can then optimise the underlying structures to make the game run faster. I make no apology for this. There are hundreds of Chess games available online to play; this project is about understanding what is happening under the hood. With that being said, let us begin.

The Chess project is what you would expect. You can see how the game looks when running in Screenshot 8.1. You can choose to play a two-player game or a game against the AI. At the moment, the AI will not make a move after the initial playbook moves have been actioned. It will throw an error. This is what our step-by-step guide below will do. Whenever you select a piece, the game will highlight all the options available to you. Simply select one of these spaces and the piece will move. At the top left of the screen, there is an indicator to let you know whose turn it is. The human player will always use the white pieces. If you wish to change how many moves ahead the AI looks, you can do this by selecting the gameobject named Player2Ai, which is parented to the Canvas_Game gameobject. Find the component named Chess Player AI (Script) on Player2Ai and modify the Search Depth. Be careful though as the larger the look ahead, the deeper the search and the longer you will have to wait for the Minimax algorithm to return a result. The game will for all intents and purposes look like it is frozen. Put a breakpoint in the code and see what is happening.

SCREENSHOT 8.1   Chess project.

STEP-BY-STEP GUIDE

Open the Unity project named GameAi that accompanies this book. Navigate through the folder system to the Chapter8_ChessAI folder. It is located in the Assets folder. Click on the Chapter8_Chess scene. Run the application. You can currently only play a two-player game.

So, to begin coding the AI, open the Scripts folder and locate the ChessPlayerAI. cs file. As always, you will find a file containing the complete code solution commented out in the same folder. This is named ChessPlayerAI_Solution.cs.

CHESSPLAYERAI.CS

All the action for this tutorial takes place in this file. The ChessPlayerAI class inherits from the ChessPlayer class, where a lot of the core functionality is located. Be sure to take a look at this file too.

TakeATurn()

Scroll down and find the `TakeATurn()` function. We are not going to change any code here, but it is important to see where our Minimax algorithm is called from. Locate the following section of code:

```
Move bestMove = new Move();
if (chessOpenings != null && chessOpenings.
IsAnotherMoveAvailable())
{
    //Play opening.
    bestMove = chessOpenings.GetNextMove();
}
```

This first part of this if statement is to deal with the playbook for Chess openings. We will enter this section of code whilst there are moves remaining in the chosen opening. This speeds up the start of the game and also puts the AI in a good position. The playbook that has been coded for this project is very simple. We choose a random opening and then move the pieces in the order specified regardless of what the human opponent is doing.

In the else section, we get to see where the Minimax algorithm is called. Before we call this however, we need to know how many pieces are still on the board, so we do a quick function call to calculate this.

```
else
{
    //Do the MiniMax Algorithm.
    GetNumberOfLivingPieces();
    score = MiniMax(chessBoard, ref bestMove);
}
```

Minimax()

Scroll a little further down the code file and you will see the `Minimax()` function. Again, we will not be changing anything in this function. The reason for this is that by working with the minimise and maximise parts of the algorithm separately, it makes debugging a little easier. This is purely a choice made to ease the understanding of the processes. When debugging, you know which player you are dealing with just by seeing which function you are currently in – `Minimise()` or `Maximise()`. The AI is always looking to maximise their score and minimise the human player's score. If, after we have this working, you feel like you would prefer to combine the two functions (`Maximise()` and `Minimise()`) into a single function to match the pseudocode provided in Image 8.10, then do give it a go.

The `MiniMax()` function has a single line of code:

```
return Maximise(boardToTest, searchDepth, ref bestMove, MaxInt);
```

This line of code calls the `Maximise()` part of the Minimax algorithm. Within `Maximise()` we will be calling the `Minimise()` part of the Minimax algorithm. And within the `Minimise()` function, we will be calling `Maximise()` to give us the recursion required.

Maximise()

This function looks to return the board that results in the highest value from its branch in the tree. We only score the board though if it is at the desired search depth. Remember, we score the board at the bottom of the tree and pass this value up. We do not score every board we come across.

Let us get started. Locate the following lines of code and delete them.

```
//Todo: Add code here.
return 0;
```

The first thing we do is to check if we are at the desired depth, and if so we return the score of this board.

```
if (currentSearchDepth == 0)
{
    return ScoreTheBoard(boardToTest);
}
```

If we are not at the desired depth, we need to delve deeper. So, before we launch into the iterative nature of the Minimax algorithm, we need to set what our best value currently is. This is for the AlphaBeta modification of the algorithm. It is set to a very low number to ensure the first board score that returns to this function will be a greater value and thus stored.

```
int bestValue = -MaxInt;
```

We need to use a copy of the current board as we will be moving pieces. We do not want to move a piece on the original board; otherwise, things will get very confused.

```
ChessBoard tempBoard = new ChessBoard();
tempBoard.CopyInternalBoard(boardToTest);
```

For each board configuration, we want to make all the moves that are available. Create a list of all the moves to iterate through later.

```
List<Move> moves = new List<Move>();
GetAllMoveOptions(tempBoard, colour, ref moves);
```

We only want to process the available moves if we have some. If we have no moves, we jump past the next section of code and return the current board value.

```
if (moves.Count > 0)
{
    for (int i = 0; i < moves.Count; i++)
    {
```

One of the parameters passed into the `Maximise()` function is the `parentLow` variable. This is the lowest score from the `Minimise()` function that called this function. We only want to do further checks if our best highest score is less than the parent's low score, otherwise stop. Remember that this function is looking to get the highest score from all descendants. This means that the current score can only get higher, and if the calling `Minimise()` function is only going to select this branch if it scores less than its current best, we are wasting our time. This is AlphaBeta pruning taking effect.

```
if (bestValue > parentLow)
{
    return bestValue;
}
```

We are still below the value stored in `parentLow`, so let us make the next move on this version of the board and pass it deeper down the game tree.

```
else
{
```

The first thing to do is to modify the board by moving the desired piece into position.

```
tempBoard.CopyInternalBoard(boardToTest);
tempBoard.MovePiece(moves[i].from_Row, moves[i].from_Col,
moves[i].to_Row, moves[i].to_Col);
```

Now we can pass this board deeper down the Minimax tree by calling the `Minimise()` function with this board configuration. We also need to minus one from the search depth as we are digging one depth deeper. Notice that we are also passing through a reference to the best move. This is so we can store the best move across all branches of the tree and use it in our `TakeATurn()` function. The `best-Value` is our current highest score. This is received by the `Minimise()` function as the `parentHigh` variable.

```
int value = Minimise(tempBoard, currentSearchDepth - 1, ref
bestMove, bestValue);
```

After we return from the `Minimise()` part of the algorithm, we need to test if the value returned is greater than what we already have stored. If so, we should update our current best value.

```
if (value > bestValue)
{
    bestValue = value;
```

If we are at the starting depth, we should also store the move that got us the good score.

```
if (currentSearchDepth == searchDepth)
{
    bestMove = moves[i];
}
```

Close off the remaining four brackets, then return the best value to the calling `Minimise()` function.

```
return bestValue;
```

Remember this is only half of the Minimax algorithm. We still need to handle the minimise portion of it. And this is what we will do next.

Minimise()

Scroll down to the next function in the file and it should be the `Minimise()` function. A lot of what we are about to implement matches what we have just done with the `Maximise()` function. Locate the following lines of code, delete them and follow the instructions below.

```
//Todo: Add code here.
return 0;
```

Always check if we have reached the depth of the tree that we were looking for. If we have, then score the board at this depth and return the value to the function that called us.

```
if (currentSearchDepth == 0)
{
    return ScoreTheBoard(boardToTest);
}
```

We are not at the desired depth, so we need to keep making moves and delving deeper down the tree. To incorporate the AlphaBeta modification, we need to store what the best value is for this branch. We always start with a high number as the `Minimise()` function is looking for the lowest value and starting high ensures we overwrite it with the first board processed.

```
int bestValue = MaxInt;
```

We do not want to modify the current board; otherwise, things get broken very fast. So, make a copy of the current board.

```
ChessBoard tempBoard = new ChessBoard();
tempBoard.CopyInternalBoard(boardToTest);
```

For each board configuration, we want to move all the pieces that have moves available. Create a list of all the moves to iterate through later.

```
List<Move> moves = new List<Move>();
GetAllMoveOptions(tempBoard, colour, ref moves);
```

Only if we have moves available do we want to dig deeper down the Minimax tree. If we have no moves, we can jump past the next section of code and return the current board value.

```
if (moves.Count > 0)
{
    for (int i = 0; i < moves.Count; i++)
    {
```

One of the parameters passed into the `Minimise()` function is the `parentHigh` variable. This is the highest score from the `Maximise()` function that called this function. We only want to do further checks if our best lowest score is greater than the parent's high score, otherwise stop. Remember that this function is looking to get the lowest score from all descendants. This means that the current score can only get lower, and if the calling `Maximise()` function is only going to select this branch if it scores greater than its current best, we are wasting our time. This is essentially the AlphaBeta pruning taking effect as it stops us from making moves and delving deeper down the tree for results that are not going to benefit us.

```
if (bestValue < parentHigh)
{
    return bestValue;
}
```

We are still above the value stored in `parentHigh`, make the next move on this version of the board and pass it deeper down the game tree.

```
else
{
```

Next, we reconfigure the current board by moving the desired piece into position.

```
tempBoard.CopyInternalBoard(boardToTest);
tempBoard.MovePiece(moves[i].from_Row, moves[i].from_Col,
moves[i].to_Row, moves[i].to_Col);
```

Now we can pass this board deeper down the Minimax tree by calling the `Maximise()` function with the new board layout. We also need to minus one from the search depth as we are digging one depth deeper. Notice that we are also passing through a reference to the best move. This is so we can store the best move across all branches of the tree and use it in our `TakeATurn()` function. The `bestValue` is our current lowest score. This is received by the `Maximise()` function as the `parentLow` variable.

```
int value = Maximise(tempBoard, currentSearchDepth - 1, ref
bestMove, bestValue);
```

Store the lower value between that returned and the currently stored best value.

```
bestValue = Mathf.Min(bestValue, value);
```

Close off the remaining three brackets and return the best value to the calling `Maximise()` function.

```
return bestValue;
```

That's it!

As always, if you find you have compilation errors, be sure to check the solution located in the same folder. It will have additional debug code that you can use when debugging too.

FUTURE WORK

There is so much left to do with this project. The first of which is to implement some optimisations so that the Minimax search runs faster. This will make the game more fun to play. When you are done with that, here are a couple more suggestions:

Modify the piece weightings:

- Changing the weightings of the pieces will alter the way the AI plays the game. Make a Pawn more valuable than a Rook and see what happens.

Modify how we score the board:

- Locate the ScoreTheBoard() function and change the way we do this. Try a variety of different approaches (Number of pieces, number of moves, positioning etc.) and see what works best.

Write a single Minimax() function:

- Combine the Minimise() and Maximise() functions to create a single Minimax() function.

Modify the opening playbook:

- Rather than choosing a random playbook, take a look at choosing one based upon the human player's first move. This will make our AI look more intelligent and put them in a stronger position.
- At the start of a game, if the human player diverts from the expected moves stored in the playbook, allow the AI to switch into move selection using the Minimax algorithm earlier. To do this, the opening playbook will need to store the expected moves of the opponent as well as the moves for the AI.

9 Genetic Algorithms

Sometimes referred to as Evolutionary Algorithms, Genetic Algorithms are search and optimise techniques based upon Charles Darwin's principle of the survival of the fittest. It is a multi-stepped approach to finding a solution to a given problem. These steps include selection, reproduction and mutation. In essence, by combining solutions that are not quite good enough over multiple generations we can evolve to a good solution.

Before we get into the nuts and bolts of this approach, let us take a step back and consider genetics and evolution from the perspective of nature. After all, that is what this approach is attempting to replicate. As an example, we are going to look at the humble giraffe. The one thing we know about a giraffe is that it has a long neck so it can reach foliage that is high up. But what if the giraffe started off with a short neck? And the long-neck variety was a mutation. Take a look at Image 9.1. Do you see the problem for the short-necked variety of giraffe?

IMAGE 9.1   The long-necked giraffe.

Over time, all that low hanging vegetation gets snapped up, and it is only the giraffes with the longer necks that get to eat. Slowly the short-necked giraffes die out and only their long-necked cousins remain. If this were repeated over millions of generations of giraffes, you end up with the giraffe we see today. That is survival of the fittest right there. This process is depicted in Image 9.2. Imagine this loop continues through the entire lifespan of the giraffe species.

DOI: 10.1201/9781003305835-9

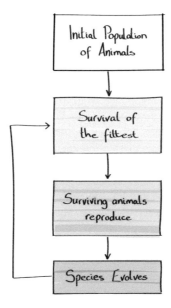

IMAGE 9.2   Natural selection.

I will level with you here. I have no idea if that is how the giraffe got its long neck, but it is a great example of how genetic algorithms work. We have a problem: *How do I eat the vegetation that is high up?* And we evolved a solution: *The long-necked giraffe.*

How is any of this relevant to games you ask? Well, generic algorithms are a great way to evolve solutions to problems when we do not know what the correct solution should be. Or, to find solutions we had not thought of and probably did not expect. For large multiplayer games, it is quite probable that the quality assurance folks that test your game could never hope to test every single edge case that might arise. It is also quite probable that we do not even know what some of those edge cases even are. Genetic algorithms are a great way to help find any potential flaws that players of different skill levels might abuse.

Genetic algorithms are also a great way to optimise your AI as well. Let us take driving games as an example. These games typically have a lot of cars with multiple setups for each one. That is a lot of data. Instead of having a human developer play through every setting for every car to determine what the best setup should be, we could use generic algorithms to do the work for us. We simply randomise the car setups to create the initial population and have each version race around the track to determine how good it is. The number of cars is a judgement call, but let us say 50 different setups for this example. Lap time is a good gauge of how well this combination of settings did, so we can use that as our score. When all 50 cars have completed the lap, we then select which ones will be used as the parents for the next generation, combine them in some manner and then repeat the process.

We can let this go on until we have a setup that can drive a lap of the track in the desired time.

This would work if the original random setups included the parts to make up the best solution. As the values are initially random, we cannot know for sure that this is the case. So that is where mutation comes into play. Remember our long-necked giraffe friend?

So, after all cars of a particular generation have completed a lap, and we have combined them to create new setups, then we can add the possibility of mutation. We could say 1% of the new settings get randomly modified. This adds some variety into the gene pool and ensures that if our initial population does not have the optimal settings, over time it could mutate them.

Image 9.3 shows how a genetic algorithm functions. Take a look back at Image 9.2, which showed the natural selection loop. Can you see the similarities? I have colour coded to make it clear.

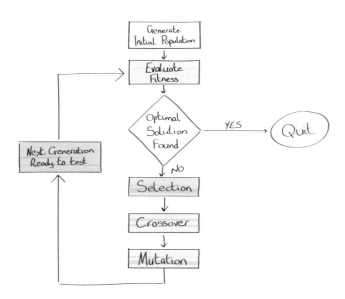

IMAGE 9.3   Genetic algorithm alternative to natural selection.

Right, that is the overview, we are about ready to jump into the nitty gritty of how genetic algorithms work, but before we do let us create a fictional game for us to use in the explanations. The game is called 'Royal Battle 1866'. It is a battle Royale style game in a steampunk setting, where the members of different Royal families go at it. Battles take place in an arena, with 20 characters going head-to-head, and the last man or woman standing is the winner. Each character can have the equipment listed in Image 9.4.

Index	Equipment	Ability
0	Gas mask	No damage from gas
1	Jetpack	Fast movement
2	Armour	Strength bonus
3	X-Ray goggles	See enemy locations
4	Grenades	Ranged attack
5	Whip	Melee attack
6	Pistol	Single distance shot
7	Gas cannisters	Dropped. Give off noxious fumes

IMAGE 9.4   Royal Battle 1866 equipment.

So, with our example game prepared, let us get back to genetic algorithms.

INITIAL POPULATION

Before everything else, we need to create the initial population. We do this through encoding, which is where we construct our chromosomes. A chromosome is a group of attributes that describe a solution. In the race-car example above a chromosome would be a single car setup. We had 50 cars, so would need 50 chromosomes to describe each of their settings.

We could have the initial population to be 100% randomly generated, but if we have an idea of the desired result, we could set the population to reflect this. It should be noted however that if the chromosomes are all very similar, the results from evolution will not be great. So I would suggest if you are pre-setting the chromosomes, throw a few random ones in there to mix things up.

ENCODING

Encoding is the term used to describe the digital description of your chromosomes. There are many ways we could go about encoding, and it really depends upon the problem you are trying to solve. Each element in a chromosome is a gene. We will use the term gene and attribute interchangeably. Three such approaches to encoding are binary encoding, permutation encoding and value encoding.

Using the binary encoding approach, a chromosome could simply be an integer with different bits flipped. Each bit would represent whether a particular attribute was enabled or disabled. Image 9.5 gives an example of this.

Chromosome 1   10110111001000000010
Chromosome 2   11110001111101010001

IMAGE 9.5   Chromosomes made up of bits.

Using the permutation encoding approach, the order of each element is important. Problems such as The Travelling Salesman problem can be solved using this type of encoding, as each city is only visited once and the best solution to the problem is the order of the visits that take the least amount of time. Image 9.6 demonstrates how all chromosomes have the same values, but it is the order of those values that is evolved.

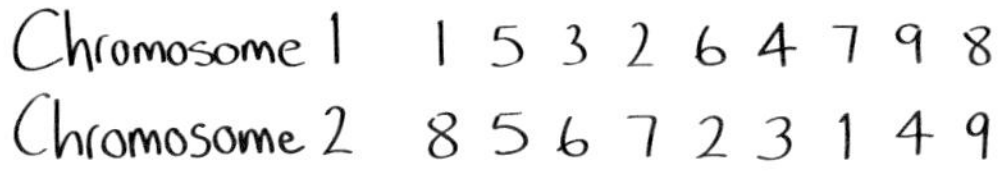

Chromosome 1   1 5 3 2 6 4 7 9 8
Chromosome 2   8 5 6 7 2 3 1 4 9

IMAGE 9.6   Chromosomes made up of the same values.

Value encoding is an approach that allows any data type to occupy an element of the chromosome. This could be a numerical value, a string, an enumeration or even a struct of many values. Image 9.7 depicts three such chromosomes. The first uses real numbers, the second uses an enum we have created and the third uses a struct.

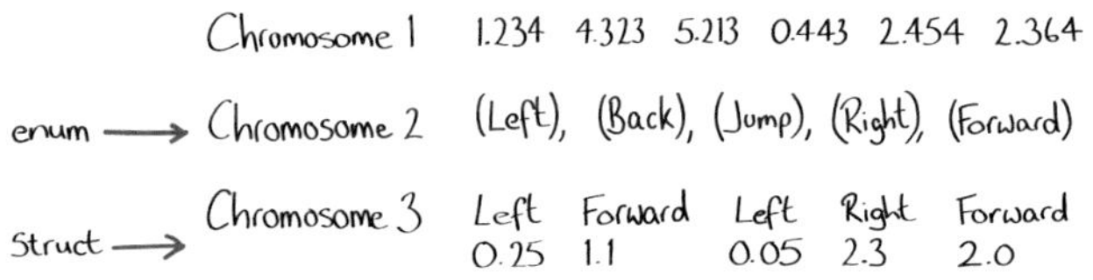

Chromosome 1   1.234 4.323 5.213 0.443 2.454 2.364

enum ⟶ Chromosome 2   (Left), (Back), (Jump), (Right), (Forward)

Chromosome 3   Left   Forward   Left   Right   Forward
struct ⟶   0.25   1.1   0.05   2.3   2.0

IMAGE 9.7   Chromosomes made up of floats, enums and structs.

EXAMPLE GAME: GENERATING INITIAL POPULATION

For our fictional title – Royal Battle 1866, we will be using a binary approach. Each chromosome will be an 8-bit integer, with each bit representing one of the equipment types described in Image 9.4. The design of this chromosome is to have all utilities grouped together and all weapons grouped together. It does not have to be this way and is entirely your decision. We will explore this decision a little later. A single chromosome might look something like Image 9.8.

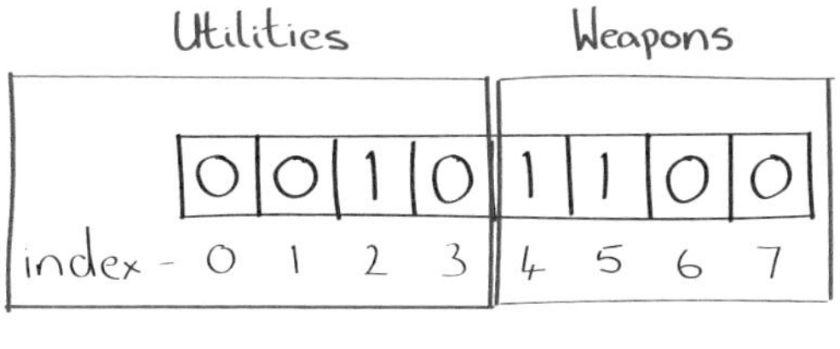

Utilities   Weapons

0 0 1 0 1 1 0 0
index - 0 1 2 3   4 5 6 7

IMAGE 9.8   Chromosome design for Royal Battle 1866.

Looking back again at the equipment table, you will see there is a column entitled index. This refers to the index in the chromosome. So, in the example chromosome in Image 9.8, you can see that the character will only be equipped with armour, grenades and a whip as the bit is set to a one at indexes 2, 4 and 5. All other elements have the bit set to zero and will not have the relevant piece of equipment available to them.

We need 20 characters though, so we will need to randomly generate 20 chromosomes that will be used in our game. This gives us our initial population, which can be seen in Image 9.9.

Chromosome	Gas Mask	Jet Pack	Armour	X-Ray goggles	Grenades	Whip	Pistol	Gas cannisters
1	1	0	1	0	1	0	1	0
2	1	1	0	1	0	0	0	0
3	0	0	0	0	0	1	0	0
4	0	1	0	0	1	0	0	1
5	0	0	1	0	0	0	0	1
6	1	1	0	0	1	0	0	0
7	0	0	0	0	0	1	0	1
8	1	0	1	0	1	0	0	1
9	0	1	0	0	1	0	0	0
10	0	1	0	0	0	1	1	1
11	0	1	1	1	0	0	0	0
12	0	1	0	0	0	0	1	1
13	1	1	1	0	1	1	0	1
14	0	1	0	0	1	0	0	1
15	0	0	1	0	1	0	0	0
16	1	1	0	0	1	1	0	1
17	0	1	0	0	0	0	0	0
18	1	0	0	0	0	1	1	0
19	0	0	1	0	0	0	0	0
20	0	1	0	1	1	1	0	0

IMAGE 9.9   Royal Battle 1866 initial population.

FITNESS

The fitness of a chromosome is a value that represents how well it did at solving the problem. With the race-car example, the fitness was lap time, and with the travelling salesman problem, the fitness is the shortest time it takes to visit all cities one time. Each problem will require its own form of fitness, and how you calculate this can be crucial. It is also worth noting that how you calculate your fitness scores will ultimately be reflected in the chromosomes that come through.

Back to Royal Battle 1866. I want to evolve characters that are stealthy killers. For this, I am going to focus on survival time and damage done. Of course, the number of kills is an obvious choice, but we are not too bothered by how many kills they make, we want them to inflict damage and survive. If we were to focus on the number of kills, then the chromosomes that win out would probably be more likely to enter the fray as soon as an enemy is spotted. We could run the genetic algorithm multiple times with different fitness criteria to evolve the attributes for different character types with different play styles.

For this example, the fitness score will be calculated using the following:

$$Fitness = survival\ time + damage\ inflicted$$

Take a look at Image 9.10 to see the (entirely made up) results after a single battle in the arena.

Chromosome	Gas Mask	Jet Pack	Armour	X-Ray goggles	Grenades	Whip	Pistol	Gas cannisters	Fitness
1	1	0	1	0	1	0	1	0	60
2	1	1	0	1	0	0	0	0	50
3	0	0	0	0	0	1	0	0	5
4	0	1	0	0	1	0	0	1	25
5	0	0	1	0	0	0	0	1	15
6	1	1	0	0	1	0	0	0	30
7	0	0	0	0	0	1	0	1	10
8	1	0	1	0	1	0	0	1	25
9	0	1	0	0	1	0	0	0	5
10	0	1	0	0	0	1	1	1	20
11	0	1	1	1	0	0	0	0	20
12	0	1	0	0	0	0	1	1	15
13	1	1	1	0	1	1	0	1	85
14	0	1	0	0	1	0	0	1	20
15	0	0	1	0	1	0	0	0	10
16	1	1	0	0	1	1	0	1	80
17	0	1	0	0	0	0	0	0	5
18	1	0	0	0	0	1	1	0	15
19	0	0	1	0	0	0	0	0	10
20	0	1	0	1	1	1	0	0	70

IMAGE 9.10   Royal Battle 1866 chromosome fitness.

SELECTION

The selection process is all about selecting which chromosomes should be used as parents for the next generation. Those selected will go into what is called the 'parent pool'. You can have as many or as few chromosomes in the parent pool as you like, but there are a couple of things to consider. If the parent pool has too few chromosomes, the gene pool will be limited, resulting in the next generation of chromosomes all being very similar. Going in the opposite direction and having too many chromosomes in the parent pool and you might as well just put them all through. You will see below that low scoring chromosomes *should* have the ability to go through to the parent pool, but if you have too many spaces available, you could very well end up with all of the chromosomes from the previous generation making it through to the parent pool, rendering the process of selection redundant. A good target to aim for is the same number of chromosomes as used in a generation. This means there is space for every chromosome from the previous generation, but in practice you will have multiple copies of the fitter chromosomes in the parent pool.

So back to the actual selection of parents. You might be thinking that you simply take the chromosomes with the highest fitness scores and remove the rest. That is certainly an approach to use and is called Rank Selection, which we discuss below; however, if we solely take this approach, we would be losing vital attributes that the lower scoring chromosomes contain. So, given we cannot just take the highest scoring chromosomes, we need a more nuanced approach to selecting which chromosomes should be used as parents for the next generation. And lucky for us there are quite a few tried and tested approaches.

TOURNAMENT SELECTION

This approach is one where you select a number of chromosomes at random and the highest scoring one is copied across to our pool of parent chromosomes. This may initially seem like it is doing exactly what I just described not to do, however on closer inspection, this approach allows for low scoring chromosomes to be selected too. The highest scoring chromosome just needs to be higher than those it is completing against. It is important to note that the same chromosome can win multiple tournaments and have multiple versions in the pool of parent chromosomes.

In Image 9.11, three chromosomes have been selected at random, and the highest scoring chromosome wins. It has a copy placed in the list of parent chromosomes. All these chromosomes are returned to the pool of chromosomes, allowing for them all to be selected again. Even the winning chromosome can be selected again.

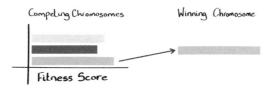

IMAGE 9.11   Tournament selection.

Image 9.12 shows a second tournament, but this time the three chromosomes selected all scored low fitness values. In fact, they are all worse than the lowest scoring chromosome in Image 9.11. The highest scoring chromosome from this group has a copy placed in the list of parent chromosomes, and they all get returned to the pool of chromosomes to await the next tournament and their chance at selection.

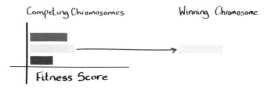

IMAGE 9.12   Tournament selection.

The number of chromosomes selected for each tournament is up to you. If you have a population of 20 chromosomes and you have tournaments of 10 chromosomes, you are reducing the chance of low-scoring chromosomes progressing. A good number to aim for is around the 10% mark. So, if there were 50 chromosomes in each generation, then each round of tournament Selection would consist of 5 randomly selected chromosomes.

ROULETTE WHEEL SELECTION

This is an approach that takes inspiration from the casino game. Each chromosome has a slice of the roulette wheel assigned to it, but the size of the slice is proportionate to its fitness score. Chromosomes with higher values get larger slices of the wheel, making it more likely that they will be selected.

We spin the wheel once for each parent required. That is, if we want a pool of 50 parent chromosomes, we need to spin the wheel 50 times. Wherever the ball stops, we take a copy of the corresponding chromosome. This approach allows for both high- and low-scoring chromosomes to be selected but gives those with the higher scores more of a chance to progress.

Let us look at an example. Image 9.13 gives a population of four chromosomes that have all had their fitness scores calculated. We are only using four to make the example easier to follow.

ID	Chromosome	Fitness	% of Wheel
1	01101011	169	14.4
2	11000010	576	49.2
3	01000111	64	5.5
4	10011001	361	30.9
Total		1170	100.0

IMAGE 9.13   Population of four chromosomes.

The last column in Image 9.13 shows the ratio of the wheel that each chromosome will have – based upon their fitness. This is simply each chromosome's fitness divided by the total fitness, multiplied by 100.

For example, chromosome 1:

$$(169 / 1170) * 100$$

Depicting this information as the roulette wheel, see Image 9.14. We now generate a random number and see which slice of the roulette wheel it falls in.

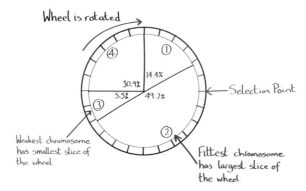

IMAGE 9.14   Roulette wheel selection.

To select a slice of the wheel, we simply generate a random number between zero and one hundred. This is the position the ball stops on the roulette wheel. For chromosome 1 to be selected, the value selected needs to be below 14.4. For chromosome 2 to be selected, the value needs to be between 14.5 and 63.6. This is because the ball needs to pass over the slice of the wheel occupied by chromosome 1 before it reaches the 49.2% occupied by chromosome 2.

STOCHASTIC UNIVERSAL SAMPLING SELECTION

Similar to roulette wheel selection is stochastic universal sampling selection. The difference with this approach is that only one spin of the wheel is required to fill the pool of parent chromosomes. Instead of the ball spinning around the whole wheel, it stops at uniform intervals, and at each stop, the chromosome whose slice we stopped on is copied across to the parent pool.

As with the roulette wheel approach, each chromosome gets a portion of the wheel based on their fitness ratio. The interval size, or step size, around the wheel is based upon how many chromosomes are required for the parent pool. We simply divide the total fitness by this number. What results is that if we wanted 100 chromosomes in our parent pool and a chromosome has a fitness ratio of 4.5, we will take through 4 or 5 copies of this chromosome. If the ratio is 50.2, we will take 50 copies. We are unlikely to require 100 parents, but whatever the required number is, the number of copies made of a chromosome is determined by their fitness ratio.

Visually I prefer unwinding the wheel, so each chromosome's portion of the wheel is laid side by side. It looks like a row of blocks, where the size of each block corresponds to its proportion of the wheel. See Image 9.15 where there are eight chromosomes to choose from, each with a different size that reflects its fitness ratio. Eight selections are required for the parent pool. Image 9.15 also makes it easier to see how the steps give a uniform sampling. So, the larger grey chromosome gets three copies going through to the parent pool, whereas the green chromosome gets two copies.

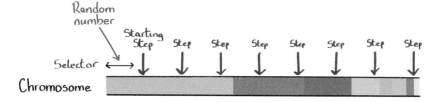

IMAGE 9.15   Stochastic universal sampling selection.

As can be seen from Image 9.15, we do not just start sampling at zero. To make it fair, we choose a random number within the range of the step size and sample at that point. For each subsequent step, the step size is added to the previous position.

RANK SELECTION

As discussed at the start of the selection section of this chapter, discarding lower scoring chromosomes wholesale is not a great idea, and that is what rank selection does. This approach will lose vital portions of the solution by taking the best and discarding the rest, but it does become useful toward the end of evolution. When we are nearing a solution and all the fitness scores are converging, rank selection becomes a suitable choice.

In Image 9.16 I have ordered the chromosomes by rank. A cut-off fitness value has been selected and all those below are removed. The cut-off is a choice you will need to make, but for this example, the top 30% will be selected for the parent pool.

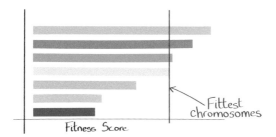

IMAGE 9.16   Rank selection.

The number of copies of each successful chromosome to be used in the parent pool is just a matter of dividing how many chromosomes are required by how many chromosomes made the cut. Then simply make that number of copies of each successful chromosome.

LINEAR RANKING SELECTION

Expanding on the idea of rank selection but allowing for chromosomes that do not score the highest to also go through to the parent pool, we have linear ranking selection.

First, we order the chromosomes from highest fitness score right down to lowest. Then we decide how many categories we are going to have. A category is all chromosomes with a fitness score within a range. For example, we could have six categories which are in the following ranges:

$$\text{Range 1}: \quad > 100$$
$$\text{Range 2}: \quad 76 \rightarrow 100$$
$$\text{Range 3}: \quad 51 \rightarrow 75$$
$$\text{Range 4}: \quad 26 \rightarrow 50$$
$$\text{Range 5}: \quad 11 \rightarrow 25$$
$$\text{Range 6}: \quad 0 \rightarrow 10$$

We then decide how many chromosomes from each range we will select to go through to the parent pool. This will largely depend on how many are required for the parent pool but will always follow the same approach. The top range will get the most, with each lower group getting a reduced amount. Image 9.17 gives a visual example of this.

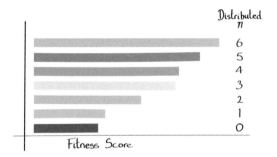

IMAGE 9.17   Linear rank selection distribution.

Chromosomes chosen from a range should be randomly selected from the chromosomes that fall into that category. It is reasonable to expect some chromosomes will be chosen multiple times and others miss out.

ELITIST SELECTION

Elitist selection is the process of choosing the very best chromosome(s) and automatically putting them through to the next generation. Those chosen as elites still exist in the pool of chromosomes to be selected from, but unaltered copies go straight through to the next generation. That means they do not go through the crossover stage or the mutation stage.

The benefit of using this approach, combined with another selection approach, is that we guarantee we do not lose the current best solution(s) through selection and crossover. The downside of this approach is that if too many elites go through the gene pool can quickly diminish and a solution converges on what is the *current* best solution, not the *optimal* solution. 'Current best' means simply that – current best. It does not mean it is the best solution to the problem, just the best solution out of the chromosomes that were tested. My advice would be to use his approach sparingly.

EXAMPLE GAME: SELECTION

For Royal Battle 1866, I have decided to use the tournament approach. From the chromosomes we will select five at random and then compete them against each other. Take a look back at Image 9.10 to see what each chromosome scored.

The first five selected were chromosomes 2, 5, 19, 17 and 8. The relative fitness has been depicted in Image 9.18 in the same format as the earlier explanations. As you can see, chromosome 2 easily wins this tournament and has a copy of itself progress through to the parent pool.

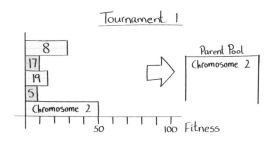

IMAGE 9.18   Tournament selection round 1.

Let us do one more tournament. This time we will select a random five chromosomes to do battle. Those chosen were chromosomes 2, 12, 15, 1 and 13. Take a look at Image 9.19 to see their relative fitness. Chromosome 13 wins this battle and has a copy of itself placed into the parent pool.

What is important to note here is that chromosome 2 was re-selected. After the previous tournament, all chromosomes are returned, meaning all are available for re-selection, including the winning chromosome. Notice that chromosome 2 did not win this tournament though. Chromosome 13 was selected, which had a greater fitness.

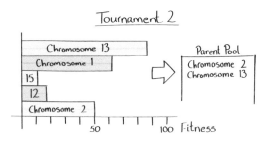

IMAGE 9.19   Tournament selection round 2.

After repeating this process until the parent pool was full, we ended up with the parent pool depicted in Image 9.20. We went with 20 chromosomes for the parent pool as that is the number of chromosomes in each generation. As explained earlier, there are multiple of the higher scoring chromosomes, but some of the lower scorers also made it through.

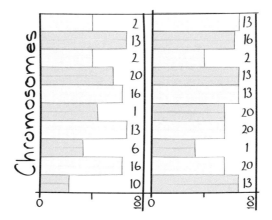

IMAGE 9.20   Parent pool.

We are now ready to breed our parents to produce the chromosomes that make up the next generation. This is the process of crossover.

CROSSOVER

The crossover step is essentially the breeding phase. We take chromosomes from our pool of parents and combine them in some manner to create child chromosomes. These new chromosomes carry over the attributes of their parents.

The number of children required for the next generation should be the same number used in the previous generation. If you decide to go with elitist selection, make sure those chromosomes go through unaltered. And remember to deduct the number of elites from the required children. So, if we need 50 children and we have 2 elites, the 2 elites go straight through, leaving 48 children to be generated.

To generate a child chromosome, we need at least two parents, but unlike in nature, in the digital world we can use as many parents as we like to generate a child. It is possible to generate multiple children from the same parents at the same time but is entirely reasonable to create a single child and then reselect parents for the next child.

First, we select our parents, which can be done by random selection, or by going through them all in turn. Random selection does not guarantee all parents will be used, which is why it is sometimes called a pool of prospective parents. By going through all parents in turn means that all children will be generated from both the high-scoring parent chromosomes as well as low-scoring ones.

Personally, I prefer the following approach. When using a parent pool with the same number of chromosomes as in each generation, then it is a good idea to use two parents to create two children. Randomly select parents, then remove them from the parent pool. This ensures all parents are used, but they are paired randomly. This approach will result in the required number of children chromosomes being generated and all of the parent chromosomes being used.

Right, it is time to look at how we can transfer the attributes of the parent chromosomes across to a child chromosome.

1-POINT CROSSOVER

Select a single point within the parent chromosomes and copy the attributes before this point from parent A and the attributes after this point from parent B. Combined these attributes make up the chromosome for a single child.

As I said before, I like to ensure all a parent's attributes progress to the next generation, so from two parents two children are generated. The second child takes the first part from parent B, and the second part from parent A, the opposite of its sibling. Image 9.21 depicts how the children are generated with a single crossover point. The first parent is coloured white, and you can see where its attributes have been placed in the two children. Likewise, the second parent is blue.

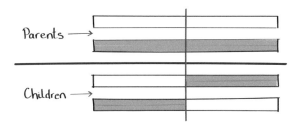

IMAGE 9.21   Single-point crossover.

To further demonstrate this process, Image 9.22 shows the same crossover using the same colour coding, but this time with the bits that make up the attributes of the chromosome.

$(Parent)$ Chromosome A: | 01 10 01 10 | 01 00 01 00 |
$(Parent)$ Chromosome B: | 11 01 00 00 | 11 10 11 01 |

$(Child)$ Chromosome C: | 01 10 01 10 | 11 10 11 01 |
$(Child)$ Chromosome D: | 11 01 00 00 | 01 00 01 00 |

IMAGE 9.22   Single-point crossover (with attributes).

Remember, you can select any point at which to crossover. The examples go with the midpoint, but it could simply have been a third of the way along or some other point.

N-Point Crossover

This approach expands upon the previous one but allows for multiple crossover points. These points can be spread out or bunched up. Take a look at Image 9.23, which demonstrates how to crossover n points.

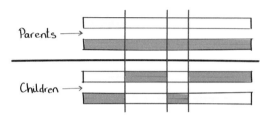

IMAGE 9.23 n-Point crossover.

Image 9.24 used the same example but includes the bits that represent the data transferred from parent to child.

(Parent) Chromosome A: `01 10|01 10|01|00 01 00`

(Parent) Chromosome B: `11 01|00 00|11|10 11 01`

(Child) Chromosome C: `01 10|00 00|01|10 11 01`

(Child) Chromosome D: `11 01|01 10|11|00 01 00`

IMAGE 9.24 n-Point crossover (with attributes).

The number of crossover points and size of the intervals between them is your call and wholly dependent upon the design of the chromosomes.

Let me explain that a little. Look back at the chromosome design for Royal Battle 1866 in Image 9.8. The first four elements are utilities, and the second four elements are weapons. It makes sense to have the crossover between these. So, if I expanded this to include an additional eight elements that could be used for character abilities, I would now have a 16-bit chromosome. My crossover points could be after the fourth bit, and after the eighth bit, resulting is a crossover of four|four|eight.

There is a problem with the example I just gave. Did you spot it? Crossing over between utilities and weapons would never modify those sections. Children would get the exact configuration for weapons as one of its parents had. All weapon configurations for all parents might be inadequate, but we have now implemented a crossover function that ensures we cannot evolve improvements in that area. Parents will keep passing along their inadequate genes. Mutation could have a role to play, which we will discuss in the next section.

UNIFORM CROSSOVER

Uniform crossover is the same as *n*-point crossover, with one difference. The interval between points is exactly the same. As with the previous approaches, images have been included to help explain this (see Images 9.25 and 9.26).

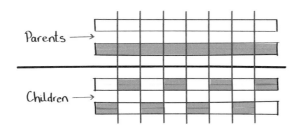

IMAGE 9.25 Uniform crossover.

This approach does not care how you have designed your chromosomes, it simply crosses over every *X* number of genes. This approach can really mix up the chromosomes from generation to generation, but when evolution has got itself into something of a rut, this may be exactly what is required to shake things up.

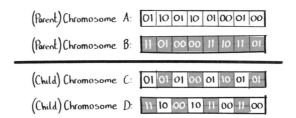

IMAGE 9.26 Uniform crossover (with attributes).

SUMMARY

The important thing with designing the crossover step is to know what you are crossing over and how you want it to work. Design it on paper first. It will save you headaches later.

There are approaches that have not been discussed in this chapter that are used for more bespoke problems. These have not been included as they are not particularly useful for games development, but if you are interested, try looking into a crossover approach called 'Enhanced Edge Recombination' which is used when solving the Travelling Salesman Problem with genetic algorithms.

EXAMPLE GAME: CROSSOVER

For Royal Battle 1866, we will be using the approach described at the start. Two parents will be selected at random, and they will be crossed over to create two children. These parents are then discarded.

We will be using a n-point crossover, to allow us to split up the weapon genes into two sets and the utilities into two sets. If we did a single-point crossover down the middle, child chromosomes would simply be switching around the whole weapon section and whole utilities section. We need a little more variety than that. The crossover will look like Image 9.27.

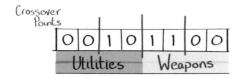

IMAGE 9.27   Crossover for Royal Battle 1866.

Take a look back at Image 9.20 to see the pool of parents. The first two chromosomes selected to act as parents were 20 and 13. From this pairing, two child chromosomes were generated. Image 9.28 uses different colours to help demonstrate which attributes came from which parent.

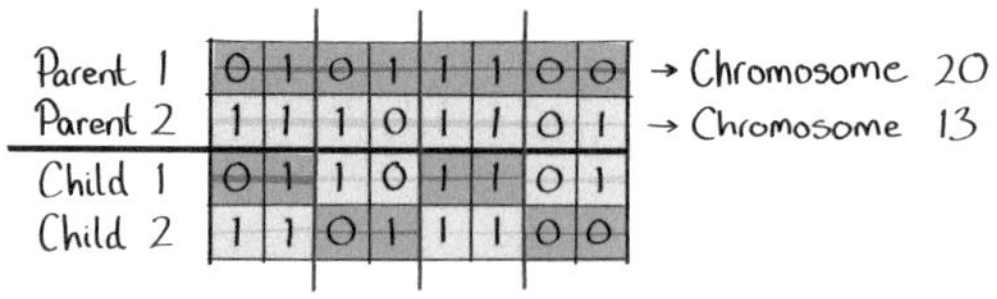

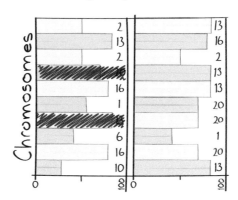

IMAGE 9.28   Children generated from chromosomes 20 and 13.

The parent pool has now been reduced by two chromosomes as 20 and 13 do not get returned. Image 9.29 is the current parent pool.

IMAGE 9.29   Updated parent pool after chromosomes 20 and 13 crossover.

From this updated parent pool, we then select another two parents. This time the chromosomes selected were 6 and 16. These get crossed over in the same manner as before and generate two more children. See Image 9.30.

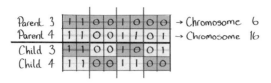

IMAGE 9.30   Children generated from chromosomes 6 and 16.

Again, these parents do not return to the parent pool, giving us now 16 parents to randomly select from. Image 9.31 shows what the updated parent pool now looks like.

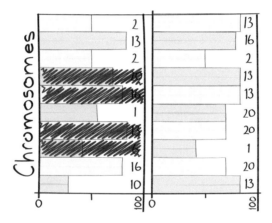

IMAGE 9.31   Updated parent pool after chromosomes 6 and 16 crossover.

This approach continues until all parents have been removed from the pool and we have the correct number of child chromosomes for the next generation.

MUTATION

Mutation is nature's way of adding variety into the gene pool. Remember the giraffe with the long neck? After we have crossed over the parents and we now have our next generation of chromosomes, we go through one final step – mutation.

Mutation should be used sparingly. If you do it too often, then the evolved solutions will be lost, as you are randomly changing attributes. You should aim for a low probability of mutation occurring, say 1% or 2% of the time.

The process of mutation is simple. Select a chromosome and select an attribute within it to change to an alternative. This could be a random choice or in the case of the attributes being bits, switch it to the other state. Image 9.32 shows this occurring using chromosomes made up of bits.

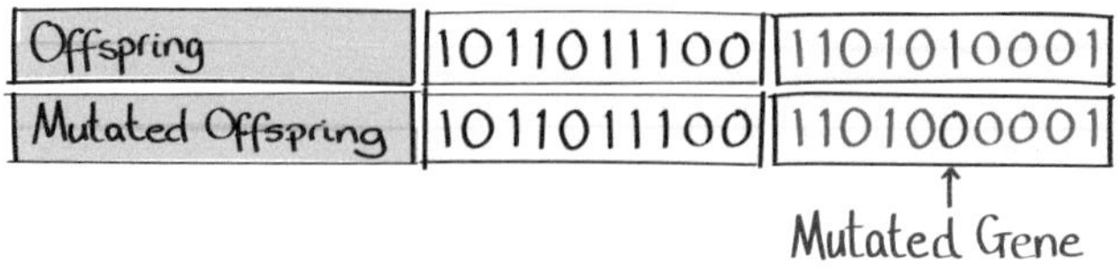

IMAGE 9.32   Mutated attribute.

When using random mutation, it is reasonable for the new value to be the same value as it started with. Imagine you are using bits as in Image 9.32, a bit can either be a zero or a one. As there are only ever two choices, it is quite probable that a bit already set to zero gets set back to zero. It may sound like a waste of time, but it is random after all. If you want it to always mutate to a different value, then there is a little extra coding to ensure that this takes place.

EXAMPLE GAME: MUTATION

In Royal Battle 1866, we will mutate 1% of attributes. As we have 8 attributes per chromosome, and we have 20 chromosomes, that gives us 160 attributes, meaning 1.6 attributes will be mutated.

For this generation, only one will be mutated, and for demonstration purposes child chromosome 1 has been selected. This child was generated from parents 20 and 13, which can be seen in Image 9.28. It has a single attribute selected and replaced with a random alternative. It happens that the attribute was originally a 1, and the alternative was a 0. Image 9.33 shows the mutated version of child 1.

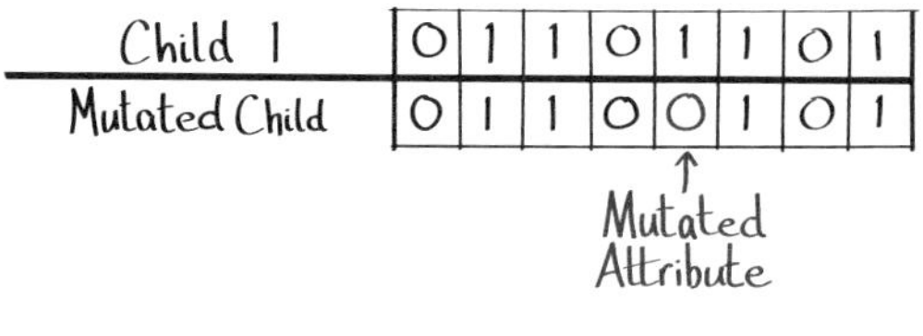

IMAGE 9.33   Mutation of a single attribute in child chromosome 1.

The mutated version of the chromosome replaces the original unmutated version in the next generation. Now we re-run the game and score this generation's chromosomes to determine their fitness scores, before repeating the process of selection, crossover and mutation again.

FINAL THOUGHTS

Genetic algorithms are not always the best method of finding a solution to a problem and the solutions evolved may be somewhat unpredictable. In fact, they are the most suitable approach to finding solutions where elements of the problem itself may be unpredictable. Earlier we discussed using genetic algorithms in multiplayer games, and that was because the human element of the problem was the unpredictable element.

Another thing to consider is the amount of time it takes to evolve an optimal solution. Taking the race car example, if each lap of the track takes around 60 seconds to complete and we have 50 cars to test each generation, that means a single loop of the genetic algorithm will take 50 minutes. If it takes hundreds of generations (and bear that in mind it may take thousands), then you are looking at a lot of hours before you reach the solution. And therefore, genetic algorithms are not a good option for a released title. However, they are useful for titles in development to evolve to solutions that *can* be used in the final product.

Throughout this chapter, we have looked at numerous different approaches to selection and multiple ways to crossover chromosomes, but regardless of what approaches are chosen, it is important to note that if the fitness function is not appropriate to the problem, your choices will not matter.

GENETIC ALGORITHMS – PRACTICAL

PROJECT OVERVIEW

This project takes the form of a spaceship flying from the left edge of the screen to the right-hand side of the screen. There is a finish line to the right that the ship needs to reach to complete the challenge. There are two versions of the game available – a user-controlled version and a genetic algorithm version.

In the user-controlled version, the player can rotate the ship using the arrow keys and thrust in the current direction by pressing the spacebar. This functions correctly out of the box. In the Genetic Algorithm version of the game, 50 ships will spawn to the left of the screen, and each uses their own chromosome of instructions to navigate the environment. Initially they will all do badly, but if the genetic algorithm functions correctly, they will collectively learn how to navigate their way to the finish line. Only the first generation of ships will spawn at the moment. We need to go through the step-by-step guide below before the algorithm will evolve further solutions. When running, this project will look like Screenshot 9.1.

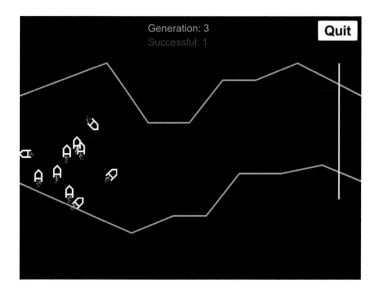

SCREENSHOT 9.1   Genetic algorithm ships.

The following guide is going to focus on the actual functions of the genetic algorithm (Selection, Crossover, Mutation) rather than how to build a genetic algorithm from scratch. The reason for this is that every problem will require a very different implementation of a genetic algorithm and is less transferable. Also, I feel it is more important for a tutorial to get right into the important code, so we can see immediate results.

Right, let us get on with it then.

STEP-BY-STEP GUIDE

Open the Unity project named GameAi supplied with this book. Navigate through the folder system to the Chapter9_GeneticAlgorithms folder. It is located in the Assets folder. Click on the Chapter9_GeneticAlgorithms scene. Run the application. It is not much fun when all the AI crash. But to kick things off this time, we are going to look at a couple of classes that require no code changes. It is always a good idea to familiarise yourself with a codebase before jumping right in and the functions we will be looking at have a huge effect on the rest of the code.

GENE.CS

The gene class has already been coded for our use, but it is important for us to understand what is going on internally. So open Gene.cs and take a look.

The first thing you should notice is an enumeration called `GAInstruction`. This is used in a gene to instruct the ship to carry out an action. These are to either thrust forward or to rotate.

```
public enum GAInstruction
{
    Thrust,
    RotateLeft,
    RotateRight,
    None
};
```

Within the Gene class itself you can see that it is simply made up of two data types. There is a float used to determine how long this gene is active before moving on to the next gene in the chromosome and the actual instruction.

```
public float fDuration = 0.0f;
public GAInstruction eInstruction = GAInstruction.None;
```

Now we know what is involved in a single gene we can move on to the chromosome class.

CHROMOSOME.CS

Again, there is no need for us to code this class as it has been provided, but we should still take a quick look. Open the Chromosome.cs class.

The first line of code to take note of is the static integer that controls the number of genes used in each chromosome. We have gone with 50, but you could increase or lower this if you like.

```
public static int kNumberNofGenes = 50;
```

We then have a list of genes.

```
public List<Gene> genes = new List<Gene>();
```

It really is that simple. There are some setup functions that follow that have been added to simplify things later. These allow us to clear the data stored, generate random values or to copy data from another chromosome.

GA.cs

Now we can start looking at the actual algorithmic side of this tutorial. There are quite a few functions to look at, and not all of them are used in this project, but I have stepped through coding them to make this chapter more useful beyond this demo. I will let you know which ones are not going to be used when we come to them, and you can choose to skip them if you like.

So, the first function we are going to look at is `GenerationComplete()`. This encapsulates the evolution side of the genetic algorithm. Open GA.cs and scroll down until you find this function. As with all previous tutorials, the complete code is available in a commented out solution file. GA_Solution.cs is found in the same folder as GA.cs.

GenerationComplete()

This function is called whenever we have completed a generation. This is when all ships have either crashed or crossed the finish line.

Find the following line of code and delete it:

```
//Todo: Add code here.
```

The first thing to do is to check if we have gone through the maximum number of generations. We do not want this application to run forever.

```
if (iCurrentGeneration < kMaxNumberOfGenerations)
{
```

Next, we calculate this generation's fitness values:

```
CalculateFitness();
```

Then evolve the next generation:

```
Evolve();
```

At this point, we are ready to run another generation of ships. So let us call the function to do just that:

```
RestartGA();
```

Simply close off the if statement with a single bracket and we are good to move on to the next function.

CalculateFitness()

We are not going to go through the code for this function as you can code this in a multitude of ways. What we have done in this game is to use the distance from the starting position to the finish line as the maximum distance. We then divide the current distance by the maximum distance. This results in a zero to one value. One would represent the ship being at the start position and zero at the finish line.

As we want larger numbers to represent higher fitness values, we need to subtract this value from one to flip the result. What we now have is a value of one if the ship is at the finish line and lower values the closer it crashes to the starting line. Let us now take a look at the selection functions.

Selection()

`Selection()` is used as a container for calling the selection function we are going to use. In this example, we have chosen to use Elite selection and Tournament selection, but you could easily replace them with another selection approach if you so choose. By using this function, we only need to change the contents within when we try out different selection algorithms.

Locate this function and remove the following line of code:

```
//Todo: Add code here.
```

Next, add the following functions calls:

```
EliteSelection();
TournamentSelection();
```

That's it. However, as I said before, you could switch these out for another selection approach. These could be either of the following:

```
RouletteWheelSelection();
```

Or

```
StochasticSelection();
```

Initially I recommend using the first option of Elite and Tournament, but after we have this application running, go ahead and try the different approaches and compare results. Let us now take a look at what is involved in each of these selection functions.

EliteSelection()

To determine whether any of our chromosomes from the previous generation are considered elite, we need to iterate through each one and check their fitness scores. Locate the following comment, remove it and add the subsequent code snippets.

```
//Todo: Add code here.
```

Iterating through our chromosomes sounds like we need a loop. So, let us start by adding a for loop.

```
for (int currentChromosome = 0; currentChromosome <
kNumberofChromosomes; currentChromosome++)
{
```

Remember what we said above? A fitness of one means we reached the finishing line, so a fitness of 0.9 is good. We are going to consider any ship with a fitness greater than 0.9 is elite. Let us check if we are over this value.

```
if (chromosomeFitness[currentChromosome] >= 0.9f)
{
```

We have a ship that we consider Elite, so let us copy this into our list of selected chromosomes.

```
selectedChromosomes[iNumberOfEliteSelections].Copy(chromosomes
[currentChromosome]);
```

We need to keep track of how many elite selections we have made so we do not copy over them in our Tournament selection.

```
iNumberOfEliteSelections++;
```

Close off the two brackets.

As we are going to be crossing over our chromosomes in pairs, check if we have an odd number of elite selections. If we do, take an additional copy of the last chromosome to make it an even number.

```
if (iNumberOfEliteSelections % 2 == 1)
{
selectedChromosomes[iNumberOfEliteSelections].Copy(selectedChr
omosomes[iNumberOfEliteSelections - 1]);
```

Remember to increment the count by another one.

```
iNumberOfEliteSelections++;
```

Close off the last bracket and we are finished. Using this approach, we are not hard-coding how many elites are allowed to be chosen. Instead, we are taking as many chromosomes as possible from the previous generation that are considered elite. This means as our generations get better at solving the problem, the more elite solutions will be taken. This forces convergence.

TournamentSelection()

Scroll down to the tournament selection function. It will only contain the following comment:

```
//Todo: Add code here.
```

Delete this line and replace it with the following code snippets.

The first decision as the programmer here is to decide how many chromosomes we are going to compete against each other. We have gone with five, but feel free to increase or decrease this.

```
int combatantCount = 5;
```

Instead of storing the entire highest scoring chromosome data, we are going to store its index in the list.

```
int highestIndex;
```

Tournament selection requires us to iterate the required number of chromosomes needed after *Elite* chromosomes have been stored. We do this by instead of starting our loop at zero, we start it at the number of elites already stored. This is why we kept track of how many elite chromosomes were stored in the `Elite()` function described earlier. Let us do that now:

```
for (int currentChromosome = iNumberOfEliteSelections;
currentChromosome < kNumberofChromosomes; currentChromosome++)
{
```

Instead of selecting five chromosomes and juggling the code for comparisons, we are going to select a single random chromosome and store this as our current highest. Then we will write a loop to select another random chromosome, which we then test against. Whichever is highest is kept. We then go around our loop again and choose another random chromosome. This continues until we have tested the required number of combatants.

Right, let us choose our first combatant.

```
highestIndex = Random.Range(0, 100) % kNumberofChromosomes;
```

Add a for loop to loop through the required number of combatants.

```
for (int i = 0; i < combatantCount; i++)
{
```

Within the loop get the index for the next combatant.

```
int index2 = Random.Range(0, 100) % kNumberofChromosomes;
```

Test to see which of our two chromosomes scores higher. The one we have stored or the new one. If it is the new one, replace our highest stored index with the index of the winner.

```
if (chromosomeFitness[index2] > chromosomeFitness[highestIn
dex])
{
   highestIndex = index2;
}
```

Close off the combatant loop with a single bracket.

We need to add the winner of the tournament to the list of selected chromosomes, so using the highest index we can copy it into the list.

```
selectedChromosomes[currentChromosome].Copy(chromosomes[highes
tIndex]);
```

Close off the tournament selection for loop with a single bracket.

RouletteWheelSelection()
This function is not being called in our solution. So, feel free to skip this function and come back to it after you have the game working.

Scroll down the GA.cs file until you locate this function. Delete the following comment before implementing subsequent steps.

```
//Todo: Add code here.
```

For roulette wheel selection, we need to know what the overall fitness of our combined chromosomes is. To do this we need to create a variable to hold the data and loop through all our fitness values, accumulating them as we do. Add the following code:

```
double totalFitness = 0.0f;
for (int currentChromosome = 0; currentChromosome <
kNumberofChromosomes; currentChromosome++)
{
   totalFitness += chromosomeFitness[currentChromosome];
}
```

Next, we need to create a variable to store the index of the current chromosome. This will store index zero up to the maximum as we loop through selecting chromosomes as we go.

```
int currentIndexInSelectedList = 0;
```

We will be looping until we have the required number of chromosomes. We know that this is 50 as it is what we stored in `kNumberofChromosomes` earlier. For this loop, we will be using a while loop:

```
while (currentIndexInSelectedList < kNumberofChromosomes)
{
```

So, next we need to generate a random position where the ball stops on the wheel. We will be doing this by getting a random number between zero and one hundred. We will also be converting the total fitness into percentage terms soon.

```
double stopPositionOnTheWheel = Random.Range(0.0f, 100.0f);
```

The probability of a particular chromosome being selected is its slice of the wheel added to all previous slices of the wheel. Obviously before we start this process, the probability needs to be set to zero.

```
double probability = 0.0f;
```

So, for us to determine if a particular chromosome is selected or not, we need to iterate through each of the chromosomes we have.

```
for (int currentChromosome = 0; currentChromosome <
kNumberofChromosomes; currentChromosome++)
{
```

Now we get the probability of this chromosome. This is in effect the slice of the roulette wheel this chromosome possesses. On the first pass through the probability will just be the size of the slice for the first chromosome. For subsequent iterations, we will need to add the current probability to that already stored.

For example, the first chromosome (chromosome A) has a 10% slice of the wheel. The stop position of the ball is 15%. Chromosome A's probability is less than the required number, so we move on to the next chromosome. Chromosome B has an 8% slice of the wheel. This gets added to the probability already stored by chromosome A, giving us a probability of 18%. This is greater than the stop position of the ball (15%), so we take chromosome B as a parent.

This may not seem intuitive at first, as the chromosome with the smaller slice got selected, but remember this is what we want. We need a variety of good and bad chromosomes to make it through the selection process. We do not know if a low scoring chromosome contains good elements. Also, if you go back to Image 9.14 and take a look at slice 3, which had the smallest slice. It would take the ball randomly stopping between 63.6% and 69.1%. These may be high numbers, but they describe a small section of the roulette wheel.

So, let us add the probability calculation:

```
probability += (chromosomeFitness[currentChromosome] /
totalFitness) * 100.0f;
```

As we now have the probability of this chromosome being selected, let us check if the probability is higher than the position the ball stopped at.

```
if (probability > stopPositionOnTheWheel)
{
```

If our current probability value is greater than the position selected on the wheel, then we need to take a copy of the chromosome stored at this index and place it into the selected chromosome list.

```
selectedChromosomes[currentIndexInSelectedList].Copy(chromosom
es[currentChromosome]);
```

Remember to increment the current index so that we will exit the while loop when we have selected the required number of parent chromosomes.

```
currentIndexInSelectedList++;
```

Then exit this loop.

```
Break;
```

The last thing to do is to close off the three brackets. Do not forget to add a semicolon to the final bracket, which closes off the while loop.

StochasticSelection()

This function is also not being called in our solution. So again, feel free to skip this function and come back to it after you have the game working.

Scroll down the GA.cs file until you locate the `StochasticSelection()` function. Delete the following comment before adding the code snippets that follow:

```
//Todo: Add code here.
```

As with other selection approaches, we need to know what the accumulated fitness of our chromosomes is. To do this we need to create a variable to hold the data and loop through all our fitness values, combining them as we do. Add the following code:

```
double totalFitness = 0.0f;
for (int currentChromosome = 0; currentChromosome <
kNumberofChromosomes; currentChromosome++)
{
    totalFitness += chromosomeFitness[currentChromosome];
}
```

Stochastic selection steps through the available options. Take a look back at Image 9.15 if you would like to see this process depicted. In terms of code, we need to know how large the step size is, we do that like this:

```
double stepSize = (double)(totalFitness /
kNumberofChromosomes);
```

We start randomly within the first step, so let us calculate that next:

```
double currentStep = Random.Range(0,100) % (int)stepSize;
```

To keep track of which chromosomes we are accessing at any point, we need to store their indexes. The index in the list of selected chromosomes is called `current-Child` and the index in the lists for the chromosomes from the last generation is called `currentParent`.

```
int currentChild = 0;
int currentParent = 0;
```

We will be using a variable to store the accumulated fitness of all chromosomes assessed thus far. Before we enter the stochastic loop, we need to set this to be the fitness of the first parent chromosome's fitness.

```
double currentFitness = chromosomeFitness[currentParent];
```

We are now ready to start our selection loop. We are going to be using a do loop for this:

```
do
{
```

At each iteration, we need to check if the value of the current step is less than the current fitness value stored.

```
if (currentStep <= currentFitness)
{
```

If the step is less than the current fitness value, we can take a copy of the parent chromosomes stored at this index and put it into the list of selected (children) chromosomes.

```
selectedChromosomes[currentChild].Copy(chromosomes[currentPar
ent]);
```

Whenever we store a chromosome in our list of selections, we need to move the index on by one position. Remember, we called this index `currentChild`. So let us increment this now.

```
currentChild++;
```

Now that we have copied the parent chromosome at this position, we also need to move the current step position on by the step size.

```
currentStep += stepSize;
```

To finish off this if statement, close off the bracket and add an else bracket to allow us to handle the movement between the chromosomes we are assessing.

```
}
else
{
```

Within this else bracket, we have found a current step position that is greater than the current fitness. We need to move on to the next parent chromosome and add the fitness of this to the current variable.

```
if (++currentParent < kNumberofChromosomes)
{
    currentFitness += chromosomeFitness[currentParent];
}
```

Close off the else block with a bracket and then close off the while loop.

```
} while (currentChild < kNumberofChromosomes);
```

This concludes the process of selecting parent chromosomes using the stochastic approach. Next, we will be moving on to combining the parents we have selected.

Crossover()

Locate the `Crossover()` function and delete the following comment before adding the code snippets that follow:

```
//Todo: Add code here.
```

To begin, let us clear all the information stored for the last generation of chromosomes.

```
ClearChromosomes();
```

In the event of us using elite selection, we need to copy those chromosomes across without any modifications. So, add the following loop:

```
for (int currentChromosome = 0; currentChromosome <
iNumberOfEliteSelections; currentChromosome++)
{
    chromosomes[currentChromosome].Copy(selectedChromosomes[cur
rentChromosome]);
}
```

For our version of a crossover function, we are going to select two parent chromosomes at a time and generate two child chromosomes at a time. We will iterate over each gene and decide whether to cross them or stick with the current gene. This is a multi-point crossover approach, but in this example, we are going to do something a little different. We will be ensuring the crossover occurs after every two genes but allowing for the target child to be altered as we cross over. For example, parent chromosomes A and B generate children chromosomes C and D. For every two genes, we generate a random value, and if this is less than the crossover rate, we put the gene at this index from A into D and B into C. If the random value is greater than the crossover rate, then we put the gene at this index from A into C and B into D.

Let us get started with this. Add the following loop to iterate through the chromosomes two at a time. Notice that we start the loop at the number of elite chromosomes we have.

```
for (int currentChromosome = iNumberOfEliteSelections;
currentChromosome < kNumberofChromosomes; currentChromosome +=
2)
{
```

Inside this loop we need to iterate through the genes. Again, we will do this with pairs of genes.

```
for (int currentGene = 0; currentGene < Chromosome.
kNumberNofGenes; currentGene += 2)
{
```

Next, we generate a random value and check if it is below the crossover rate.

```
if (Random.Range(0, 100) < kCrossoverRate)
{
```

As the value is less than the crossover rate, we need to put the genes into the opposite children. First, we deal with parent chromosome A into child chromosome D.

```
chromosomes[currentChromosome].genes[currentGene].Copy(selecte
dChromosomes[currentChromosome].genes[currentGene]);
chromosomes[currentChromosome].genes[currentGene + 1].Copy(sel
ectedChromosomes[currentChromosome + 1].genes[currentGene +
1]);
```

Second, we deal with parent chromosome B into child chromosome C.

```
chromosomes[currentChromosome + 1].genes[currentGene].Copy(se
lectedChromosomes[currentChromosome + 1].genes[currentGene]);
chromosomes[currentChromosome + 1].genes[currentGene + 1].Copy
(selectedChromosomes[currentChromosome].genes[currentGene +
1]);
```

Close off the if block with a bracket and add an else bracket to handle crossovers when we do not actually cross over.

```
}
else
{
```

As the value is greater than the crossover rate, we need to put the genes into the corresponding children. First, we deal with parent chromosome A into child chromosome C.

```
chromosomes[currentChromosome].genes[currentGene].Copy(selecte
dChromosomes[currentChromosome].genes[currentGene]);
chromosomes[currentChromosome].genes[currentGene + 1].Copy(s
electedChromosomes[currentChromosome].genes[currentGene +
1]);
```

Next, we deal with parent chromosome B into child chromosome D.

```
chromosomes[currentChromosome + 1].genes[currentGene].Copy(sel
ectedChromosomes[currentChromosome + 1].genes[currentGene]);
chromosomes[currentChromosome + 1].genes[currentGene + 1].Copy
(selectedChromosomes[currentChromosome + 1].genes[currentGene
+ 1]);
```

All that remains is for us to close off the brackets for the above blocks of code. You should need to add three of them.

Mutation()

Scroll down the GA.cs file until you locate the `Mutation()` function. Delete the following comment before adding the code snippets that follow:

```
//Todo: Add code here.
```

The way we are going to handle mutations is to iterate through each gene in each chromosome and generate a random number. If this random number is less than the mutation rate, then we mutate that particular gene.

To begin we need to create a loop to iterate through each chromosome:

```
for (int currentChromosome = 0; currentChromosome <
kNumberofChromosomes; currentChromosome++)
{
```

Then we need another loop to iterate through each gene in the current chromosome:

```
for (int geneIndex = 0; geneIndex < Chromosome.
kNumberNofGenes; geneIndex++)
{
```

Now we can generate the random number and check if the value returned is below the mutation rate.

```
if (Random.Range(0.0f, 100.0f) < kMutationRate)
{
```

If we need to mutate this gene, we can call the pre-coded `GenerateRandomGene()` function.

```
chromosomes[currentChromosome].genes[geneIndex].
GenerateRandomGene();
```

It is as simple as that. All that remains is for us to close off the brackets for the above blocks of code. You should need to add three of them.

You could play around with the mutation rate, or even move the mutation check higher up the code so that we check whether to mutate on a chromosome level, rather than a gene level. Feel free to have a play and investigate the resulting differences.

FUTURE WORK

There are so many moving parts in a genetic algorithm. Try modifying some of the following and see what differences it produces:

- Change the selection approaches used (Tournament, Roulette Wheel, Stochastic etc.).
- Change the crossover approach (Single point, Multi-point etc.).
- Only allow mutation until you have a number of successful chromosomes (50%, 75%, 90% etc.).
- Tweak the crossover rate.
- Tweak the mutation rate.

If you feel confident with the Unity game engine, modify the environment. Make it more complicated and see how a genetic algorithm solves the problem.

10 Neural Networks

The approach of using neural networks is yet another idea the AI world has taken from the natural world. A neural network is actually found in the brain, the proper term for an AI version is an 'artificial neural network'; however, for the remainder of this chapter, we will be using the term 'neural network' interchangeably with both varieties. The concept of a system based upon the way the brain functions was conceived back in the 1940s but fell out of favour. It returned to favour in the 1980s with the introduction of 'learning' which changed things … more on this later.

There is a lot of explanation to go through before we can use a neural network in a game example. We will get there, but first we need to understand the concept of a neural network and how we process the data it holds.

BIOLOGY

There are billions of neurons that control the flow of electrical signals in our brains and a single neuron can be connected to thousands of other neurons. This network of neurons is what we call a neural network. A single neuron is made up of several different elements. Take a look at Image 10.1 and we will have a quick look at what is involved. The soma is the body of the cell, which has multiple dendrites that receive chemical stimuli from thousands of other neurons. This passes through the synaptic gap where a chemical reaction takes place that either excites or inhibits the input. If this collective stimulus is enough to trigger the neuron, the axon carries an electrical signal from the soma to the axon terminals, where a chemical stimulus is released to other neurons.

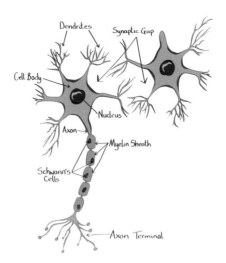

IMAGE 10.1   A neuron in the brain.

DOI: 10.1201/9781003305835-10

The artificial version of a neuron can be seen in Image 10.2, which depicts a digital neuron at its most basic level. It consists of two inputs (dendrites), weights (synaptic gap) and an output (axon terminals). Again, the correct term is 'artificial neuron' but from this point on we shall be using the term 'neuron' when referring to the AI variety as well as the biological variety. The first version of a neuron we are looking at is a single-layer perceptron. This version can solve linearly separable problems, but not non-linear problems. Later we will be looking at a multi-layer perceptron, which can solve non-linear separable problems.

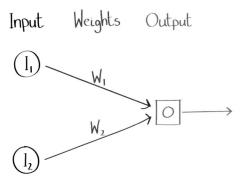

IMAGE 10.2   A single-layer perceptron with two inputs.

SINGLE-LAYER PERCEPTRON

There can be any number of inputs, but each must have a corresponding weight. Inputs are multiplied by these weights and then summed to give an overall input to the neuron. The weights themselves serve two purposes, to either increase or decrease the likelihood of a neuron firing. The weights are where the knowledge of a particular task resides and can be modified as a network learns.

To look deeper into an artificial neuron, we need to consider activation functions. An activation function is where we take the summed input and run it through a process to determine what the output should be. Image 10.3 shows an expanded version of a neuron; this time with three inputs, but it also delves into how the overall input is calculated.

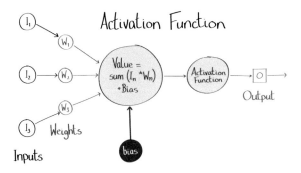

IMAGE 10.3   Activation (an artificial neuron with three inputs).

As you can see, each input is multiplied by its corresponding weight, and then all three are added together. To get the output, we need to run this accumulated value through an activation function. Images 10.4–10.6 show the most commonly used activation functions. The input value is plotted along the horizontal axis, and then the output is the corresponding value on the vertical axis where the red line intersects.

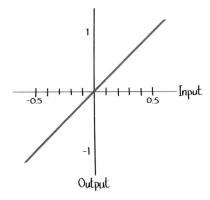

IMAGE 10.4   Linear activation function.

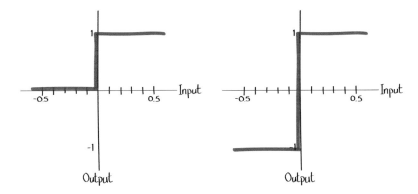

IMAGE 10.5   Unsigned and signed step activation functions.

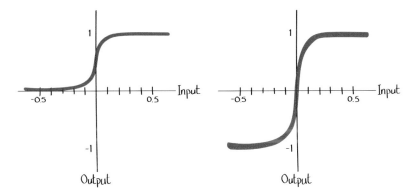

IMAGE 10.6   Unsigned and signed sigmoid activation functions.

So, at this point it makes sense to jump into an example or two so we can really see how a neuron works. Taking the example neuron in Image 10.3, let us plug in some input values. We are going to use 0.5, 1.0 and 0.9. The weights will be 0.5, −0.8 and 0.8. Do not worry where these values come from for now. They are just for demonstration purposes. In an actual game, the inputs may represent things like, distance to enemy, distance to pick-up, current health etc. Take a look at Image 10.7.

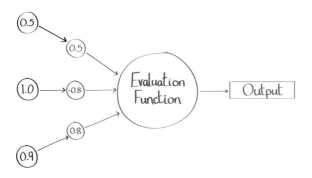

IMAGE 10.7   Neural network example.

Next, we need to calculate the total input value. We do this by multiplying each input by its corresponding weight and then accumulating the results.

$$= (0.5 * 0.5) + (1.0 * -0.8) + (0.9 * 0.8)$$
$$= (0.25) + (-0.8) + (0.72)$$
$$= 0.17$$

The output was not depicted in Image 10.7 and for good reason. The output would depend upon the activation function used. This is where we select one of the functions seen in images 10.4, 10.5 and 10.6, or something entirely different. Let us take a look at what the output will be using each of these activation functions.

If we went with the linear activation (Image 10.4), we would have an output around 0.2. If we had used one of the step activations (Image 10.5), we would have an output of 1.0. The Sigmoid activation functions (Image 10.6) would be somewhere around the 0.7. All of these are estimates, but feel free to take a look at the different activation graphs and plot an input of 0.17.

Let us look at another example. This one involves logic gates. A logic gate takes a number of inputs and outputs a result of true or false; 0 or 1 in this example. Image 10.8 shows the different inputs and the resulting outputs for an AND logic gate. This gate expects both inputs to be true (1) to output true (1). If either, or both inputs are false (0), then the output will be false (0).

Input		Output
i_1	i_2	
1	1	1
0	0	0
1	0	0
0	1	0

IMAGE 10.8   AND logic gate problem.

If we plot the outputs from an AND logic gate onto a two-dimensional graph, where the horizontal axis is input i_2 and the vertical axis is i_1, you get what we have in Image 10.9. There are four outputs, and those coloured black are outputs that resulted in false, and the one that is red is the condition resulting in a true output. So, if i_1 is set to 1 and i_2 is set to 1, we get the red output indicated in the top right of the graph. All other outputs resulted in false and are depicted as black.

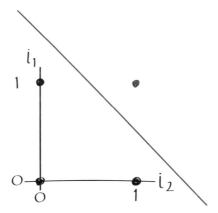

IMAGE 10.9   AND logic gate output.

There is something interesting we can do with this graph. We can separate the outputs that are red (true) from those that are black (false) with a single straight line. This means the problem is linearly separable, which is something our simple neuron can solve. The solution to making the neuron output the correct value when the inputs are those stated in Image 10.8 is all about the activation function. Ignoring the activation functions described above, what simple mathematical check could we use to take the two inputs of i_1 and i_2 and output the results seen in Image 10.8 (either a 1 or 0)?

It is actually a trivial problem when you think about it. The activation function needs to sum the inputs and if the accumulated total is greater than one, we output one, otherwise we output zero. Image 10.10 shows the neuron required to solve the

AND logic gate problem. **Note:** We have no weights in this example to simplify the problem, but for consistency you can consider the weights as being set to 1.0. This means the input multiplied by the weight results in the same value we started with, for example 1.0 (input) × 1.0 (weight) = 1.0.

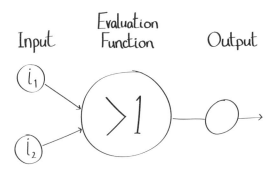

IMAGE 10.10   Neuron to solve the AND logic gate.

Let us take a look at another logic gate. This time the OR logic gate. Image 10.11 shows the inputs and expected outputs. As you can see, if either (or both) of the inputs are true (1), the output will be true (1).

Input		Output
i_1	i_2	
1	1	1
O	O	O
1	O	1
O	1	1

IMAGE 10.11   OR logic gate problem.

Drawing these outputs in graph form in the same way we did for the AND logic gate, you get what is seen in Image 10.12. There are three outputs that have true (1) results. These are depicted as red dots. Notice again that it is possible to draw a straight line between the red (1) outputs and the black (0) outputs.

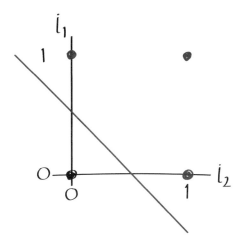

IMAGE 10.12   OR logic gate output.

The activation function required for a neuron to return the correct output is simple enough. Have a think about it, and then take a look at Image 10.13, which shows the neuron that will solve the OR logic gate problem.

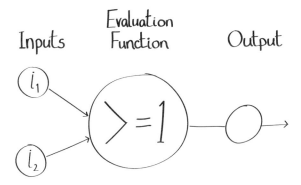

IMAGE 10.13   Neuron to solve the OR logic gate.

A logic gate problem that you might think could be solved in the same manner is the Exclusive OR (XOR) logic gate. Unlike the OR logic gate, the XOR only returns a result of true (1) if one input is true (1). If both are true, then the XOR gate returns a result of false (0). Image 10.14 shows all possible inputs and outputs for this logic gate.

Input		Output
i_1	i_2	
1	1	O
O	O	O
1	O	1
O	1	1

IMAGE 10.14   XOR (exclusive or) logic gate problem.

Plotting the details from Image 10.14 onto a graph results in what can be seen in Image 10.15. Notice this time that it is not possible to draw a straight line between the outputs that are red (1) and black (0). This means the problem is not linearly separable. Remember at the start of this chapter we said that a single-layer perceptron could only solve linearly separable problems? Well, here is a perfect example. Feel free to draw out a neuron and see if you can come up with a solution.

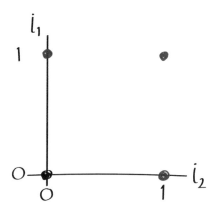

IMAGE 10.15   XOR logic gate output.

The solution to the XOR gate problem is for our simple neuron to expand from being a single-layer perceptron and to become a multi-layer perceptron.

MULTI-LAYER PERCEPTRON

A multi-layered neuron expands in the way the name implies – it allows for multiple layers. We can now have hidden layers. Take a look at Image 10.16, which shows a multi-layered perceptron with three inputs, one hidden layer consisting of six nodes and two outputs. Up to this point, it has only made sense to have one output node, but as we move towards actual game usage, you will find more outputs can be required.

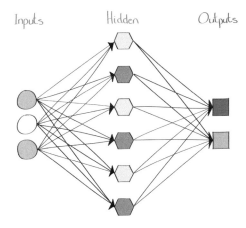

IMAGE 10.16   A multi-layered perceptron.

One hidden layer is usually adequate to solving a problem; however, there is nothing stopping you from having as many layers as you like. Each layer adds a lot of complexity, and when you get into debugging these systems, you will find that it is difficult enough to follow what is happening with one layer of hidden nodes to want to fight with multiple hidden layers.

Let us get back to the problem of the XOR logic gate. Image 10.17 is the multi-layer perceptron solution to the problem. The activation function used in each of the hidden nodes and the output nodes is one that returns true (1) on a combined input of greater than zero, otherwise it returns false (0). In other words, if the combined input into a node is less than zero, the signal pushed forward inhibits, whereas on a combined input greater than zero the signal pushed forward excites.

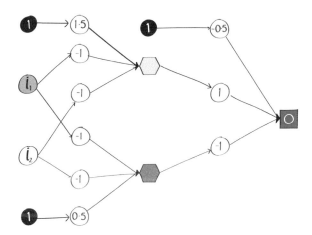

IMAGE 10.17   A multi-layer perceptron to solve the XOR logic gate problem.

One thing you might notice from Image 10.17 are the three black circles – each of these is a bias. A bias just acts as an additional input that cannot be modified. Essentially it ensures a minimum input. All nodes can have a bias but depending on the problem you are attempting to solve; it may not be necessary. In the calculations below, the bias is always the first element.

Let us step through this network and solve the four options seen in Image 10.14.

The first entry has the values: $i_1 = 1$ and $i_2 = 1$.

The combined inputs to the first hidden node are calculated like this:
$(1 * 1.5) + (1 * -1) + (1 * -1) = -0.5$

The combined inputs to the second hidden node are calculated like this:
$(1 * 0.5) + (1 * -1) + (1 * -1) = -1.5$

As you can see, both nodes have a combined input less than zero. This means the signal passed from these nodes into the next layer will be 0. That is, the values used for the inputs into the output layer will be these activation values, not the combined input.

So let us take a look at the calculation for the inputs into the output node. It looks like this: $(1 * -0.5) + (0 * 1) + (0 * -1) = -0.5$

Notice we used the activation values in the calculation? This is an important thing to take on board, because if you mistakenly used the combined input and passed that value through as the input values into the next layer, you would not get the correct results.

The combined input into the output node is less than zero; therefore, the output from this pass through the network will be 0. This is good. Check back with Image 10.14 and you will see this is the result we wanted.

Next, we will run through the second entry in the table, which has the values: $i_1 = 0$ and $i_2 = 0$.

The combined inputs to the first hidden node are calculated like this:
$(1 * 1.5) + (0 * -1) + (0 * -1) = 1.5$.

The combined inputs to the second hidden node are calculated like this:
$(1 * 0.5) + (0 * -1) + (0 * -1) = 0.5$.

As you can see, both nodes have a combined input greater than zero. This means the signal passed from these nodes into the next layer will be 1.

If we now take a look at the calculation for the inputs into the output node, you get the following: $(1 * -0.5) + (1 * 1) + (1 * -1) = -0.5$.

The combined input into the output node is less than zero; therefore, the output from this pass through the network will be 0, which again is the correct result.

Now it is the turn of the third entry in the table, which has the values: $i_1 = 1$ and $i_2 = 0$.

The combined inputs to the first hidden node are calculated like this:
$(1 * 1.5) + (1 * -1) + (0 * -1) = 0.5$.

The combined inputs to the second hidden node are calculated like this:
$(1 * 0.5) + (1 * -1) + (0 * -1) = -0.5$.

As you can see, the first hidden node has a combined input greater than zero. This means the signal passed from this node into the next layer will be 1. The second node has a combined input less than zero, so the signal it passes forward into the next layer will be 0.

Let us take a look at the calculation for the inputs into the output node:
$(1 * -0.5) + (1 * 1) + (0 * -1) = 0.5$

The combined input into the output node is greater than zero; therefore, the output from this pass through the network will this time be 1, which is the correct result.

Finally, we get to the fourth entry in the table, which has the values: $i_1 = 0$ and $i_2 = 1$.

The combined inputs to the first hidden node are calculated like this:
$(1 * 1.5) + (0 * -1) + (1 * -1) = 0.5$.

The combined inputs to the second hidden node are calculated like this:
$(1 * 0.5) + (0 * -1) + (1 * -1) = -0.5$.

In exactly the same manner as the previous entry in the table, the first hidden node has a combined input greater than zero and the second node has a combined input less than zero. This means the calculation for the inputs into the output node looks like this:
$(1 * -0.5) + (1 * 1) + (0 * -1) = 0.5$.

The combined input into the output node is greater than zero; therefore, the output from this pass through the network will be 1.

If any of this explanation was tricky to follow, it might help to draw out the network on a piece of paper and fill in the values as you progress through it. I am sure when you see it on paper, it will all come together.

LEARNING

A neural network needs to be able to learn for it to be of any use. This is what is commonly referred to as machine learning. For a neural network to learn, it is a good idea to have some idea what the results of the network should look like. If we know this, then we can compare the output from the network to the desired result and modify our weights accordingly. This is called supervised learning. If we do not know what the result should be we need to get creative. Unsupervised learning could use a generic algorithm approach to evolving the weights to the correct values or use a clustering approach. We will be looking at both supervised learning, using back propagation and unsupervised learning, using genetic algorithms in the following section. Before we do though, there are a couple of things we need to address. A neural network can have as many input nodes, hidden nodes and output nodes as required. It is the problem you are solving that drives the construction of a network. A neural network that attempts to identify human faces is going to require far more nodes than a neural network designed to play a game like SNAKE.

INPUT ISSUES

Inputs of different scales should be brought into line; otherwise, the one with the greater range will drown out the lower. For example, in a platform game, an input for the distance to the next platform that returns 2 metres next to an input for the nearest pick-up that returns 200 metres will cause problems. These should be converted into a comparable scale. One easy way to do that is to divide the distance by the maximum distance, resulting in a 0–1 value for each.

HIDDEN LAYERS

How many nodes should a hidden layer have? This is a good question with no definitive answer. I have seen networks with double the number of nodes on the input layer, half the number of nodes on the input layer and one and a half times the number of nodes on the input layer. All these networks solved the task they were created to solve. It is a case of trial and error. Start small and increase the size of the network if it is not up to the job.

ADJUSTING WEIGHTS

A network learns by modifying its weights. It is as simple as that really. We need to go through a lot of training until we reach the values that give us the desired outputs, but it is not any more complicated than that. We are first going to look at Back Propagation, followed by a genetic algorithm approach. For both approaches, we need to set up the network with initial values for the weights.

As we have no idea what the values of the weights in our network should be, we should randomly set them. You usually want to start with small values, somewhere in the range of −0.75 to +0.75 should be fine. These values will be modified as training progresses, so we want to be sure there are no wild outliers before we begin. We may very well end up with some values that are substantially out of this initial range, but we will let the network figure that out for itself.

BACK PROPAGATION

Back propagation is the idea by which we work through the network backwards from the output layer to the input layer and modify each weight by a small amount as we go. This adjustment will bring it closer to the weight value required to get the overall output from the network we are looking for. This is supervised learning as we know what the output should look like. The back propagation process can be seen in Image 10.18. Each section will be detailed below. This process continues until the overall output from the network is within some predefined tolerance we set.

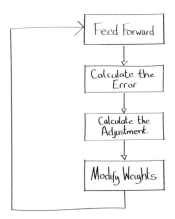

IMAGE 10.18 Back propagation process.

FEED FORWARD

Progression through the network from input layer, through hidden layer(s) until we reach the output layer, is the act of feeding forward the data. This single pass through the network is called an epoch, and we may need many such iterations before the network is trained.

TERMINOLOGY: EPOCH

A single iteration through the network from input layer to output layer.

CALCULATING THE ERROR

To know how much we need to adjust the weights, we need to know how far away the output was from the desired result. We can do this by taking the actual result from the desired result, leaving us with the error.

$$error = actual - desired$$

CALCULATING THE ADJUSTMENT

To determine how accurately the network will learn, we need to set a learning rate. If this is a low value, the network learns slower but incrementally gets to the correct values. If it is too large, the learning can jump past the correct values and will have to re-learn in the opposite direction.

The adjustment to each weight is equal to the learning rate multiplied by the error, multiplied by the activation value from that particular node (the value this node sent forward through the network).

$$\text{Weight adjustment} = \text{Learning rate} * \text{error} * \text{activation value}$$

We can now go ahead and add this adjustment to the weight's current value. This will modify the weight in a manner that will help get the overall output of the network closer to the target output.

If we need to fine tune the network, we can reduce the size of the learning rate over time.

GENETIC ALGORITHM

When using a genetic algorithm approach to learning, the genes within the chromosomes will be the weights from the network. We need to create a number of chromosomes to populate our initial population, which then follows the process described in Chapter 9 – Genetic Algorithms. This process has been duplicated in Image 10.19.

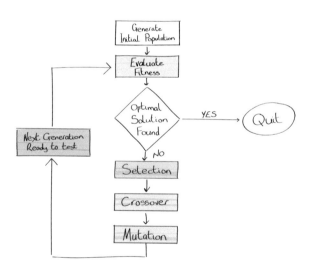

IMAGE 10.19   Genetic algorithm process.

In a fully connected network, each chromosome has the following number of elements:

$$\# \text{Inputs} * \# \text{Hidden Nodes} * \# \text{Outputs}$$

TERMINOLOGY: FULLY CONNECTED

All nodes from a previous layer are connected to all nodes on the next layer.

Let us take a look at the network example from Image 10.16. It has three input nodes, six hidden nodes and two output nodes.

$$3 \times 6 \times 2 = 36$$

These elements have random starting values just as described earlier for standard weights. Then we run an epoch for each of the chromosomes, calculate their fitness and follow the standard approach for selection, crossover and mutation detailed in the previous chapter. We repeat this process and evolve our weights until the overall output from the network is within the predefined tolerance we set.

GAME EXAMPLE: SNAKE

So far the problems solved have been good for explaining the mechanics behind a network, but not that useful to games. So that is what we are going to look at in this section. We will be looking at the classic game – SNAKE and developing an AI to control a snake. The idea is the snake will learn how to play the game over time and its score will increase as the network navigates it around its tail and towards the pick-ups.

For this version of SNAKE, we will be using 12 inputs. All will be in the range of 0.0–1.0 to ensure none of them can smother the input of another. These inputs will cover movement direction, distance to a pick-up and distance to a collidable cell.

For movement there are four possible directions a snake can go in. These inputs will be either a one or a zero depending on whether the cell in the direction specified can be moved to. Look at Image 10.20, the head of the snake is the green cell. The input nodes for movement in the directions of UP, LEFT and DOWN will all be one as they are valid options. Movement in the RIGHT direction however is where the tail of the snake is, so that input node will be zero.

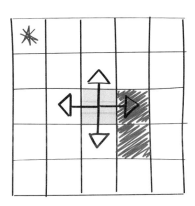

IMAGE 10.20   SNAKE movement input.

For a snake to know whether it is doing a good job, we will be using the score, and the score is based upon the number of pick-ups collected. So, the distance to the pick-up is another input we require. We will stick with the four-directional approach for this as well, and the inputs will be in the range of 0.0–1.0; 1.0 indicating the pick-up is in the next cell in that direction, or a lesser value the further away it is; 0.0 indicates it is not in that direction at all. Take a look at Image 10.21, which has the pick-up in the top left corner.

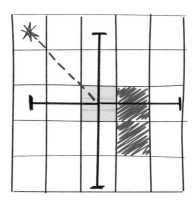

IMAGE 10.21   SNAKE pick-up distance input.

The final set of inputs is the distance to a collision in each direction. We want our snake to stay away from walls and its own tail, so this again is an important input for the network to have. This input works in the same manner as the pick-ups, in that it is a 0.0–1.0 value, with a 1.0 indicating a collision in the next cell in the specified direction. Image 10.22 shows the head of the snake reaching out in all four directions.

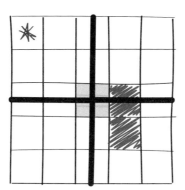

IMAGE 10.22   SNAKE collision input.

So, we have our 12 inputs, next we need to determine how many nodes in the hidden layer there will be. We will be going with four nodes on one hidden layer. We can start with a low number of hidden nodes and then increase them if we do not see the results we want. Finally, we need our output nodes. This is simple. The snake can move in four directions, so we need four outputs. The output with the highest value will be the direction the snake moves in.

Now we have all the details we need to depict the actual network. Image 10.23 is what a network with the above details would look like. Each one of the connecting lines in the image has a weight. Using the calculation we described above, this gives us 12 inputs multiplied by 4 hidden nodes multiplied by 4 outputs. That is 12*4*4, giving us 192 weights. So, our chromosomes will have 192 elements to them. Our SNAKE neural network is not complicated but dealing with that amount of numbers can be mind boggling. Imagine if we increase the inputs to allow for more intelligence.

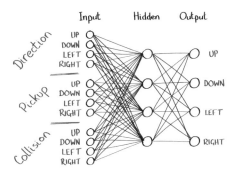

IMAGE 10.23   Neural network for a SNAKE.

Now we run the game (we will do this in the tutorial section of this chapter) – see Screenshot 10.1. For each move, we pass through the details to the input nodes and then move in the direction of the highest scoring output node. We allow the snake to play until it dies. When all snakes in our population have completed a run through, we can use the scores they achieved as their fitness values. As described in the Genetic Algorithm chapter, we then select potential parents, crossover chromosomes to generate children and then add random mutation. When we have a full population for the next generation, we repeat the process. We just need to determine the criteria for ending the learning. Something simple like training continues until a snake can score 100 points or more.

To begin with the snakes will all be rubbish. They will crash into walls, into their own tails and fail to collect pick-ups. Over multiple generations though, the snakes will get better at the task. If you were to take a look at the weights periodically throughout the training, it will just look like a bunch of random numbers, and nonsensical to us. This is fine – as long as the network understands them. If we knew what these values needed to be we would not have needed to train the network in the first place, would we?

FINAL THOUGHTS

It may come as a surprise, but neural networks are not a particularly useful approach to use for game AI. The results can be unpredictable, which goes against the idea of games being an authored experience. Designers will expect the agents you code to act in a manner suitable to the experience they are constructing. Neural networks at their most basic description are pattern-matching algorithms. They are great for facial recognition or dealing with lots of data. They certainly have their uses in the field of artificial intelligence, but they have not been overly used in the development of agent behaviour.

With that being said, there are some games that have used this approach and have proven to be successful. Extremely complicated board games such as Go can use this approach to assess the myriad of options and strategies Go offers a player on every turn. But the fact that there are not a plethora of published games shouting about how they have used neural networks really tells you all you need to know.

NEURAL NETWORKS – PRACTICAL

PROJECT OVERVIEW

This project is a version of the classic SNAKE game described in the theory part of this chapter. The snake starts the game with only a head and a tail and each time it collects a pick-up, its body grows. Crashing into the walls of the environment or into your own body will kill the snake, so the challenge increases the better you do at the game.

There are two modes of play available. You can play a one player game, using the arrow keys to navigate the environment, or you can watch the AI play a game. Screenshot 10.1 shows the game in action. As the project currently stands, the AI version will just stand still when selected. This is because we are yet to set up some important parts of the network. When you have followed the step-by-step guide below, it will run fine.

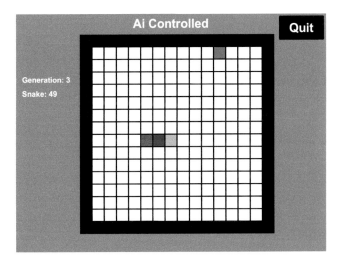

SCREENSHOT 10.1   Classic SNAKE game.

The AI makes its decisions using a neural network and evolves better weights for the network using a genetic algorithm approach. This approach has been chosen over a back propagation approach because when using back propagation, you need to know what the desired result is. This is hard to know in games where the actual playing of the game can result in vastly different outcomes.

When we have the AI running. Watch the debug output to see how well the neural networks are progressing. For each generation we will output the highest scoring snake's fitness. This is a floating-point value where the first part is the number of pick-ups, and the second part (after the decimal point) is the number of moves made. It scores 0.0001 for every move. So, for example, a snake that scores 5.0101 has collected 5 pick-ups and survived for 101 moves.

The AI snakes will also move extremely fast. This is intentional. Time does not have an impact upon the decision-making process, so speeding up the movement reduces the amount of time it takes to progress through generations of snakes. The one player version of the game moves at a reasonable speed.

STEP-BY-STEP GUIDE

Open the Unity project named GameAi supplied with this book. Navigate through the folder system to the Chapter10_NeuralNetworks folder. It is located in the Assets folder. Click on the Chapter10_NeuralNetworks scene. Run the application. It is not much fun when the AI just sits there. Is it?

First, we need to write the code for our neural network before it can be used to direct the movement of the snake. If you remember from the theory portion of this chapter, a network consists of layers, which themselves consist of neurons. Navigate to the Neuron.cs and we shall start to make our network functional. As always, if you get stuck, take a look at the solution code files, which are located in the same folder.

NEURON.CS

At the top of this file, you will find a couple of member variables already set up. There is an integer to hold the number of inputs to this neuron, a list to hold the weights and the bias to use.

```
public int numberOfInputs;
public List<float> weights = new List<float>();
public float fBias = 1.0f;
```

The list will be populated in the constructor for the neuron. The constructor is the only function in this file and has the same name as the class –Neuron. Go ahead and locate this function.

Neuron()

Locate the following line and remove it:

```
//Delete Me.
```

The number of inputs will be passed into the constructor as a parameter, along with a value to use as a bias. We may not use the bias for this project, but it has been added to demonstrate how it can be incorporated.

Set up the number of inputs and the bias.

```
numberOfInputs = numOfInputs;
fBias = bias;
```

Loop through the inputs and add a random weight to our list in the range of −1 to 1.

```
for (int i = 0; i < numOfInputs; i++)
{
    weights.Add(Random.Range(-1.0f, 1.0f));
}
```

There is another function in this class for accessing the bias. This is a self-explanatory function, so is not detailed further. We now have our neuron class set-up navigate to the Layer class.

LAYER.CS

Like the neuron, we have a couple of member variables already set up for us. These consist of an integer to hold the number of neurons in this layer and a list to hold those neurons.

```
int numberOfNeurons;
List<Neuron> neurons = new List<Neuron>();
```

There are more functions in this class than there were in the neuron class. We need access to the neurons, specific weights and to access how many neurons there are. These functions have been provided with the necessary code and require no modification. We are however going to modify the Layer() constructor. Locate this function and remove the following line:

```
//Delete Me.
```

Layer()

To set up a layer we need to know how many neurons the layer will hold. We also need to know how many inputs each of the neurons will have. We need to know this because it is in the layer constructor that will be creating the neurons and calling the neuron constructor.

To begin, store the number of neurons passed in as a parameter in our member variable.

```
numberOfNeurons = qtyOfNeurons;
```

Next, we create the number of neurons required and store them in our list. We are going to pass through 0 as the bias to each neuron. This means that the bias will not modify the result at all.

```
for (int i = 0; i < numberOfNeurons; i++)
{
    neurons.Add(new Neuron(qtyOfInputsPerNeuron, 0.0f));
}
```

So, that was simple enough. Next, we will move on to the Network itself.

NETWORK.CS

The Network class is the container for all the layers that our neural network will hold. It is responsible for the setup of these layers and the processing of them. To achieve this there are some member variables required. These are for storing the number of inputs our network can accept, the number of hidden layers and how many neurons are in these layers, and finally how many outputs there should be.

```
int numberOfInputs;
int numberOfOutputs;
int numberOfHiddenLayers;
int numberOfNeuronsPerHiddenLayer;
```

Beneath you will find the list used to store our layers.

```
List<Layer> layers = new List<Layer>();
```

Right, let us get to the interesting stuff. Navigate down to the Network constructor. Locate the following comment and delete it:

```
//Delete Me.
```

Network()

The parameters passed in are important, so the first thing we do is store these values in our member variable counterparts.

```
numberOfInputs = qtyInputs;
numberOfOutputs = qtyOutputs;
numberOfHiddenLayers = qtyHiddenLayers;
numberOfNeuronsPerHiddenLayer = qtyNeuronsPerHiddenLayer;
```

When creating a neural network, the input layer is not actually a part of the network. That is determined by whatever is using the network. However, the network must know how to handle the inputs and have the appropriate number of weights for the data to be passed to the first hidden layer.

Before we jump into creating hidden layers, we need to check if there are any. If not, we can just move onto the output layer.

```
if (numberOfHiddenLayers > 0)
{
```

We have at least one hidden layer, so let us handle the creation of the first one. This is a special layer in terms of all the hidden layers, as it is the one that uses an external source to determine how many inputs this layer has.

```
layers.Add(new Layer(numberOfNeuronsPerHiddenLayer,
numberOfInputs));
```

Subsequent hidden layers take the number of neurons per hidden layer (passed in as a function parameter) as both inputs and outputs.

```
for (int i = 0; i < numberOfHiddenLayers - 1; ++i)
{
    layers.Add(new Layer(numberOfNeuronsPerHiddenLayer,
numberOfNeuronsPerHiddenLayer));
}
```

The last layer to add is the output layer. This takes the number of neurons per hidden layer as inputs and outputs the required number of outputs (specified via the function parameters).

```
layers.Add(new Layer(numberOfOutputs,
numberOfNeuronsPerHiddenLayer));
```

We now need to close off this section of code with a bracket but also add an else bracket for the possibility of there being no hidden layers.

```
}
else
{
```

A network without any hidden layers passes the data through to the output layer. This will progress through one set of weights. As was discussed in the theory portion of this chapter, there are problems that cannot be solved with single-layered networks.

```
layers.Add(new Layer(numberOfOutputs, numberOfInputs));
}
```

Update()

Scroll down the file until you locate the `Update()` function. Locate the following comment, delete it and follow the steps below:

```
//Delete Me.
```

When processing the input data through a network, we will be using a simple for loop to progress along each layer. We are using the number of hidden layers for this, but also adding one to this count to include the output layer.

```
for (int i = 0; i < numberOfHiddenLayers + 1; ++i)
{
```

Each layer needs to have its inputs set up correctly. On the first pass through this loop, we can assume that the inputs are correct. They were passed in as a function parameter and should be the data required for a network of this configuration. However, if we are not dealing with the first layer (the input data to the first hidden layer), then we need to move the stored outputs from the previous layer to the input data for the current layer.

First check if we are dealing with the first layer.

```
if (i > 0)
{
```

We are not looking at the first layer, so clear the inputs used on the last iteration of this loop.

```
inputs.Clear();
```

Work through the outputs, adding them to the input list.

```
for (int index = 0; index < outputs.Count; index++)
{
    inputs.Add(outputs[index]);
}
```

Close the check for the first layer with a single bracket.

```
}
```

Every iteration of this loop, that is, every layer we process should start with the output data empty. We will fill this in as we process the layer. Do this now.

```
outputs.Clear();
```

We are now ready to process the current layer of the network. We need to loop through each neuron and multiply the corresponding weight to it. The total goes through the activation function.

OK, create a loop to iterate through the neurons.

```
for (int j = 0; j < layers[i].GetNumberOfNeurons(); j++)
{
```

We need a couple of local variables to keep track of things. These are the net input and a count for the number of inputs. The second of these is just to make our code easier to read.

```
float netInput = 0.0f;
int inputCount = layers[i].GetNeurons()[j].numberOfInputs;
```

For each neuron, we will be multiplying each input by the corresponding weight. This is important to note. As this is a fully connected network, all inputs (or outputs from the previous layer) go into all nodes on the next layer. This means there should be the same number of weights as input nodes. Do not worry though, we have already set this up. Our network looks exactly like Image 10.23.

```
for (int k = 0; k < inputCount; ++k)
{
```

Using our net input variable, we should add the current input multiplied by the current weight to the current total.

```
netInput += layers[i].GetNeurons()[j].weights[k] * inputs[k];
}
```

After all inputs have been processed for this neuron, we need to incorporate the BIAS. Again, we are not doing anything with the BIAS here. We are simply adding zero to the total, but it is included in case we want to modify our network to use a BIAS.

```
netInput += layers[i].GetNeurons()[j].GetBias();
```

We now have our total for this neuron. It is passed through the sigmoid function before being stored in our output list.

```
outputs.Add(Sigmoid(netInput));
```

The last thing to do is to close off the brackets. There should be two of them.

```
    }
}
```

There are additional functions found in the Network class such as the function to get the weights. These are self-explanatory, so we will not be going over those. All the code is there for you to look through.

We now have our neural network code. The next step is for us to create a network suitable for solving the problem at hand. This is done in the NNGrid.cs file, so let us go and take a look.

NNGRID.CS

This file is where everything is brought together. It is where the snakes are all created, where the networks for each snake are created and processed. It is where the input to move a snake is handled, whether that be AI or user controlled. There is a lot to this file, but we will only be looking at the functions relevant to neural network functionality. There are genetic algorithm functions at the bottom of this file, but given we have a whole chapter dedicated to this area, along with its very own tutorial, I would suggest working through that chapter before you tackle this one.

At the top of the file, you will find a collection of constant variables already set up. This is where you can change the number of snakes in the project, and the number of nodes and layers.

```
const int kNumberOfNNSnakes = 50;
const int kNumberOfInputNodes_Snake = 12;
const int kNumberOfHiddenNodes_Snake = 4;
const int kNumberOfOutputNodes_Snake = 4;
```

```
const int kNumberOfWeights_Snake = (kNumberOfInputNodes_Snake
* kNumberOfHiddenNodes_Snake) + (kNumberOfHiddenNodes_Snake *
kNumberOfOutputNodes_Snake);
```

Feel free to play around with these after you have completed this tutorial. Changing the number of input nodes requires additional code. We are looking at four inputs for positioning, four inputs for the pick-up and four inputs for movement direction. This is where the 12 comes from. Again, look back at Image 10.23 to see what our network looks like.

SetUpNeuralNetwork()

This function is relatively trivial. We have handled the hard work of creating a network in our Network.cs file. What we need to do here though is to create a network for each snake. We will do this by looping for the required number of snakes. Delete the following:

```
//Delete Me.
```

And add this loop:

```
for (int i = 0; i < kNumberOfNNSnakes; i++)
{
    neuralNetworks.Add(new Network(kNumberOfInputNodes_Snake,
kNumberOfOutputNodes_Snake, 1, kNumberOfHiddenNodes_Snake));
}
```

UpdateSnakeAI()

Locate the following comment. Delete it and progress to the steps below:

```
//Delete Me.
```

In the `DoMovement()` function, there is a check to see how much time the snake has to locate the next pick-up. If the count has reached zero, the snake is killed. This is to allow our application to continue when a neural network has come up with a solution that never collects pick-ups but manages to avoid collisions. The count (`levelTime`) is reset to 10 seconds every time the snake collects a pick-up.

To reduce the time remaining, we need to add the following:

```
levelTime -= Time.deltaTime;
```

Unsurprisingly we need to process the inputs that we will feed into the network. So let us create a list to store these values.

```
List<float> inputs = new List<float>();
```

As we said above, four of the inputs are to do with positioning. Take a look back at Image 10.20. We will check each of the movement directions (Up, Down, Left and Right) and set the input to 1.0 for an empty tile and 0.0 for a collidable tile. We will be looking more in depth at the function `GetNNInputForPosition()` below.

```
inputs.Add(GetNNInputForPosition(MovementDirection.Up));
inputs.Add(GetNNInputForPosition(MovementDirection.Down));
inputs.Add(GetNNInputForPosition(MovementDirection.Left));
inputs.Add(GetNNInputForPosition(MovementDirection.Right));
```

The next four inputs are for the pick-up. Take a look back at Image 10.21. If a pick-up is to be located above and to the right, both inputs will have a value set in the range of 0.0–1.0. If the pick-up is in the next tile, then that direction will be set to 1.0. For directions away from the pick-up, the input value here will be set to zero. Do not worry though, we will be looking at `GetNNInputForPickup()` in more detail below.

```
inputs.Add(GetNNInputForPickup(MovementDirection.Up));
inputs.Add(GetNNInputForPickup(MovementDirection.Down));
inputs.Add(GetNNInputForPickup(MovementDirection.Left));
inputs.Add(GetNNInputForPickup(MovementDirection.Right));
```

The last four inputs are for collisions. Take a look back at Image 10.22 to see how this looks. For each direction, the higher the number, the better the option. The values range from 1.0 to 0.0. A collidable cell right next to the snake's head will return 0.0. As with the other functions for calculating the input, we will be looking at `GetNNInputForCollision()` below:

```
inputs.Add(GetNNInputForCollision(MovementDirection.Up,
NNTileType.Blocked));
inputs.Add(GetNNInputForCollision(MovementDirection.Down,
NNTileType.Blocked));
inputs.Add(GetNNInputForCollision(MovementDirection.Left,
NNTileType.Blocked));
inputs.Add(GetNNInputForCollision(MovementDirection.Right,
NNTileType.Blocked));
```

Call the `Update()` function in Network.cs, passing through the input values just calculated.

```
List<float> outputs = new List<float>();
neuralNetworks[currentChromosome].Update(inputs, ref outputs);
```

From the four outputs – one for each direction (UP, DOWN, LEFT and RIGHT). Whichever one has the higher value is the best direction our neural network has decided we should move in. We need to check these conditions before storing the proposed movement direction.

```
if ((outputs[(int)MovementDirection.Up] > outputs[(int)
MovementDirection.Down]) && (outputs[(int)MovementDirection.
```

```
Up] > outputs[(int)MovementDirection.Left]) && (outputs[(int)
MovementDirection.Up] > outputs[(int)MovementDirection.
Right]))
{
    proposedMovementDirection = MovementDirection.Up;
}
else if ((outputs[(int)MovementDirection.Down] > outputs[(int)
MovementDirection.Up]) && (outputs[(int)MovementDirection.
Down] > outputs[(int)MovementDirection.Left]) &&
(outputs[(int)MovementDirection.Down] > outputs[(int)
MovementDirection.Right]))
{
    proposedMovementDirection = MovementDirection.Down;
}
else if ((outputs[(int)MovementDirection.Left] > outputs[(int)
MovementDirection.Up]) && (outputs[(int)MovementDirection.
Left] > outputs[(int)MovementDirection.Down]) &&
(outputs[(int)MovementDirection.Left] > outputs[(int)
MovementDirection.Right]))
{
    proposedMovementDirection = MovementDirection.Left;
}
else
{
    proposedMovementDirection = MovementDirection.Right;
}
```

Finally, we need to pass this decision through to the function that handles the actual movement of the snake.

```
DoSnakeMovement();
```

GetNNInputForPosition()

For this function, we are only interested in whether the head of the snake will be colliding with an obstacle if it were to move one cell in the desired direction. As ever, to begin with, locate the following lines and delete them:

```
//Delete Me.
return 0.0f;
```

We are going to be as succinct as possible with this function, which means we will be using a local variable to store the tile in the proposed direction.

```
NNTileType tileTypeToCheck = NNTileType.Empty;
```

Open a switch statement to handle the different directions and set the local variable to be the tile in this direction.

```
switch (dir)
{
```

```
case MovementDirection.Up:
    tileTypeToCheck = gridLayout[snake[0].row, snake[0].column
- 1];
break;

case MovementDirection.Down:
    tileTypeToCheck = gridLayout[snake[0].row, snake[0].column
+ 1];
break;

case MovementDirection.Left:
    tileTypeToCheck = gridLayout[snake[0].row - 1, snake[0].
column];
break;

case MovementDirection.Right:
    tileTypeToCheck = gridLayout[snake[0].row + 1, snake[0].
column];
break;

default:
Break;
}
```

Now that we have the tile details in the proposed direction, we need to ensure that it is empty or contains a pick-up (a cell containing a pick-up is essentially empty in terms of collisions). If it is empty, then we can return 1.0 indicating a positive result.

```
if (tileTypeToCheck == NNTileType.Empty || tileTypeToCheck ==
NNTileType.PickUp)
{
    return  1.0f;
}
```

If we reach this point in the code, it means that we are looking at a tile that is an obstacle. So, we should return 0.0 indicating an undesirable direction.

```
return 0.0f;
```

GetNNInputForPickup()

For this function, we are only interested in the distance from the pick-up location to the location of the snake's head. So let us jump right into it. Locate the following lines and delete them:

```
//Delete Me.
return 0.0f;
```

Store the row and column position of the pick-up for ease of readability in the code below.

```
float pickUpPosCol = (float)pickupPosition.column;
float pickUpPosRow = (float)pickupPosition.row;
```

Store the row and column position of the snake's head for ease of readability in the code below.

```
float headPosCol = (float)snake[0].column;
float headPosRow = (float)snake[0].row;
```

Open a switch statement to handle the different directions.

```
switch (dir)
{
```

First, we handle a prospective move in the UP direction. We are calculating the return value by taking the row where the snake's head is located from the row where the pick-up is located. We then divide this by the board dimensions to get a zero to one value and then take this away from 1.0. We are left with a higher score the closer the pick-up is to the head.

```
case MovementDirection.Up:
    if (pickUpPosRow <= headPosRow)
    {
        return (1.0f - (headPosRow - pickUpPosRow) / (float)
kSnakeBoardDimensions);
    }
break;
```

To handle a prospective movement in a DOWN direction. We do the same as we did with an UP direction, but this time we take the row where the pick-up is located from the row where the snake's head is located.

```
case MovementDirection.Down:
    if (pickUpPosRow >= headPosRow)
    {
        return (1.0f - ((pickUpPosRow - headPosRow) / (float)
kSnakeBoardDimensions));
    }
break;
```

When handling a horizontal movement, we look at the columns rather than the row, which we used for vertical movement. So, to handle a prospective movement in a LEFT direction we calculate the return value by taking the column where the snake's head is located from the column where the pick-up is located. We then divide this by the board dimensions to get a zero to one value and then take this away from 1.0. We are left with a higher score the closer the pick-up is to the head.

```
case MovementDirection.Left:
    if (pickUpPosCol <= headPosCol)
    {
        return (1.0f - (headPosCol - pickUpPosCol) / (float)
kSnakeBoardDimensions);
    }
break;
```

To handle a prospective movement in a RIGHT direction. We do the same as we did with an LEFT direction, but this time we take the column where the pick-up is located from the column where the snake's head is located.

```
case MovementDirection.Right:
    if (pickUpPosCol >= headPosCol)
    {
        return (1.0f - ((pickUpPosCol - headPosCol) / (float)
kSnakeBoardDimensions));
    }
break;
```

There should be no need to handle any other input, but it is good practice to include a default case.

```
default:
break;
}
```

At the very bottom of this function, we return 0.0. We will only reach this line of code if the pick-up was not located in the proposed direction. Returning a zero value indicates there was nothing here.

```
return 0.0f;
```

GetNNInputForCollision()

This function is designed to return a value between 0.0 and 1.0 for the distance to the nearest collidable tile in a specified direction. We are only interested in the distance between the current cell to the head position, as the body will only be placed if a valid head movement was made.

As usual, locate the following lines and delete them:

```
//Delete Me.
return 0.0f;
```

We need two local variables to help with this task. The first is to keep track of a collision occurring. As soon as the collided variable is set to true, we no longer need to check any further cells. The second variable is to store how many cells we looked at before finding a collision.

```
bool collided = false;
int i = 0;
```

Open a switch statement to handle the different directions.

```
switch (dir)
{
```

The first case to deal with is the UP direction.

```
case MovementDirection.Up:
```

We need to keep searching until we find a collision. Remember that the environment is surrounded by collidable tiles, so we will hit something eventually.

```
while (!collided)
{
```

Increment the variable that holds how many cells we have checked.

```
i++;
```

Check if the cell on the grid in this position is a type of collision, and if so, set our collision flag to true.

```
if (gridLayout[snake[0].column, snake[0].row - i] ==
typeOfCollision)
{
    collided = true;
}
```

Otherwise, we need to check if we have collided with part of the snake's own body.

```
else
{
```

Start a loop that will iterate through all segments of the body and check if the head is in the same cell as them. Notice we start the for loop at 1 so we do not test the head of the snake against itself.

```
for (int j = 1; j < snake.Count; j++)
{
    if (snake[0].column == snake[j].column && snake[0].row - i
== snake[j].row)
```

```
    {
        collided = true;
        break;
    }
}
```

Close off the else section with a bracket and close off the while loop with another bracket. Then add a break to exit the switch statement.

```
    }
}
break;
```

Next, we move on to the DOWN direction. This is exactly the same as the UP direction, with a change in how we apply the i variable. For DOWN we add it to the row, whereas for UP we deducted it from the row. Type in the following code:

```
case MovementDirection.Down:
    while (!collided)
    {
        i++;
        if (gridLayout[snake[0].column, snake[0].row + i] ==
typeOfCollision)
        {
            collided = true;
        }
        else
        {
            for (int j = 1; j < snake.Count; j++)
            {
                if (snake[0].column == snake[j].column &&
snake[0].row + i == snake[j].row)
                {
                    collided = true;
                    break;
                }
            }
        }
    }
break;
```

Next, we move on to the LEFT direction. This is exactly the same as the previous directions, apart from we make modifications to the column rather than the row. Type in the following code:

```
case MovementDirection.Left:
    while (!collided)
    {
        i++;
```

```
            if (gridLayout[snake[0].column - i, snake[0].row] ==
typeOfCollision)
            {
                collided = true;
            }
            else
            {
                for (int j = 1; j < snake.Count; j++)
                {
                    if (snake[0].column - i == snake[j].column &&
snake[0].row == snake[j].row)
                    {
                        collided = true;
                        break;
                    }
                }
            }
        }
break;
```

Finally, we handle the RIGHT direction. This is the same as the LEFT direction, with a change in how we apply the i variable. For LEFT, we deduct it from the column, whereas for RIGHT we add it to the column. Type in the following code:

```
case MovementDirection.Right:
    while (!collided)
    {
        i++;
        if (gridLayout[snake[0].column + i, snake[0].row] ==
typeOfCollision)
        {
            collided = true;
        }
        else
        {
            for (int j = 1; j < snake.Count; j++)
            {
                if (snake[0].column + i == snake[j].column &&
snake[0].row == snake[j].row)
                {
                    collided = true;
                    break;
                }
            }
        }
    }
break;
```

There should never be any other type of direction to handle, but it is good practice to include a default case.

```
default:
break;
}
```

We just need to return our zero to one value. First, we need to calculate what the maximum number of moves should be. The maximum distance we can move in the environment is the dimension (number of cells) of the grid minus two for the collidables at each side.

```
float maxDistance = kSnakeBoardDimensions - 2;
```

If we divide the number of cells we checked (i in this example) by the maximum, we will get a zero to one value, with 1.0 being at the maximum distance. However, we would like for 1.0 to be a positive outcome to match the other input functions. To do this we simply need to take our result from 1.0. This will give us a 1.0 if the nearest collidable is far away.

```
return 1.0f - ((float)i / maxDistance);
```

FUTURE WORK

There are plenty of changes you could make to the genetic algorithm portion of the snake's learning, but we are not going to focus on that here. Refer to the genetic algorithm chapter, which I am sure will give you plenty of ideas for modifications you could incorporate.

In terms of the neural network portion of the snake's learning, you could do one of the following:

- Play around with the Bias. What difference does this make?
- Consider what other inputs may be useful to the decision-making process. Add them to the input calculations (modifications will be required to the network to handle this change).
- Add additional nodes to the hidden layer. Did this produce better results?
- Add an additional hidden layer. Does this produce better results?

Index

Note: Locators in *italics* represent figures.